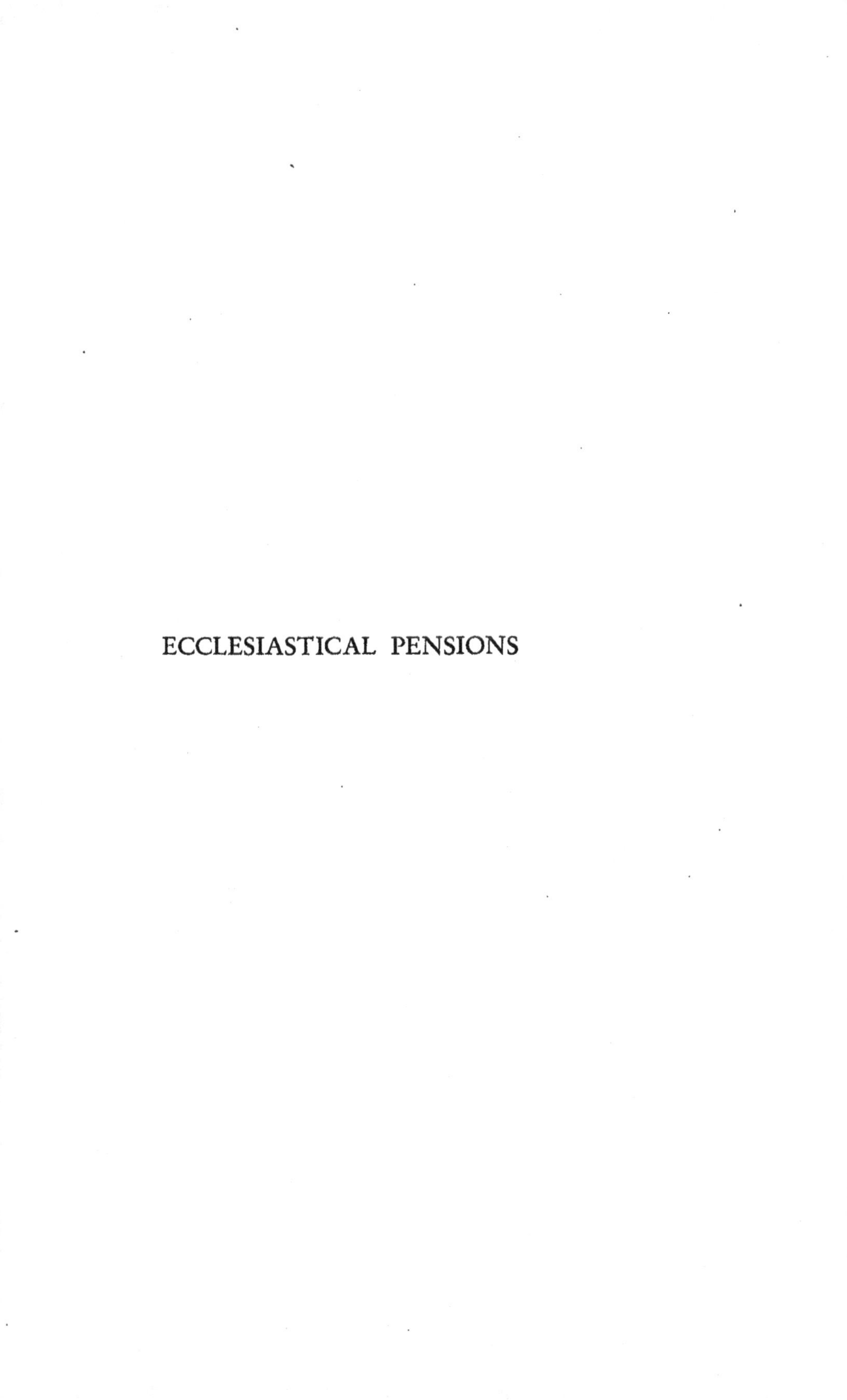

ECCLESIASTICAL PENSIONS

THE CATHOLIC UNIVERSITY OF AMERICA
CANON LAW STUDIES
No. 157

ECCLESIASTICAL PENSIONS

AN HISTORICAL SYNOPSIS AND COMMENTARY

BY

SYLVESTER FRANCIS GASS, M.A., J.C.L.
Priest of the Archdiocese of Milwaukee

A DISSERTATION

Submitted to the Faculty of Canon Law of the Catholic University of America in Partial Fulfillment of the Requirements for the Degree of

DOCTOR OF CANON LAW

THE CATHOLIC UNIVERSITY OF AMERICA PRESS
WASHINGTON, D. C.
1942

NIHIL OBSTAT:

EDUARDUS J. ROELKER, S.T.D., J.C.D.,
Censor Deputatus.
Washingtonii, D. C., die XXIX Maii, 1942.

IMPRIMATUR:

✠ MOYSES ELIAS KILEY, S.T.D.,
Archiepiscopus Milwauchiensis.
Milwauchiae, die XXIX Maii, 1942.

PRINTED IN THE UNITED STATES OF AMERICA
BY THE WATKINS PRINTING CO., BALTIMORE

TO

MY FATHER AND MOTHER

TABLE OF CONTENTS

Foreword ... ix

PART ONE—INTRODUCTION

Definition and Division ... 1
Historical Developments Leading Toward the Ecclesiastical Pension ... 9

PART TWO—HISTORICAL SNYOPSIS

Chapter I

Origin and Development of Ecclesiastical Pensions to the Decree of Gratian (1140) ... 13
Section A. Prior to the Institution of Benefices ... 13
Section B. Pensions on Benefices ... 18
Article 1. The Active Subject of Ecclesiastical Pensions 20
Article 2. The Object of Ecclesiastical Pensions ... 21
Article 3. The Passive Subject of Ecclesiastical Pensions ... 21
Article 4. Conditions for the Establishment of Ecclesiastical Pensions ... 22
Article 5. The Termination of Ecclesiastical Pensions 23

Chapter II

Ecclesiastical Pensions From the Decree of Gratian (1140) to the Council of Trent (1545) ... 24
Article 1. The Active Subject of Ecclesiastical Pensions 24
Article 2. The Object of Ecclesiastical Pensions ... 28
Article 3. The Passive Subject of Ecclesiastical Pensions 30
Article 4. Conditions for the Establishment of Ecclesiastical Pensions ... 33
Article 5. The Termination of Ecclesiastical Pensions 37

Chapter III

Ecclesiastical Pensions From the Council of Trent to the Promulgation of the Code of Canon Law... 40
Article 1. The Active Subject of Ecclesiastical Pensions 40
Article 2. The Object of Ecclesiastical Pensions ... 45

Article 3. The Passive Subject of Ecclesiastical Pensions 47
Article 4. Conditions for the Establishments of Ecclesiastical Pensions 54
Article 5. Rights and Obligations of the Pensioner 63
Article 6. The Termination of Ecclesiastical Pensions 68

PART THREE—COMMENTARY

CHAPTER IV

THE ACTIVE SUBJECT OF ECCLESIASTICAL PENSIONS 79
Article 1. The Holy See 79
Article 2. Local Ordinaries 80
a) *Sede plena* 81
b) *Sede vacante* 82
c) *Sede impedita* 84
Article 3. Cardinals in Their Own Titles and Deaconries 91

CHAPTER V

THE OBJECT OF ECCLESIASTICAL PENSIONS 92
Article 1. The Competence of the Holy See 92
Article 2. The Competence of the Local Ordinary 94

CHAPTER VI

THE PASSIVE SUBJECT OF ECCLESIASTICAL PENSIONS 98
Article 1. Moral Persons 98
Article 2. Physical Persons 98
a) Laymen 98
b) Clerics 100
Scholion. The Effects of canonical irregularity on the capacity to acquire ecclesiastical pensions 112

CHAPTER VII

PERSONS WHO CANNOT ENJOY ECCLESTICAL PENSIONS 115
Article 1. Members of Religious Institutes 115
Scholion. Quasi Religious 118
Article 2. Those Guilty of Crime 119
Article 3. Laicized Clerics 120

CHAPTER VIII

CONDITIONS FOR THE ESTABLISHMENT OF ECCLESIASTICAL PENSIONS 121
Article 1. The Time of Reserving the Pension 121
Article 2. Just Cause 124
Article 3. Formalities 130
a) Interested parties 132
b) The decree 136
Article 4. The Amount of the Pension 138

CHAPTER IX

RIGHTS AND OBLIGATIONS OF THE PENSIONER 150
Scholion. The superfluous income of the pension..... 155

CHAPTER X

THE TERMINATION OF ECCLESIASTICAL PENSIONS 157
a) Alienation 158
b) Termination by default of the benefice 160
c) Prescription 160
d) Expiration of the term of the pension 162
e) Cessation of poverty 162
f) Resignation of pension 163
g) Promotion of pensioner 163
h) Solemn religious profession 164
Scholion. Simple religious profession 166
i) Departure from the clerical state 167
j) Penalties 169
k) Death 171
Scholion. The effects of canonical irregularity on the capacity to retain ecclesiastical pensions..... 172
CONCLUSIONS 173
BIBLIOGRAPHY 175
ABBREVIATIONS 187
BIOGRAPHICAL NOTE 189
ALPHABETICAL INDEX 191
CANON LAW STUDIES 199

FOREWORD

That the Church should be concerned about even the temporal welfare of her members is a fact quite in accord with her nature. Although instituted by Christ for the ultimate eternal salvation of mankind, nevertheless according to man's physico-spiritual nature as well as the status of the Church as a visible society she interests herself also in the temporal needs of her members in the measure in which they will aid her communicants in attaining their final end. By virtue of her divine mission she vindicates for herself the right to have edifices and other sacred places, to possess all temporal means required for her needs and pious works.

It is a commonplace to observe that the temporal welfare of those members who take an intimate part in ministering the faith unto mankind has always had a foremost place among the solicitudes of the Church. When Christ sent the seventy-two disciples to preach and to prepare the people for His coming, He instructed them to equip themselves very lightly and outlined the mode of conduct they were to observe, concluding with the words, "the labourer is worthy of his hire."

The clergy of the early Church were regularly provided for out of the goods of the Church as held and administered by the bishop. Roman law, while making provisions for clerical sustenance, does not contain any positive enactments with regard to ecclesiastical pensions. The only question of extraordinary sustenance that might have arisen during that early period would have been in connection with a bishop who was hindered from receiving the ordinary means of subsistence accruing from his see. It is precisely an instance of this kind, appearing in the fifth century, which is generally pointed to as the first record of an ecclesiastical pension.

From the sixth century onward the goods of the Church were more and more withdrawn from the common holding and the administration of the local bishop. By the eleventh century the ecclesiastical benefice was rather universally established. The cleric occupying a benefice derived his sustenance from the fruits of such a benefice. Some provision, however, had to be made for ecclesiastics who were not incumbents of benefices, but who as clerics nevertheless had a right to maintenance out of church property. One of the more common modes of such support was the ecclesiastical pension.

A consideration of the meaning and divisions of pensions will be followed by a brief résumé of the manner of providing sustenance for clerics during the first five centuries of the Church.

A history of the ecclesiastical pension can be divided into three periods. That which is prior to the Decree of Gratian (about 1140) reveals a pension of a kind, given especially to indigent bishops. This period, however, is more important because it witnessed the development of the benefice, on which the strictly understood ecclesiastical pension properly depends. During the next period, that is, from the Decree of Gratian to the Council of Trent (1545-1563), there is seen the extensive and at times somewhat erratic development of the pension. The great Council of reform considered the abuses that had crept into the pension's administration, and legislated accordingly. The final period to be considered deals principally with the stabilization of the institution. The norms enacted by the Fathers of Trent were studied by canonists and moralists and applied in numerous decisions handed down by the Sacred Congregation of the Council and the Sacred Roman Rota. Subsequent particular legislation, instead of providing new material for possible future general enactments, for the most part reaffirmed the Tridentine legislation.

The main part of this study will consider the law of ecclesiastical pensions according to the Code of canon law. While retaining much of the former law, the Code has clarified certain heretofore doubtful points.

The ecclesiastical pension is less common today than formerly. The subsistence granted by clerical mutual aid societies, both in Europe and in the United States, is not precisely the pension contemplated in canon law. The latter is an extension of the Pauline principle that those who serve at the altar ought to have their share with the altar, and those who preach the gospel should have their living from the gospel. The former, although more practical in regions where well endowed benefices are not abundant, are in many respects not unlike purely secular mutual insurance corporations.

The writer wishes to take this occasion to express his profound gratitude toward His Excellency the Most Reverend Samuel Alphonsus Stritch, D.D., Archbishop of Chicago, formerly of Milwaukee, and to His Excellency the Most Reverend Moses Elias Kiley, S.T.D., Archbishop of Milwaukee, for the opportunity afforded him for graduate studies and for their kind interest. A word of special thanks is also due to the Reverend Raymond L. Newell, J.C.L. The writer acknowledges with heartfelt appreciation the helpful direction of the Faculty of the School of Canon Law of the Catholic University of America; to them and to all other friends who have in any way been of assistance in the preparation of this study the writer feels deeply grateful.

PART ONE
INTRODUCTION

DEFINITION AND DIVISION

The word "pension" is derived by some from the latin *pendeo,* in the sense that it hangs from, rests or depends upon the benefice from which it is drawn, much as usufruct is dependent upon proprietorship.[1]

Others derive the term from *pendo,* denoting a payment at annual intervals.[2] This is quite in accord with the usage of the term in Roman law; for there it commonly signified the individual partial payments of a sum due, made on specified days,[3] and especially the discharge of obligations arising from transactions of letting and hiring,[4] particularly in emphyteusis (lease of land in perpetuity),[5] where it is used interchangeably with *canon, vectigal, reditus,* to denote rent or a fixed sum.[6] To denote rent in *superficies* (the Ro-

[1] " . . . dicitur pensio à pendeo, quia dependet formaliter à beneficio à quo detrahitur, sicut ususfructus à proprietate."—Fagnanus, *Commentaria in quinque libros decretalium* (Romae, 1661), in c. "Ad audientiam," 35, *de rescriptis* [I, 3], n. 49. Cf. Barbosa, *Iuris ecclesiastici universi libri tres* (Lugduni, 1660), Lib. III, c. 11, n. 2. André, *Cours alphabétique et méthodique de droit canonique* (Paris, 1844-46), II, 815.

[2] Barbosa, *Iuris ecclesiastici universi,* Lib. III, c. 11, n. 2; Du Cange, *Glossarium ad scriptores mediae et infimae latinitatis* (ed. nova, Parisiis, 1733-1736), V, 361.

[3] *Vocabularium iurisprudentiae romanae* (Berlin: Walter de Gruyter, 1894-1936), vol. IV, fasc. II, p. 600, § 1. Henceforth cited as *VIR.* Dirksen, *Manuale latinitatis fontium juris civilis Romanorum* (Berolini, 1837), p. 694, "Pensio," § 1.

[4] *VIR.* IV, 600. C. (4.65) 19.

[5] Cf. Gaius, *Institutionum commentarii quattuor* (ed. B. Kuebler, Lipsiae: B. G. Teubner, 1928), 3, 45. Cf. I. (3.24) 3.

[6] Sherman, *Roman Law in the Modern World* (2. ed., New York: Baker, Voorhis & Co., 1922-1924), II, n. 602, note 5. Cf. e.g., C. (11.65) 4; C. (4.66) 2; C. 11 (74.2); C. (4.65) 16; D. (6.3) 1-3.

man long lease of land for purposes of building) the term *pensio* is likewise used, synonymously with *solarium*.[7] Besides the general sense of rent, however, the term also had other special connotations, such as, "charge" or "amount of payment" in a sale,[8] "claims" of a creditor with respect to his debtor,[9] and a refund credited to an account.[10]

The term *pensio* was also very commonly used instead of *stipendium* to denote tributes or taxes.[11] The term appears in legislation concerning private citizens and their relationships with phases of military activity. Thus, the word denoted requisition for transport and repairs of arms.[12] In another place *pensio* was used in reference to charges or contributions which householders were forbidden to demand on the occasion of quartering soldiers, as this was a duty of the householder.[13]

In modern secular law the term in cne of its meanings has been carried over with much of the same sense as in Roman law, denoting either a payment for the use of a thing, or again, rent payed for the use and occupation of another's house.[14]

[7] Sherman, *op. cit.*, II, 609, note 49. Richer (*Dictionarium juris civilis, canonici et feudalis necnon delectus legum feudalium* [Taurini, 1792]), pointing to D. (12.6) 55, states: "Pensio proprie est merces inhabitationis aedium alienarum." Cf. e.g., C. (4.32) 14; C. (4.65) 3; C. (11.70) 1; C. (1.5) 8.5; C. (8.14) 7; D. (6.1) 73.1; D. (6.1) 74; D. (43.18) 2.

[8] C. (11.3) 2.1-3.

[9] C. (4.63) 1.

[10] C. (9.27) 5.

[11] C. Th. (16.2) 36; C. (11.66) 2.2. Cf. Constitution of the Emperor Honorius against the Donatists (414).—Baluzius, *Nova collectio conciliorum* (Parisiis, 1683), I, 358. In canon law cf. St. Gregory I (590-604), Ep. II, 38: *Petro subdiacono Siciliae* (592). — *Monumenta Germaniae Historica* (Berlin: Weidmann, Hannover: Hahn, Leipzig: Karl W. Hiersemann, 1877-), *Epistolae*, I, pars 1, *Gregorii I Papae registrum epistolarum, Libri I-IV* (ed. Paulus Ewald, 1887), 134, 136. Henceforth the general collection will be designated *MGH*. Cf. also Nicholas V (1447-1455), indult to Amedeo VIII, duke of Savoia, *apud* Moroni, *Dizionario di erudizione storico-ecclesiastica* (Venezia, 1840-1879), LXI, 159-160; Benedict XIV (1740-1758), Concordat with Ferdinand VI, *apud* Moroni, *ibid.*, LXVIII, 150. Henceforth cited as Moroni, *Dizionario*.

[12] C. (12.50) 22.

[13] C. (12.40) 9. 4.

Thus far from a consideration of the etymology of the word it can be seen that the term is used to refer to what accrues to a person from his own holdings. There is another sense in which the term refers to what one obtains from the goods of another.[15]

This is the sense of the ecclesiastical pension: one which is imposed upon the revenues of the Church, whatever they may be.[16] It is the imposing of an obligation to pay a certain revenue to a third party.[17] In the sense in which it will be primarily considered in this study, a pension may be described in a general way as a definite portion of the income of a benefice.[18]

An ecclesiastical pension may be defined as the right to receive each year a part of the fruits from a benefice not one's own (or from other ecclesiastical revenues), established for a just cause by an ecclesiastical superior in behalf of a cleric.[19]

Ecclesiastical pensions can be divided broadly into temporal, spiritual, and mixed. Temporal pensions are payments for services whether rendered by lay persons (lay or civil pensions), e. g., papal guards,

[14] Shumaker-Longsdorf, *The Cyclopedic Law Dictionary* (2. ed., Chicago: Callaghan and Company, 1922), p. 755, adducing Calvini, *Lexicon juridicum*.

[15] Bersano, *Tractatus de compensationibus* (Mediolani, 1691), c. 2, q. 8, n. 1-2.

[16] Prompsault, *Dictionnaire raisonné de droit et de jurisprudence en matière civile ecclésiastique* (Paris, 1849), III, 95.

[17] D'Angelo, *Tasse e pensioni nel codice di diritto canonico* (2. ed. cor. et ampl., Torino: L. I. C. E., 1927), p. 117.

[18] Hinschius, *Das Kirchenrecht der Katholiken und Protestanten in Deutschland* (Berlin, 1869-1897), vols. I-IV, *System des katholischen Kirchenrechts* (Berlin, 1869-1888), II, 412. Henceforth cited as Hinschius.

[19] Ius percipiendi singulis annis partem fructuum ex alieno beneficio (vel aliis proventibus ecclesiasticis) auctoritate competentis Superioris ecclesiastici cuipiam clerico iusta de causa constitutum.—Cf. Wernz, *Ius decretalium* (Romae et Prati, 1898-1905), II, 321, III, who, however, does not explicitly mention the cleric as the exclusive recipient of a pension; Reiffenstuel (*Ius canonicum universum* [Paris, 1864-1882], Lib. III, tit. 12, n. 84—hereafter cited as Reiffenstuel), De Angelis (*Praelectiones juris canonici* [Romae, 1877-1887], Lib. III, tit. 12, 7°) as also Ferraris (*Bibliotheca canonica*, etc. [Romae, 1885-1892], "Pensio," n. 5) omit "*singulis annis*." Sipos (*Enchiridion iuris canonici* [Pécs, "Haladás R. T.", 1926], p. 734) adds to "*ex alieno beneficio*" the parenthetical "*(vel aliis proventibus ecclesiasticis)*."

knights, and other employees of the Church,[20] or by clerics, but for services of a material, rather than a strictly spiritual nature involving power of orders or jurisdiction, e. g., organists, sacristans, chanters, procurators. Spiritual pensions are conferred upon clerics while rendering services of a spiritual nature but not pertaining to a benefice, e. g., salaries of preachers, assistants in parishes,[21] chaplains. Mixed pensions are those conferred upon clerics usually in consideration of services rendered in the past.[22]

From the mode of conferring, it can be *in titulum ordinationis,* as a subsidiary title of ordination to sacred orders,[23] or *in titulum beneficii,* accruing from the fruits of some benefice on which it is imposed.[24] On the other hand, a pension can be conferred *in stipendium, a)* for a present spiritual ministry to which, however, no benefice is joined, e. g., preaching, or *b)* for temporary maintenance, e. g., while a cleric is continuing studies, or *c)* most properly, for spiritual ministrations performed, e. g., for an aged cleric, or one otherwise incapacitated.

A clerical pension is called *pensio beneficialis* when it is drawn

[20] Cf. Pius XI, motu propr. *De pensionibus ordinandis,* 31 dec. 1937—*Acta Apostolicae Sedis, Commentarium Officiale* (Romae, 1909-), XXX (1938), 33-50. Henceforth cited as *AAS*.

[21] Cf. Ferreres, *Compendium theologiae moralis* (14. ed., Barcinone: Eugenius Subirana, 1928), I, 695; Hannan, *The Canon Law of Wills* (Philadelphia: The Dolphin Press, 1935), n. 313, p. 199.

[22] Cf. St. Alphonsus Liguori, *Theologia moralis* (ed. nova . . . cura et studio P. Leonardi Gaudé, C.SS.R., Romae: ex typographia Vaticana, 1905-1912), Lib. III, n. 491, q. 6; La-Croix, *Theologia moralis* (Venetiis, 1761), Tom. II, Lib. IV, art. 6, q. 170-186, n. 1116; F. Suarez, *Opera omnia* (ed. nova a Carolo Berton, Parisiis, 1856-1878), Lib. IV, *de simonia,* c. XXVI, n. 5.

[23] Cf. canon 979, § 4; Wernz-Vidal, *Ius canonicum* (Romae: Universitas Gregoriana, 1927-1938), IV, pars 1 *(De rebus),* n. 225, II; Cappello, *Tractatus canonico-moralis de sacramentis* (1.-4. ed., Taurinorum Augustae: Marietti, 1932-1939), II, pars 3, n. 426, stating that the pension of canon 1429, § 1 is not sufficient as title of ordination.

[24] Cf. c. 6, X, *de clericis non residentibus,* III, 4; c. 30, X, *de praebendis et dignitatibus,* III, 5; Reiffenstuel, Lib. III, tit. 5, nn. 86, 87. "Pensions are not benefices even though they are paid out of the income of a benefice, unless they are government pensions established by concordat in lieu of resti-

on the fruits of a benefice, while if derived from other ecclesiastical goods it is known as *pensio communis*.[25]

From the viewpoint of duration ecclesiastical pensions can be temporary or perpetual. The former [26] are such as have been decreed to run only for a time, either predetermined or conditioned by future circumstances, such as completion of studies or recovery of health, when the cleric will be able to take up or resume the active ministry.[27] Temporary pensions never last beyond the life of the incumbent of the benefice.[28] Perpetual pensions are either relatively or absolutely perpetual. Relatively perpetual pensions are reserved for the life of the pensioner, the obligation to pay them passing to the successors in the benefice.[29] Absolutely perpetual pensions are imposed in such a way that the obligation to pay them passes to all incumbents of the benefice so burdened, and with the death of one pensioner are to be transferred to a new pensioner.[30] Absolutely perpetual pensions are likewise those reserved for moral persons, parishes, seminaries, and the like. The Code makes no mention of absolutely perpetual pensions. Only the Holy See is competent to reserve them, as it has done in the past.

Authors have discussed at great length whether a pension may be considered as a benefice. A distinction was made between a pension assigned by title (*in titulum beneficii*) and one assigned as remun-

tution of confiscated benefices; Ferreres, *Theol. Mor.*, I, 695-697."—Hannan, *The Canon Law of Wills*, p. 193, note 124. For the distinction between benefices and pensions, *v. infra*, p. 5-8.

[25] Noval, *Commentarium codicis iuris canonici, Liber IV, De processibus* (Romae: Marietti, 1920-1932), part. II-III, n. 589. To be cited: *De processibus*, II.

[26] This is the *pensio personalis* of canon 1412, 4°, according to Blat, *Commentarium codicis iuris canonici* (Romae: Collegio Angelico, 1921-1938), Lib. III, part. 2-6 (ed. 2, 1934), n. 315.

[27] Cf. Hinschius, II, 413.

[28] Canon 1429, § 1.

[29] Cf. canon 1429, § 2. Commissio Pontificia ad codicis canones authentice interpretandos, *Dubia*, 20 maii, 1923, IX.—AAS, XVI (1924), 116. This Commission will be referred to as C. P. I.

[30] Wernz, *Ius decretalium*, II, n. 321, III; De Angelis, *Praelectiones*, Lib. III, tit. 12, n. 7; Sipos, *Enchiridion iuris canonici*, p. 734; Ferraris, "Pensio," nn. 2-4; D'Angelo, *Tasse e pensioni*, p. 118-119.

eration (*in stipendium*). The former might occur where a church enjoyed an abundant revenue but was without a regular minister. The legitimate authority could then designate it as a perpetual benefice, e. g., a perpetual vicarship for a cleric to whom would be assigned a portion of the fruits of that church to be received annually.[31] It was expressly taught that a definite pension by title of benefice could be established on the revenues of a church, and thus on one benefice another could be erected, as long as enough remained for the first beneficiary to sustain him fittingly and as long as it was not done in fraud,[32] which was forbidden by Innocent III (1198-1216) in the Fourth Council of the Lateran (1215).[33] The older authors rather commonly concluded that a pension conferred *in titulum* is properly and truly an ecclestiastical benefice, citing a chapter in the Decretals.[34] Nor does it matter whether such an arrangement is called pension rather than benefice, when as a matter of fact such a pension, given *in titulum* and conferring a perpetual right to the fruits of ecclesiastical goods, is adequately covered by the definition of a benefice.[35] They are pensions in the full sense of the word, and yet the rules for benefices apply to them as well.[36] Pallottini, however, denies this,[37] and adduces as his authorities Boniface VIII (1294-

[31] Cf. c. 6, X, *de clericis non residentibus*, III, 4.

[32] Fagnanus, in c. "Ad audientiam" [31], X, *de rescriptis* [I, 3], nn. 41-47, pointing to many other authors; Reiffenstuel, Lib. III, tit. 5, nn. 86-87; Ferraris, "Pensio," n. 3.

[33] C. 32=c. 30, X, *de praebendis et dignitatibus*, III, 5: "Illud autem penitus interdicimus, ne quis in fraudem de proventibus ecclesiae, quae curam habere debet proprii sacerdotis, pensionem alii quasi pro beneficio conferre praesumat."

[34] C. 6, X, *de clericis non residentibus*, III, 4. As expressly holding this view, suffice it to mention Covarrubias (1512-1577), *Liber quaestionum practicarum* (Lugduni, 1594), c. 36, n. 10, "Quoties . . . "; Fagnanus, in c. "Ad audientiam" [31], X, *de rescriptis*, [I, 3], nn. 44, 46, where he infers with others that in rescripts pertaining to benefices mention must be made of such a pension. Cf. Ferraris, "Pensio," n. 6; Reiffenstuel, Lib. III, tit. 5, n. 90.

[35] Fagnanus, *ibid.*, nn. 44, 45, citing numerous other authors; Reiffenstuel, *ibid.*, n. 91.

[36] Hinschius, II, 413, note 6. Reiffenstuel, *ibid.*, n. 90.

[37] *Collectio omnium conclusionum et resolutionum quae in causis propo-*

1303) [38] and a decision of the Sacred Congregation of the Council.[39]

With reference to the other group of pensions—those granted *in stipendium* or the temporary, personal pensions—hardly any author maintains that these are ecclesiastical benefices.[40] Fagnanus (1598-1678)[41] maintained that in unfavorable matters they do not come under the name of benefices;[42] not so, however, in favorable matters. He substantiated his position by citing the Sacred Congregation of the Council [43] and a reply of Gregory XIII (1572-1585) to a question proposed to him by the Congregation on July 19, 1577. The Pontiff answered that in favorable matters, such as the *privilegium fori,* under consideration, a pension comes within the scope of a benefice. Whereupon the Congregation on August 8 of the same year stated that the distinction be observed and that the rescript be issued accordingly.[44]

A pronouncement of the Sacred Congregation of the Council rendered in the last century declared on the contrary that it is the most approved opinion of canonists that there is a very broad distinction between pensions and benefices, and that there is no similarity in their natures.[45]

sitis apud Sacram Congregationem Cardinalium S. Concilii Tridentini interpretum prodierunt ab eius institutione anno MDLXIV ad annum MDCCCLX (Romae, 1890), "Pensio," n. 3: "Unde pensio ecclesiastica, sive detur in stipendium sive in titulum nunquam venit appellatione beneficii."—Hereafter this work will be cited as Pallottini.

[38] " . . . si alicui usque ad certam summam provideri mandamus, ei non in pensione, sed in beneficiis ecclesiasticis tantum volumus provideri, nisi de pensione in nostris litteris mentio habeatur expressa." C. 4, *de praebendis et dignitatibus,* III, 4, in VI°.

[39] In *Elboren.* Dubiorum, 2 aug. 1721, §Pro parte vero, arguing from c. 31, X, *de rescriptis,* I, 3.

[40] "Ein kirchliches Benefizium ist die Pension nicht."—Hinschius, II, 417.

[41] In c. "Ad audientiam" [31], X, *de rescriptis* [I, 3], n. 117.

[42] Reg. 15, R. J., in VI°

[43] In c. "Cum in cunctis" [7], X, *de electione et electi potestate,* [I, 6] n. 103.

[44] In c. "Ad audientiam" [31], X, *de rescriptis,* [I, 3], n. 134. Cf. Reiffenstuel, Lib. III, tit. 5, n. 92-98.

[45] *In Faventina,* "Pensionis," 17 dec. 1836, §Hic.—Pallottini, "Pensio," n. 1, citing Lotterius, Pichler, Zondatus, Garcias, Reiffenstuel in support of this position.

The entire discussion, therefore, seems to be a matter of an insufficiently clear concept and a defective circumscription of the notes entering into a precise definition. A clerical pension, according to the definition already given,[46] is a source of income derived from a benefice not one's own. It is, moreover, generally not connected with any office, but rather given for support (*alimentorum causa*) in consideration for services rendered in the past. In the case of due remuneration for services to be rendered the term *honorarium*, emolument, compensation, or a similar one might be more correctly applied.[47] Finally, the note of perpetuity is absent from the concept of a pension, as it perdures either for the life of the pensioner or of the beneficiary. Absolutely perpetual pensions are the exceptions. The so-called *pensio in titulum beneficii* amounts to a benefice for all practical purposes, as in the case of a perpetual vicarship, and is but improperly called a pension.[48]

[46] V. *supra*, p. 3.

[47] Cf. S. C. C., *In nullius Foropompilii*, 21 aug. 1819, § Ea.—Pallottini, "Pensio," n. 2.

[48] Hinschius, II, 417. Cf. canons 1409, for the definition of a benefice; 1412, 1°, excluding a temporary parochial vicarship from the concept of a benefice; 1412, 4°, expressly stating that a personal pension is not a benefice; 1429, treating of pensions, considers only personal pensions.

HISTORICAL DEVELOPMENTS LEADING TOWARD THE ECCLESIASTICAL PENSION

In the early days of the Church all goods were held in common.[1] Under this primitive arrangement of common ownership the offerings of the faithful were deposited with the bishop and administered by him, generally with the assistance of one of his deacons, often known as the archdeacon, and more commonly in the East by a priest called the econome. St. Ignatius of Antioch († 107) mentions this phase of work of those who were, however, first of all "ministers of the mysteries of Jesus Christ." [2] It is recorded that Pope St. Lucius (253-254) before entering upon his martyrdom entrusted the administration of his flock to the archdeacon Stephen.[3] Similarly, in the life of Pope St. Sixtus (257-258) it is related that he was attended by the archdeacon Lawrence.[4] After the peace of the Church and the legal recognition of her existence the practice continued for several more centuries. As late as the sixth century it was expressly stated that it is the obligation of the bishop to provide for the poor and the disabled infirm.[5]

Although originally the goods were distributed according to individual particular needs, the practice arose around and after the year 400 of dividing the ecclesiastical goods into three or four parts. One of these parts was directed toward the support of clerics. The fourfold division was observed in the Roman provinces, elsewhere the threefold division was in vogue.[6]

1 Acts II, 44-45; IV, 32-35; V, 1-4.

2 *Epistola ad Trallianos*, II, 3: "Non enim ciborum et potuum diaconi sunt, sed ecclesiae Dei ministri."—Journel, *Enchiridion patristicum* (ed. 8. et 9., Friburgi Brisgoviae: Herder & Co., 1932), n. 48; Funk, *Patres apostolici*, (2. ed., Tubingae, 1901), I, 242.

3 *Le Liber pontificalis*, texte, introduction et commentaire par l'abbé Duchesne (Paris, 1886-1892), I, 153.

4 *Liber pontificalis*, ed. Duchesne, I, 155.

5 I Council of Orleans (511), c. 16.—Mansi, *Sacrorum conciliorum nova et amplissima collectio* (Florentiae, *postea* Parisiis, Leipzig, Arnhem, 1901-1927), VIII, 354=c. 1, D. LXXXII. To be cited as Mansi.

6 Cf. Lesne, *Histoire de la propriété ecclésiastique en France*, Mémoirs et

The continued growth of the Church, the increase of donations, the more permanent establishment of Christian communities away from the centers of population, the acquisition of real property,—all these were factors which militated against the early communal spirit. Thus it came about little by little that the goods of the Church were no longer exclusively held and administered by the bishop. This was true particularly in the West, where rural baptismal churches had their own property by the sixth century.[7]

An interesting note in the trend away from centralized holdings of ecclesiastical goods appears in north central France, where the holders of feudal estates were desirous of having resident clerics attend oratories within their territories—the so-called proprietary churches. The bishops of these praedial regions had the final voice in admitting a cleric to the praedial oratories, but the founders had the obligation of providing for his proper maintenance.[8]

By the ninth century[9] the rights granted to clerics to use for life the fruits accruing from real property and joined permanently with ecclesiastical offices came to be called benefices after the manner of the feudal fiefs or benefices. It was a consequence of the proprietary church system, and was later extended to bishoprics.[10] The term had appeared previously in canonical literature, but only in the

travaux, publiés par des professeurs de facultés catholiques de Lille (Lille, 1910), vol. 1. Stutz, *Geschichte des kirchlichen Benefizialwesens von seinen Anfängen bis auf die Zeit Alexanders III* (Berlin, 1895). Buonocore, *Il "Titulus canonicus"* (Napoli: Enrico Maria Muca, 1933), p. 154.

[7] E.g., Council of Agde (506), c. 7.—Mansi, VIII, 325. Leclerq (Hefele-Leclerq, *Histoire des conciles* [tr. from 12. German ed., Paris: Letouzey & Ané, 1908-], tom. II, part. 2, p. 984, ft. n. 1) would cite this as the earliest indication of the later ecclesiastical benefice, although this opinion must be rejected in the light of more recent information on medieval benefices.

[8] IV Council of Orleans (541) cc. 7, 31.—Mansi, IX, 114, 119.

[9] *Capitulary of Louis the Pious* (817), c. 10.—*MGH, Leges*, sect. II, *Capitularia Regum Francorum* (ed. A. Boretius, 1883), I, 277. Cf. also Council of Worms (858), c. 50.—*MGH, Leges*, sect. III, *Concilia*, II, *Concilia aevi Karolini I* (recogn. Albertus Werminghof, 1904-1908), pars 2, p. 821: *Canones Wormatiensi falso adscripti*=c. 25, C. XXIII, q. 8, palea.

[10] Wernz-Vidal, *Ius canonicum*, II *(De personis)*, n. 145; Hinschius, II, 367; Hohenlohe, *Grundlegende Fragen des Kirchenrechts* (Wien: Kommissionsverlag, 1931), pp. 80-129.

general sense of a benefit or an advantage.[11] It is not until the eleventh century, however,[12] that we find the term in its restricted sense of a "firmly rooted income joined to an ecclesiastical office and flowing from ecclesiastical property for the benefit of the incumbent."[13]

After the breakdown of the common life in cathedral and collegiate foundations, after the division of goods between the bishop and the canons, and after another division of the *massa capitularis* amongst the individual canons, the portions for the latter, called prebends, were likewise regarded as prebendary benefices to distinguish them from parochial benefices.[14]

As the common ownership and administration of ecclesiastical goods by the bishop waned and as the concept of the canonical benefice became crystallized, it became necessary also to revamp the Church's program of providing for the support of the cleric who was not an active incumbent of a benefice. One of the more important methods employed was that of the clerical pension.

[11] C. 6 [Hieronymus ad Titum], C. VIII, q. 1. Hinschius (II, 367) proves that cc. 1, 2, C. I, q. 3, which forbid the obtaining of ecclesiastical benefices by simony, although attributed to Gregory I (590-604), are much more probably enactments of Gregory VII (1073-1085); thus also Jaffé, *Regesta Pontificum Romanorum* (ed. 2., Lipsiae, 1885-1888), JL, n. 5278. Henceforth cited as JK (*ab condita ecclesia ad annum DXC*, ed. F. Kaltenbrunner); JE (*ab anno DXC ad annum DCCCLXXXII*, ed. P. Ewald); JL (*ab anno DCCCLXXXII usque ad annum MCXCVIII*, ed. S. Loewenfeld).

[12] Alexander II (1061-1073), *Epistola* (?1068)—*JK*, n. 4722; Mansi, XIX, 986-987=c. 9, C. I, q. 3: "Constituimus itaque . . . , ut nullus deinceps episcoporum beneficium ecclesiae, quod quidem canonicam (canoniam) vel praebendas seu etiam ordines vocant, pro aliquo pretio vel munere clericis audeat unquam conferre." Canonry, prebends, or orders were all included under the term "benefice." The Code of canon law (c. 1409) has removed all uncertainty as to the sense of the term.

[13] Hinschius, II, 367.

[14] C. 32 [Gregory IX (1227-1241)], X, *de rescriptis*, I, 3; c. 8 [Innocent III (1198-1216)], c. 30 [Honorius III (1216-1227)], X, *de concessione praebendae et ecclesiae non vacantis*, III, 8. Cf. Hinschius, II, 367; Thomassinus, *Vetus et nova Ecclesiae disciplina circa beneficia et beneficiarios* (Magontiaci, 1787), Pars III, lib. 2, c. 23, n. 35 (henceforth cited as Thomassinus); Schneider, *Die Entwicklung der bischöflichen Domkapitel* (Mainz, 1882), p. 41-50, 61-84.

PART II

HISTORICAL SYNOPSIS

CHAPTER I

ORIGIN AND DEVELOPMENT OF ECCLESIASTICAL PENSIONS TO THE DECREE OF GRATIAN (1140)

SECTION A. PRIOR TO THE INSTITUTION OF BENEFICES

The mode of holding goods in common, which prevailed in the early Church, took care of providing for the temporal needs of the clergy in ordinary cases; for every bishop attended to the needs of the clerics ministering under his jurisdiction. There was a problem, however, in the extraordinary case of the head of a see who for any number of reasons might have been separated from his diocese, thereby terminating his active ministry. One finds in these cases the basic elements of what were to be known in later centuries as clerical pensions: due support granted to one who had been deprived of his office and its fruits.

The first clear record of such a pension is found in the acts of the Council of Chalcedon (451).[1] In the matter of Domnus, former bishop of Antioch, session X of this Council[2] relates that Maximus, bishop of Antioch, requested of the Council that he be permitted to

[1] Thomassinus, Pars III, lib. 2, c. 29, n. 3; Hinschius, II, 412; Wernz, *Ius decretalium*, II, n. 321.

[2] Thus Mansi, VII, 269-272, although not only is there uncertainty as to the original position of this case in the acts of the Council, but even its genuineness is questioned. Codex Bohierianus places it before *actio* VII, while a Vatican manuscript places it within the same *actio*. It is placed after *actio* VII in the edition of Petrus Crabbe (1528), who adds that it was found in some older codices but ascribes it to Proculus and Albinius, German scholastics. The *actio* is wanting in the Greek Codex, nor does it appear in the codex of Monte Casino. Stephanus Baluzius finds evidence for it in the Vatican codices and the works of Cardinal Casanate transmitted to him.—Mansi, VII, 270, 638, 660. Hefele (*Conciliengeschichte* [2. ed., Freiburg

assign a certain portion of the fruits of the church of Antioch for the support of his predecessor. In this first instance of a pension several important characteristics are noteworthy. The present and former incumbents of the see could not make any agreements between themselves without the intervening authority of the Council. Maximus, on whom the burden would fall, had freely requested it. The amount sought was only as much as would assure the future support of Domnus. The cause for the pension was the fostering of peace and concord. It was conferred with the authority of the Supreme Pontiff, the consent of the Council, and the assent of the royal judges. To safeguard the occupant of the see and those entrusted to his administration of ecclesiastical goods, the amount of the pension was limited to the necessary allowances for decent sustenance.[3] The same Council acted on the controversy between the deposed Bassianus and the substituted Stephanus, both claiming the see of Ephesus.[4] It was decided that a third bishop be elected, since neither Bassianus nor Stephanus had obtained the see in accordance with the canons. They were permitted to retain the episcopal dignity, and were to receive annually out of the income of the church of Ephesus 200 gold *solidi* apiece for their sustenance.[5] Worthy of note is the fact that here, too, the pension was assigned only with the consent of the entire Council, and that the royal judges not only gave their assent but also assigned the sum of money which was then approved by the Council.[6] It will also be observed that the amount was to be paid at regular annual intervals.

im Breisgau, 1875], II, 491, n. 1) puts it at the end of session IX. Schwartz (*Acta conciliorum oecumenicorum, iussu atque mandato Societatis scientiarum argentoratensis edidit Eduardus Schwartz* [Strassburg, 1914; deinde Berolini, Lipsiae: Walter de Gruyter, 1922-], Tom. II, vol. 1, pars 3, p. xxii) assigns it to *actio* XI, stating that it is not to be found in the original edition.

Phillips (*Kirchenrecht* [Regensburg, 1855-1889], VII, 304) suggests that possibly the first record of a pension is the case of Eustathius, former bishop of Pamphylia, whose case is found in an *epistola* at the end of *actio* VII of the Council of Ephesus (431)—in Mansi, IV, 1475-1477.

[3] Thomassinus, Pars III, lib. 2, c. 29, n. 3.

[4] *Actio XI-XII.*—Mansi, VII, 271-300; Schwartz, ed., *Acta conciliorum oecumenicorum*, Tom. II, vol. 1, pars 3, pp. 44-53.

[5] Mansi, VII, 299; Schwartz, *ibid.*, pp. 52-53.

[6] Thomassinus, *ibid.*, n. 4.

In session XIV of the same Council another case between two bishops was decided. The see was given to him who appeared to have the right to it, while the other was accorded an annual pension, the amount to be regulated according to the income of the diocese.[7]

An interesting manner of supporting a dethroned bishop is narrated by Gregory, Archbishop of Tours (538/9–593/4). Faustinus, Bishop of Aix, was deposed in the Council of Mâcon (583),[8] and Bertramnus, Orestes, and Palladius, who had consecrated him, were ordered to support him and to give him 100 *aurei* each year.[9]

In the case of Bishop Contumeliosus who had been deposed by a provincial council, Pope St. Agapetus I (535-536) decreed that while the administration of the patrimony of the church was entrusted to the archdeacon, care should be taken that the Bishop be not deprived of sufficient means of livelihood.[10]

The same Pontiff made provision for those African bishops who, having abjured their Arian tenets, were received back into the true fold; but they were not allowed to engage in any functions of the church nor to aspire to higher honors.[11]

The letters of Pope St. Gregory the Great (590-604) abound with cases in which provision was made for bishops deprived of their source of support. Thus, from the very first year of his pontificate he was concerned about the bishops who had been expelled from their sees. If there was no hope of immediate restoration of their see, or at least of gathering its fruits, the other resident bishops were enjoined in the meantime to provide for their sustenance.[12]

[7] Mansi, VII, 314-358; Schwartz, *op. cit.*, pp. 60-62.

[8] *MGH, Leges*, sec. III: *Concilia*, tom. I, pp. 155-161; Mansi, IX, 931-938.

[9] Gregory of Tours, *Historia Francorum*, Lib. VIII, 20.—*MGH, Scriptores rerum merovingicarum* (ed. W. Arndt et B. Krusch, 1884), I, *Gregorii Turonensis opera*, pars 1, p. 338. Cf. Thomassinus, Pars III, lib. 2, c. 29, n. 18.

[10] *Ep. VII.*—Mansi, VIII, 856-857; JK, n. 890. Cf. Thomassinus, *ibid.*, n. 19.

[11] *Ep. II.*—Mansi, VIII, 849. Thomassinus (*ibid.*, n. 6) observes that this can hardly be called a pension: they merely shared in the *sportulae*, or daily distribution of goods.

[12] Ioannes Diaconus (IX cent.), *Vita Gregorii I*, lib. III, § 16.—Migne, *Patrologiae cursus completus, series latina* (Paris, 1844-1864), LXXV, 140; hereafter to be cited as *MPL*.

The prefect of Illyria had decreed that the bishops driven from their dioceses by war should be received and maintained by those bishops who were still in possession of their sees. The Pontiff called to their attention another mandate even greater, namely, that of the eternal Prince. These bishops should receive their oppressed brethren of the episcopate willingly and support them according to the means of their own see. The exiled bishops were to have no jurisdiction in the diocese; they were to be treated as guests, without anything even approaching a division of a diocese, receiving only that which was necessary.[13]

The biographer of St. Gregory the Great tells of three cases where bishops for reasons of health were compelled to retire from their active ministry. The Pope accepted their voluntary resignation but required that an amount sufficient for their maintenance be set aside from the income of their former sees.[14]

In these early days when the concept of a pension was not yet clearly formed, cases are found where, besides the heads of dioceses, also certain other clerics inferior to bishops enjoyed such an accommodation. When members of the cathedral clergy were assigned to another church or entered a religious order, the bishop could permit them to continue to receive by way of pension that portion of the fruits which they had been wont to receive while in the service of the cathedral. Although it seemed preferable to the III Council of Orleans (538) that such should be sufficiently provided for by their new titles, it nevertheless left the matter to the prudence of the bishops.[15]

Similarly, priests who had been suspended from the active ministry because of certain crimes, while they might never be restored

[13] Gregorius I (590-604), *Ep.* I, 43; *Ad universos episcopos per Illiricum.*—*MGH, Epistolae,* I, 69; Mansi, IX, 1065. For a similar provision cf. *idem, Ep.* XIV, 8, to Boniface, deacon at Constantinople (603).—*MGH, Epistolae,* II, 2, 427-428.

[14] Ioannes Diaconus (IX cent.), *Vita Gregorii I,* Lib. IV, § 39.—*MPL,* LXXV, 201, 202. Cf. Gregory I, *Ep.,* IX, 138, *Maximiano Episcopo Ravennae* (599).—*MGH, Epistolae,* II, 1, 136; *Ep.* XI, 29, *Anatolio Diacono Constantinopolim* [sic] (601).—*MGH, Epistolae,* II, 2, 299-300; *Ep.* XIII, 8, *Aetherio Episcopo* (602).—*MGH, Epistolae,* II, 2, 373-374.

[15] C. 18.—Mansi, IX, 171; Thomassinus, Pars III, lib. 2, c. 29, n. 20.

to office, were nevertheless to be assured a fitting maintenance. Thus Perpetuus, Bishop of Tours, forbade that two ex-pastors should ever be reinstated, but required that they should be provided for by their parishes as long as they lived.[16]

A certain deacon, Felix, charged with schism was examined by Pope St. Gregory (590-604) and found repentant. Whereupon the Pontiff entreated the Bishop of Syracuse to receive him into his church and restore him to the office of deacon, or at least allow him a portion of the emolument for his needs, adding that he himself would share in supporting the deacon by a small annual allowance from the church of Rome.[17]

The same illustrious Pontiff, in sending certain clerics to monasteries to do penance, desired that a certain amount be set aside for their maintenance, lest they be a burden to the religious community.[18]

Clerics who were ill might be provided for in a similar way. Thus St. Gregory the Great ordered Bishop Candidus to pay to an ailing cleric the "usual" sum.[19]

On another occasion Gregory reproved Maximinianus, Bishop of Syracuse, for having excommunicated an infirm abbot, for whom he commanded that necessaries be provided.[20]

By the middle of the seventh century, when rural parishes began to have considerable revenues, the bishops in selecting these parish priests to be members of the cathedral clergy, permitted them to retain the title to their parishes and the right to the fruits with the exception of such an amount as was necessary for the decent maintenance of the priest who took care of the parish. The pastors re-

[16] D'Achery, *Spicilegium sive collectio veterum aliquot scriptorum* (Parisiis, 1723), I, 303. Cf. Thomassinus, *ibid.*, n. 21.

[17] *Ep.* IV, 14 (593).—*MGH, Epistolae*, I, 1, 247; JE, n. 1285. Mansi (IX, 1165) reports this letter as III, 14.

[18] *Ep.* I, 42 (591).—*MGH, Epistolae*, I, 67. Cf. *Ep.* I, 18 (591).—*MGH, Epistolae*, I, 23-24.

[19] *Ep.* II, 11.—*MGH, Epistolae*, I, 109-110. Thomassinus (*ibid.*, c. 14, n. 2-3) regards this as merely a proper share of the fourth portion of church goods distributed amongst the clergy.

[20] *Ep.* II, 35.—*MGH, Epistolae*, I, 131. Cf. *Ep.* II, 31.—*MGH, ibid.*, 127-128.

ceived an allowance also from the cathedral, which was described as a gift, lest it be charged that they held two titles.[21]

Section B. Pensions on Benefices

The administration of ecclesiastical temporalities passed through a period of fundamental change during the Merovingian (500-752) and the Carolingian era (752-911 in Germany, 752-987 in France). In the early sixth century Pope St. Symmachus (498-514) sent a letter to Caesarius of Arles,[22] which in the opinion of Baronius reveals the origin of the ecclesiastical benefice.[23]

Historical records of clerical pensions formally depending on benefices are very few prior to the twelfth century, although paradoxically there was yet much freedom and little restricting or qualifying legislation on the matter of pensions. Thomassinus (1619-1695) suggests that this meagerness, at least for the early middle ages, was due to the yet imperfect stage attained in the development of benefices, which consisted solely [sic] of distributions. These allotments consisted of moderate provisions of food and clothing. Canons against alienation of ecclesiastical property made it impossible for one who was receiving these necessaries of life to seek the same and greater

[21] Council of Merida (666), c. XII.—Mansi, XI, 82; Thomassinus, Lib. III, pars 2, c. 29, n. 22; André, *Course alphabétique et méthodique de droit canonique*, II, 816-817.

[22] *Ep.* V, § 1.—Mansi, VIII, 212. In a footnote Mansi (*ibid.*) notes that the *Coll. Isid.* designates this document as *Decretum I*, while the Jesuit ms. in Paris of *Coll. Dionys.* allocates this as *Constitutum II Conc. sub Symmacho.* There is disagreement as to the year of issuance. For A.D. 502: Mansi, *loc. cit.*; Baronius (*Annales ecclesiastici auctore Caesare Baronio, una cum critica historica-chronologica P. Antonii Pagii* [Lucae, 1738-1742], IX, 24, n. 36); but Pagius gives reasons to show that the correct year is 513. Likewise for A.D. 513: JK, n. 764; Richter-Friedberg (c. 61, C. XVI, q. 1).

[23] "Ex quibus potes intelligere si consideras, lector, beneficiorum Ecclesiasticorum originem. Etenim cum solerent clerici ab Ecclesia per Episcopum mensibus singulis victus causa meritam stipem accipere, ut ex sancto Cypriano secundo tomo Annalium demonstratum est; postea vero factum ut aliquibus ex his Ecclesiae possessiones, quoad viverent, ab ipso episcopo concederentur, quae beneficia dici coeperunt, eo quod (ut habet Symmachus in ea epistola) benemeritus tantummodo eas concedi liceret."—*Loc. cit.* But see above, p. 10-11.

income elsewhere.[24] With lay domination growing apace during the following centuries even the thought of seeking but the necessaries of life by way of pension must have appeared, to say the least, somewhat vain according to the wisdom of the "children of this generation." The increasing secular power was overshadowing the authority of the Church in administering her temporalities. Thus it happened that not only was the Church ignored, but the favor of secular princes was often positively sought, as it offered promise of greater advantages. Needless to add, the means employed were not always free from simony.

A reform movement against this distressing situation was launched in the middle of the eleventh century under Pope Leo IX (1049-1054) who had been influenced by the reform of Cluny. He was ably assisted by his energetic archdeacon Hildebrand, who was tireless in suggesting legislation for a restoration of the early prestige of Rome also to the succeeding Pontiffs, Nicholas II (1059-1061) and Alexander II (1016-1073). Upon the death of the latter, Hildebrand was elected to the papacy and took the name of Gregory VII (1073-1085).

During all this confusion in the pre-Gratian period efforts were directed at maintaining discipline in the major canonical institutions, beginning with the authority of the papacy.[25] The juridic

[24] *Vetus et nova Ecclesiae disciplina*, Pars III, lib. 2, c. 30, n. 4. It must be noted that we are now much better informed on early medieval benefices. "On voit apparaître au IXe siècle, à côté de ces *beneficia* quelconques, des bénéfices qui prennent un charactère fixe et perpétuel et sont attribués nécessairement à un personnage dûment qualifié, pourvu d'une charge proprement dite, à laquelle est attaché ce bénéfice."—Lesne, "Les diverses acceptions du terme 'beneficium' du VIIIe au XIe s."—*Nouvelle revue historique de droit français et étranger*, 4e sér., t. III (1924), 55. Cf. Stutz, "Lehen und Pfründe"—*Zeitschrift für Rechtsgeschichte*, Germ. Abt., II, p. 220; Kan. Abt., IV, p. 506, cited by Lesne, *ibid.*, pp. 49-50, note 2. Cf. also Lesne, *Histoire de la propriété ecclesiastique en France*; Stutz, *Geschichte des kirchlichen Benefizialwesens von seinen Anfängen bis auf die Zeit Alexanders III.*; Hohenlohe, *Grundlegende Fragen des Kirchenrechts*, esp. pp. 80 ff.; Schneider, *Die Entwicklung der bischöflichen Domkapitel bis zum vierzehnten Jahrhundert*; Hinchius, II, 367; Wernz-Vidal, *Ius canonicum*, II (*De personis*), n. 145.

[25] Witness the ninth century spurious collections of Benedict the Levite

concept of the benefice was becoming more settled and definite. The development of the ecclesiastical pension appears more fully only in the following epoch of the history of canon law. There are, however, a few rather clear records of this period, which together with earlier adumbrations are worth brief consideration.

Article 1. The Active Subject of Ecclesiastical Pensions

The Pope as head of the universal Church certainly has the power to impose on benefices the obligation of directing a portion of their fruits toward the support of a needy cleric. Pope St. Gregory VII (1073-1085) used this power when he directed that a priest who had been convicted of homicide, should never again be admitted to the altar, but if he performed adequate penance, some provision ought to be made for his maintenance.[26]

When the same Pontiff confirmed (1080) the sentence of deposition pronounced by his legate against Archbishop Manasses of Rheims, he gave him an opportunity to expurgate his misdeeds in a monastery. Before setting out, however, the Archbishop was to swear that he would take no more from his church than was necessary to support himself and his three attendants.[27]

(847/857), Angilram († 791), and Pseudo-Isidore (847/857), the pre-Gregorian collections, e.g., the *Collectio Anselmo dedicata* (ca. 882), the collections of Regino of Prüm (ca. 906) and Burchard of Worms (ca. 1012), the collections of the Gregorian Reform, and the canonical collections of France toward the end of the eleventh century; cf. Van Hove, *Commentarium Lovaniense*, Vol. I, tom. 1, *Prolegomena* (Mechlinae, Romae: A. Dessain, 1928), pp. 141-159.

[26] *Lib. I, ep.* 34, *ad Remedium linculniensem episcopum* (1073): " . . . nulla sanctorum patrum auctoritas concedit ulterius sacris altaribus ministrare . . . ne stipendiis ecclesiasticis careat, . . . dignum tamen est consequi eum aliquod beneficium ab apostolica sede."—JL, n. 4806; *MGH*, *Epistolae selectae*, Tom. II, fasc. I, *Gregorii VII Regestrum* (ed. E. Caspar, 1920-1923), pars I, p. 55; Mansi, XX, 88. Thomassinus (Pars III, lib. 2, c. 31, n. 2) holds it probable that this is a pension rather than merely an arbitrary distribution.

[27] *Lib. VII, ep.* 20. " . . . et Cluniacum aut Casam Dei cum uno clerico et duobus laicis tuis stipendiis religiose victurus secedas. Quod si facere volueris, praedicto Diensi episcopo prenuntiare procures, ut in eius presentia sacramento confirmes de rebus predictae ecclesiae te nichil interim distracturum,

Bishops and prelates were apparently capable of creating pensions, provided such act was free from simony. If bishops were acting fully within their authority when they assigned ecclesiastical property in usufruct to their clerics, then, it would seem, that safeguarding the laws on alienating and diminishing benefices, they were competent to assign also limited portions to take care of the needs of other of their ecclesiastical subjects. For centuries one mode of clerical support had been the *distributiones* and *sportulae*. The pension was similar to these moderate provisions, but it differed from them in that it was to be paid at regular intervals.

Article 2. The Object of Ecclesiastical Pensions

In considering the object on which a pension might be imposed, one finds but few precise regulations in pre-Gratian times. It can be held as certain, however, that any type of ecclesiastical office or benefice could be made the object of a pension by the Pope. In the early days, Gregory I (590-604), in providing for incapacitated bishops and even priests and clerics of lower rank, arranged for payments not only from the revenues of their former churches or titles, but even from the Pope's own income. With the development of canonical benefices, which bishops and other prelates were empowered to confer, it seems not unlikely that they also obtained the power of setting aside a moderate portion of their income for the support of needy clerics. It appears, however, that this power was used for the most part only after recommendation by the Supreme Pontiff.

Article 3. The Passive Subject of Ecclesiastical Pensions

One of the notes of an ecclesiastical pension is that it is imposed for the benefit of a cleric. The instances cited as the first pensions involved bishops who had been removed from their sees because of canonical unfitness and because of intrigues.[28] In 581 at the synod of Mâcon the deposed bishop Faustinus was granted an annual pay-

nisi quantum tibi et predictis sociis competenter suffecerit."—JL, n. 5163; *MGH*, *ibid*., vol. II, p. 496; Mansi, XX, 303-304.

[28] Council of Chalcedon (451), Actiones X, XI, XII.—Mansi, VII, 269-300; Schwartz, ed., *Acta conciliorum oecumenicorum*, II, 1, pars 3, p. 40-53.

ment to be made by his consecrators.[29] For some time bishops were the more frequent recipients of pensions, although already in the fifth century Bishop Perpetuus of Tours provided by testament (474) for the lifelong maintenance of two of his deposed pastors by *sportulae* from his own goods.[30]

At the end of the sixth century Pope St. Gregory the Great is known to have arranged for the support of a repentant schismatic deacon.[31] Reference has been made to a certain priest guilty of homicide, for whom St. Gregory VII (1073-1085) recommended ecclesiastical support if he performed satisfactory penance, even though he might never again be permitted to exercise his orders.[32]

Article 4. Conditions for the Establishment of Ecclesiastical Pensions

Among the canonical causes for conferring pensions in this pre-Gratian period were principally the peace of the Church, in cases where there was dispute about rightful possession of a benefice, and the preservation of the dignity of the clerical state, lest because of poverty clerics should engage in unbecoming, worldly occupations. For clerics removed from the active ministry because of a crime a satisfactory period of penance was usually a prerequisite. While a cleric was expiating his misdeeds in a monastery provision was usually made for his keep, lest he be a burden to the religious community.

Obligations and Rights of the Pensioner

There were no special obligations imposed upon the pensioner up to this time. In the act of conferring such maintenance, it was generally made clear that those who shared in the fruits of an office had no rights whatever to share in the office or benefice itself.

[29] MGH, *Scriptores rerum merovingicarum*, I, *Gregorius Turonensis*, pars I, *Historia francorum*, p. 338.

[30] D'Achery, *Spicilegium*, I, 303.

[31] *Ep.* IV, 14.—JE, n. 1285; MGH, *Epistolae*, I, 1, 247; Mansi, IX, 1165. *V. supra*, p. 17.

[32] *Lib. I.*, *ep.* 34.—JL, n. 4806; MGH, *Epistolae selectae*, Tom. II, fasc. I, *Gregorii VII Regestrum*, ed. Caspar, vol. I, p. 55; Mansi, XX, 88. *Supra*, p. 20.

Article 5. The Termination of Ecclesiastical Pensions

The assistance or relief granted to clerics in these early days rarely extended beyond the lifetime of the pensioner. This is implied in the very notion of a pension, but was also frequently stated explicitly. St. Gregory I (590-604) decreed thus in the case of a bishop who had been compelled to retire because of severe headache.[33] Other extraordinary grants for support became extinguished when the reason for which they were given ceased to exist, as in the cases of exiled bishops when they were permitted to return to their sees, or of clerics incapacitated because of temporary illness when they had sufficiently recovered.

Cessation also occurred by entering upon a way of life incompatible with the clerical state. Thus clerics who embraced the military state lost not only their benefice but also their pensions; for, as the council of Meaux (845) put it, they cannot at the same time be soldiers for God and for the world.[34]

[33] *Ep.* XIII, 8, *Aetherio episcopo* (602): " . . . ut quousque eundem episcopum in hoc saeculo vita tenuerit."—*MGH*, *Epistolarum*, Tom. II, pars 2, p. 374.

[34] C. 37: " . . . quia non possunt simul Deo et saeculo militare."—*MGH*, *Legum*, Sect. II: *Capitularia regum francorum*, Tom. II, pars 1, n. 293, p. 407; Mansi, XIV, 827.

Chapter II

ECCLESIASTICAL PENSIONS FROM THE DECREE OF GRATIAN (1140) TO THE COUNCIL OF TRENT (1545)

The epoch of four hundred years beginning in the middle of the twelfth century is indeed the period in which the concept of the ecclesiastical pension was clarified. The definite principles established in the twelfth and thirteenth centuries, occasioned to a large extent by the simoniacal abuses rampant at the time, have been in great measure the basis, and have furnished important guiding norms for all subsequent legislation on clerical pensions.

Article 1. The Active Subject of Ecclesiastical Pensions

The Pope in virtue of his plenary apostolic power over the goods of the Church has the broadest power of reserving pensions on all kinds of benefices. This unrestricted administrative faculty of the Pope was expressly declared by Clement IV (1265-1268) in a decree of 1265,[1] and again by Clement V (1305-1314) in the Council of Vienne (1311-1312).[2]

Restrictions in matters pertaining to pensions do not apply to him, as can be deduced, for instance, from the Third Council of the Lateran (1179). In canon 7 the levying of new burdens on churches, the increase of those already existing, and the reservation of a part of the fruits for their own use is severely forbidden to bishops, abbots, and other prelates.[3] Because of his fullness of power the Pope, on

[1] C. 2, *de praebendis et dignitatibus*, III, 4, in VI°: "Licet ecclesiarum, personatuum, dignitatum aliorumque beneficiorum ecclesiasticorum plenaria dispositio ad Romanum noscatur Pontificem pertinere . . ."

[2] C. 1, *ut lite pendente nil innovetur*, II, 5, in Clem.: " . . . salva tamen in praemissis omnibus Romani Pontificis potestate ad quem Ecclesiarum personatuum, dignitatum aliorumque beneficiorum ecclesiasticorum plena et libera dispositio ex suae potestatis plenitudine noscitur pertinere."

[3] " . . . Prohibemus insuper ne novi census ab episcopis vel abbatibus, aliisve praelatis imponantur ecclesiis, nec veteres augeantur, nec partem redituum suis usibus appropriare praesumant . . . Si quis autem aliter egerit, irritum quod fecerit habeatur."—Mansi, XXII, 222=c. 7, X, *de censibus*, III, 39.

the other hand, is not bound by common law, and can suspend it.[4]

Title 12 of Book III of the Decretals has the rubric: "*Ut ecclesiastica beneficia sine diminutione conferantur.*" From this superscription and similar ones it was commonly held as certain that it is the general rule that an authority inferior to the Supreme Pontiff, when conferring a benefice, cannot reserve a pension to be paid to a third party.[5]

This obviously refers to perpetual pensions; for a study of the practice discloses that all collators inferior to the Pope did confer pensions but under definite limitations with reference to competency to reserve pensions, persons on whom and for whom pensions might be levied, the amount of the pension, the need of canonical causes for the reservation of a pension, and the like.

In the decree of the Third Council of the Lateran (1179) [6] it was forbidden to bishops, abbots and other prelates to erect new pensions, to increase existing pensions, and to levy pensions in their own favor.[7]

In 1253 Pierre de Lamballe, Archbishop of Tours, convoked a council at the abbey of Saint-Florent de Saumur. One of the enactments prohibited abbots from imposing new pensions.[8] Clement V (1305-1314) had the same prohibition inserted in the general laws

[4] C. 4, X, *de concessione praebendae et ecclesiae non vacantis*, III, 8: "Qui secundum plenitudinem potestatis de iure possumus supra ius dispensare."

[5] Cf. Ferraris, "Pensio," n. 15.

[6] C. 7.—Mansi, XXII, 22=c. 7, X, *de censibus*, III, 39.

[7] Hinschius, II, 413; Wernz-Vidal, *Ius canonicum*, II (De personis), n. 180 and note 3, p. 202; Pallottini, "Pensio," n. 37, reporting S. C. C., *Ripana*, "Pensionis," 13 feb. 1819, § Certum, citing also c. 8 [Alexander III in Concilio Turonensi, c. 1 (1163)], X, *de praebendis et dignitatibus*, III, 5. Note also c. 3, X, *de censibus*, III, 39 (*Non potest episcopus novum censum imponere monasterio*. Gregorius I Stephano Cantori, 592): " . . . Mandamus, quatenus, si ab initio hoc non fuerit, etiam labentibus temporibus aliquid noviter non permittas imponi." The generic "*census*, *Abgabe* (Hefele [*Conciliengeschichte*, V, 713])—burden" may well include pensions, as the authors just noted indicated.

[8] Council of Saumur, c. 20, *Ut abbates novas pensiones prioribus non imponant.*—Guérin, *Les conciles généraux et particuliers* (Bar-le-Duc, 1868-1869), II, 486. Henceforth cited as Guérin. Mansi, XXIII, 814-815.

of the Council of Vienne (1311-1312).9 This canon was included substantially in the statutes of the Council of Paris in 1346.[10]

Alexander III (1159-1181) wrote to the Bishop of Canterbury regarding an agreement that might be reached between two litigants, whereby the losing party might later be given some right in the church in question. The Pontiff stated that as long as the compromise is not contrary to law the bishop is not in any way to reject it, the implication being that the bishop is competent to act in such matters. The letter continues that a payment without episcopal authority made to the rector of a church on those grounds is not to go beyond the lifetime of the one who pays.[11]

Pope Innocent III (1198-1216) sent in 1207 to the Bishop of Brescia a document which has become one of the most important of all pieces of legislation on ecclesiastical pensions. It is the renowned "caput 'Nisi essent' 21, *de praebendis et dignitatibus.*" In litigation as to who was the rightful prior, one of the parties was asked by the judges to cede his rights to the priorate while the other party in the litigation as long as he remained in office was to pay to the former an annual sum of forty *librae* out of the fruits of the priorate. This arrangement was approved by the Pontiff.[12]

[9] C. un., *de supplenda negligentia praelatorum,* I, 5, in Clem.: " . . . Eadem quoque auctoritate dioecesani suffulti nullo modo permittant, quod iidem praelati prioratus, ecclesias, administrationes aut beneficia hujusmodi applicent mensis suis, pensionesve novas eis imponant, aut veteres augeant, sive quae ipsis de novo impositae, sive auctae solvantur."

[10] C. 11.—Mansi, XXVI, 22. Cf. Nicolaus de Tudeschis [Abbas Panormitanus], *Commentaria in quinque libros Decretalium* (Venetiis, 1588), in c. "Prohibemus" 7, X, *de censibus,* III, 39, n. 2; henceforth cited as Panormitanus.

[11] C. 5, X, *de transactionibus,* I, 36: " . . . Si compositio non est iuri contraria, non est loci episcopo aliquatenus reprobanda; sed census absque episcopali auctoritate cui praeest ecclesiae sub hoc praetextu solutus, vitam eius, qui solverit, non excedit."—JL, n. 13832, no date being assigned.

[12] C. 21, X, *de praebendis et dignitatibus,* III, 5: " . . . nos eam hoc adhibito moderamine toleramus, ut ad praestationem quadraginta librarum non dignitas prioratus, sed persona prioris maneat onerata, ne forte circa proventus aliqua videatur facta sectio prioratus ita, quod ipso priore defuncto successor ipsius ad praestationem quadraginta librarum minime teneatur." Feb. 7, 1207. Cf. Potthast, *Regesta Pontificum Romanorum* (Berolini, 1874-1875), n. 3003.

Hence, it seems clear that a bishop could for a reasonable cause impose a pension with the consent of the beneficiary and lasting as long as the latter remained in the benefice. According to Pallottini [13] it is the common opinion that a bishop can do this even by his own ordinary power.[14] On the other hand, notwithstanding the existence of canonical causes, it appears that a bishop by virtue of ordinary power could not reserve a pension for the life of the pensioner, so that the obligation of paying it would pass to the succeeding incumbents of the benefice.[15]

It was admitted that superiors of regulars could impose pensions on the manual benefices of their institute, the removable benefices, namely, which were joined to their monasteries and administered by vicars.[16]

As for clerics who were not prelates, express legislation against their capacity appears in a Council of Westminster (1173). Clerics were not to create pensions out of the fruits of their church in favor of others, secretly and without the assent of their bishop.[17] Such illegitimate and uncanonical pensions established by priests and simple clerics without the knowledge of the ordinary and for private interests were called private and adulterine pensions in the Synod of Rouen (1189). Those paying or accepting such would be excommunicated and deprived of all ecclesiastical benefices.[18]

[13] "Pensio," n. 17; cf. also Ferraris, "Pensio," n. 16.

[14] Glossa in c. "Audivimus" 3, *de collusione detegenda*, V, 22, v. "pensionem." Navarrus [Martinus Azpilcueta], *Opera omnia* (Venetiis, 1618-1621), consil. 43, n. 4 *De simonia;* Panormitanus, in c. "De cetero" [5, X], *de transactionibus*, n. 2.

[15] C. 21, X, *de praebendis et dignitatibus*, III, 5: " . . . ne forte circa proventus aliqua videatur facta sectio prioratus . . . " Cf. Navarrus, *De iurepatronatus*, consil. 8, n. 9.

[16] C. un., *de supplenda negligentia praelatorum*, I, 5, in Clem. Panormitanus, in c. "Nisi essent" [21, X], *de praebendis et dignitatibus*, [III, 5], n. 12.

[17] C. 28: "Pensiones aliis non faciant clerici in ecclesiis occulte et sine assensu episcopi, ut alii eisdem succedant."—Mansi, XXII, 144. Cf. on this synod and its rôle in the decretal collections, Seckel, *Deutsche Zeitschrift für Kirchenrecht*, IX (1900), 159 sq.

[18] C. 20: "Nemo privatas pensiones et adulterinas, seu portiones de ec-

The freedom of the legitimate superior in reserving pensions was to be safeguarded. Thus, the same Council of Rouen forbade the vicious practice of extorting pensions.[19] The abuse of intimidation and threats in order to obtain pensions had become so widespread that Pope Innocent IV (1243-1254) within sixteen days during January, 1245, sent three letters to different religious institutes and one to a bishop, insisting each time that no such pension could be lawfully demanded without a special mandate.[20]

Article 2. The Object of Ecclesiastical Pensions

In the definition of an ecclesiastical pension it is stated that it is derived from the fruits of another's benefice or from other ecclesiastical goods. "Other ecclesiastical goods"[21] was inserted to include extraordinary means of clerical support chiefly to cover the period when the benefice did not yet exist, or was only partially developed; but at least since the twelfth century the proper object of a pension was most commonly some kind of benefice.

The Supreme Pontiff could impose the obligation of paying a pension not only as a personal obligation resting on the incumbent of the benefice and terminating with him, but also as a real obligation on the benefice itself, so that the obligation would pass to successive incumbents of the benefice.[22]

clesia vel ecclesiasticis beneficiis, deinceps solvere vel accipere praesumat. Quod quis fecerit, omni beneficio ecclesiastico privatus, excommunicationi subjaceat."—Mansi, XXII, 584; Guérin, II, 373-374.

[19] C. 24: "Nullus . . . litibus vexare praesumat, ut sic pensionem ab eo extorqueat."—Mansi, XXII, 585; Thomassinus, Pars III, lib. 2, c. 31, n. 4.

[20] "*Magistro et fratribus ordinis de Sempingham.* Paci et tranquillitati."—Berger, *Les Registres d'Innocent* IV (Paris, 1884-1897), I, n. 865, p. 144; " . . . *Abbati et conventui monasterii Sancti Germani de Pratis Parisiensis, ordinis Sancti Benedicti.* Paci et . . . "—Berger, I, n. 909, p. 149; " . . . *Abbati et conventui monasterii Sancte Columbe Senonensis, ordinis Sancti Benedicti, ad Romanam Ecclesiam nullo medio pertinentis.* Paci et . . . "—Berger, I, n. 910, p. 149; " . . . *Episcopo Leodiensi.* Promerente tam tue . . . "—Berger, I, n. 942, p. 153. Henceforth this collection will be cited as Berger.

[21] Sipos, *Enchiridion iuris canonici*, p. 734.

[22] C. 2, *de praebendis et dignitatibus*, II, 4, in VI°; c. 1, *ut lite pendente nil innovetur*, II, 5, in Clem.

An early notice of what constituted a proper object for a pension can be inferred from canon 7 of the Third Council of the Lateran (1179), which forbade bishops, or abbots, or other prelates from imposing new pensions on churches.[23] Clement V (1305-1314) in the Council of Vienne (1311-1312) enumerated besides churches also "priories and administrations," the latter referring to vicarships of parishes that were incorporated into the institute and administered by a rector.[24] Pope Innocent IV (1243-1254) imposed pensions in favor of certain retired abbots, to be drawn from the abbeys from which they had resigned.[25]

The episcopal manse was considered as an object for a pension constituted by the Apostolic See in behalf of a bishop's vicar *in pontificalibus*, i. e., in consecrating churches and altars.[26]

It will be noticed that most of the information concerning the object of a pension is obtained from negative legislation. Such enactments were occasioned by the abuses of the eleventh and twelfth centuries, side by side with legitimate reservations of pensions. Benefices had come to be burdened for purposes of illicit and simoniacal enrichment in circumvention of the canons against the plurality of benefices.[27]

[23] Mansi, XXII, 22=c. 7, X, *de censibus*, III, 39. Incorporated into Council of Cognac (1260), c. 14.—Guérin, II, 504; Mansi, XXIII, 1036. Cf. also Council of Saumur (1253), c. 13.—Mansi, XXIII, 813.

[24] C. un., *de supplenda negligentia praelatorum*, I, 5, in Clem.: " . . . prioratus, ecclesias, administrationes aut quaevis alia beneficia." Cf. the earlier particular Council of Saumur (1253), c. 20: *Ut abbates novas pensiones prioribus non imponant.*—Mansi, XXIII, 814-815.

[25] Berger, I, n. 2594-2596, p. 387-388; II, n. 4127, p. 4.

[26] Constitution for the reformation of the clergy of Germany (Ratisbon, 1524), c. 19.—Hardouin, *Acta Conciliorum* (Parisiis, 1714-1715), IX, 1915. Hereafter cited as Hardouin. Mansi, XXXII, 1088. The pension in this case was a *pensio spiritualis*.

[27] Hinschius, II, 413, observing that such abuses existed as late as the seventeenth century, citing Leopold von Ranke, *Fürsten u. Völker v. Südeuropa*, 3. ed., 4, 116, 153. The 4. ed. appeared under the title *Die Osmanen und die spanische Monarchie im XVI. und XVII. Jahrhundert* [*Sämmtliche Werke* (Leipzig), tom. 35-36 (1877)].

Article 3. The Passive Subject of Ecclesiastical Pensions

An ecclesiastical pension, as its name implies, is one that is intended for the maintenance of a cleric. During the period under consideration the picture of the passive subject of pensions is drawn in broad strokes, showing in general lines various classes of clerics who could receive a pension, and giving also a few indications as to who were ineligible.

An instance of a pension granted to a chaplain of the Holy See is found in a letter of Pope Innocent IV (1243-1254). An abbot with his community in the diocese of Rouen had obliged themselves to an annual payment of thirty marks to a certain Albert de Ancisa, papal chaplain. The Pope confirmed the action of the abbot.[28]

In 1248 the bishop-elect of Vercelli was impeded from taking possession. Pope Innocent wrote to his legate asking him to see that a becoming and sufficient sum be given him yearly for the duration of the discord, the sum to be provided by some of the churches and monasteries within the territory of his legation.[29] On another occasion the same Pontiff provided for a former bishop, now in poverty. He was to be assisted by an annual payment of twenty pounds, "*Januensis monetae,*" to be paid by two or three monasteries or churches of the province of Milan.[30]

Abbots who had been relieved of their office could be granted pensions. In the middle of the thirteenth century a certain Cuno, papal chaplain, sometime Premonstratensian Abbot, had resigned his dignity. Whereupon Pope Innocent IV (1243-1254) ordained that he be paid on the feast of St. Matthew an annual pension of one hundred *librae parisienses* to be drawn on the holdings of the Premonstratensian monastery.[31] The pension was to be immune from

[28] "*Alberto de Ancisa, cappellano nostro.* Cum a nobis . . . " (A. D. 1250 or 1251).—Berger, III, n. 5492, p. 10.

[29] "*G. de Montelongo, subdiacono et notario nostro, Apostolicae Sedis legato.* Quanta et qualia . . . "—Berger, II, n. 4280, p. 32.

[30] Innocent IV, "*Episcopo Albiganensi et priori Sancti Michaelis et archipresbytero Vigintimiliensi.* Cum personam dilecti . . . " (1245).—Berger, I, n. 1610, p. 243. Curiously the source states that the milanese provinces are to pay in genoese currency.

[31] "*Fratri Cunoni quondam abbati Praemonstratensi, cappellano nostro.* Ante commissam tibi." (1247).—Berger, I, n. 2594, p. 387.

any demands that might be made on it.[32] Furthermore, the prior of the house at Laon, whither the abbot had retired, and also the dean of that place were charged to see that payment was duly made.[33]

On another occasion a certain Benedictine Abbot of the diocese of Limoges (Limousin) sought to resign his office, because he felt himself deficient in learning, although he had laudably administered the temporalities of his monastery. The Pope instructed the Bishop of Limoges to accept the resignation, and to assign to the retiring Abbot a becoming pension from the goods of the monastery.[34]

During the prevalency of leprosy from the twelfth to the fifteenth centuries it was not unusual that parish priests would also fall victims. Towards the close of the twelfth century Clement III (1187-1191) decreed that a certain parish priest stricken with leprosy ought to be removed from his office because of the scandal and the abhorrence of the people; but as long as he lived his needs should be satisfied according to the means of the parish.[35]

How to support parish priests who had become ill, or who had grown old and infirm has always been an important problem. It is known that in England (although there is no reason to conclude that the practice was peculiar to the Church of the Isles) the bishop often sequestered the benefice, appointing a neighboring priest as a sort of administrator, while the former parish priest was usually maintained with a part of the revenues of his former benefice.[36]

In 1286 Philip de Harwodelme, a pastor at Bigby, because of ill-

[32] " . . . *Abbati Bonimontis, Cisterciensis ordinis, Gebennensis diocesis, et magistro Wilhelmo de Orfes, canonico Gebennensi.* Ante commissam dilecto." (1247).—Berger, I, n. 2595, p. 387.

[33] " . . . *Priori domus Vallis Scolarium et . . . decano Laudunensi.* Ante commissam dilecto." (1247).—Berger, I, n. 2596, p. 388.

[34] Innocent IV (1243-1254), "*Electo Lemovicense.* Dilectus filius . . . abbas Sollempniacensis." (1249).—Berger, II, n. 4127, p. 4.

[35] C. 4, X, *de clerico aegrotante vel debilitato,* III, 6.—JL, n. 16607. Some codices, as also Jaffé, 1. ed., n. 10238, ascribe this decree to Celestine III (1191-1198). Cf. Richter-Friedberg, notes on this *caput.*

[36] Cutts, *Parish Priests and their People in the Middle Ages in England* (New York, 1898), p. 290-291.

ness and advanced age was assigned a retiring pension of twenty marks to be paid out of the income of the parish.[37]

William de Tres, Vicar of Perran Zabulo, had grown very old. In 1309 Bishop Stapledon sequestered his vicarship and appointed a coadjutor who was to pay two shillings a week for the sustenance of the aged vicar.[38]

Again in 1326 Bishop Stapledon of Exeter required Barthol de More, pastor of Kynstock by the resignation of John Mon because of infirmity, to take an oath to maintain the same John for the rest of his life. Shortly afterward it was more definitely arranged that, "lest in process of time, to the scandal of the clergy, the said John should be compelled miserably to beg, he shall receive a payment of six marks of silver, viz., 40 s. at St. Michael, and 40 s. at Easter."[39]

The pastor of St. Neot's, in the diocese of Exeter, was stricken with leprosy. Bishop Stapledon appointed Ralph de Roydene as coadjutant. Besides specific arrangements about setting aside a certain part of the house for the pastor, "Sir Ralph shall pay to the vicar every week for his maintenance in food, drink, and firing, and other small necessities, 2 s. sterling, and yearly on the feast of St. Michael, or thereabout, 20 s. for his robe."[40]

The Chichester Register lists a case in which the master and the brethren of Holy Trinity College, Arundel, asked the bishop to grant a pension to William Rateford, who had resigned the pastorate at Kurdford.[41]

Bishop Spufford of Hereford in 1422 appointed a pastor to the parish of Dilwyn to succeed Walter Robins, who, having laudably discharged his ministry, was assigned a pension of 40 s.[42]

As for clerics who had not been incumbents of benefices, instances can be found where they likewise received pensions, or at least some

[37] Quivil's *Register* (Hingeston-Randolph), p. 337; *apud* Cutts, *op. cit.*, p. 292.

[38] Cutts, *op. cit.*, p. 292.

[39] Cutts, *op. cit.*, p. 293.

[40] Stapledon's "Register," p. 342 [Hingeston-Randolph, *Prebendary*]; *apud* Cutts, *op. cit.*, p. 294.

[41] Cutts, *op. cit.*, p. 295.

[42] *Dioc. Hist. of Hereford*, p. 113-114; *apud* Cutts, *op. cit.*, p. 295.

generous provision was made for them. Thus in 1237 the bishop of Durham with permission of the Holy Father provided a common house for certain aged, infirm, and blind clerics of his diocese, and assigned "the tithe of his wills for their support."[43]

Ordinarily in considering a person eligible for a pension it was taken for granted that he was at least a subject of the ecclesiastical authority reserving the pension for him. An exception to this is found in the Register of Innocent IV (1243-1254). The bishop of Arras, notwithstanding certain restrictions imposed on him by his chapter, was permitted freely to seek counsel of the Pope about conferring pensions to externs who were otherwise worthy.[44]

A certain Durandus de Paluello, chanter of Autun was awarded a pension in virtue of a special apostolic mandate by a certain Frederick, "plebanus de Vico Pisano, papae capellanus." Pope Innocent IV (1243-1254) confirmed the pension, which consisted of 180 *librae turonenses* to be paid every year during Easter week by certain monasteries of the province of Lyon as long as Durandus lived.[45]

Article 4. Conditions for the Establishment of Ecclesiastical Pensions

A pension is the right to receive a part of the fruits of a benefice. This presupposes always that there remains a sufficient part of the fruits for the support of the incumbent of the benefice.[46] On the other hand, a pension is intended primarily to assist the needs of a cleric who would otherwise be without decent sustenance. It is recorded that a certain cleric, allegedly enjoying a sufficient income from ecclesiastical benefices, nevertheless demanded from a church

[43] Papal Letters, i, 59, *Rolls Series; apud* Cutts, *op. cit.*, p. 296.

[44] "*Episcopo Attrebatensi* [Atrebatensi]. Constitutus in nostra praesentia: pensionibus extraneorum conferendis personis ydoneis."—Berger, III, n. 7106, p. 339.

[45] "*Durando de Paluello, capellano nostro, cantori Eduensi.* Hiis que de." (1252).—Berger, III, n. 5752, p. 61. " . . . *Abbati Sancti Johannis Bisuntini, et . . . capellae Ducis Divionensis, Lingonensis diocesis, decanis.* Cum dilectus filius." (1252).—Berger, III, n. 5753, p. 61.

[46] Cf. c. un., X, *Ut ecclesiastica beneficia sine diminutione conferantur*, III, 12.

a pension out of an income which was hardly adequate to sustain the rector alone. Pope Alexander III (1159-1181) [47] forbade any further attempts, declaring that it is unbecoming and unreasonable for one who enjoys sufficient income to seek additional favors from a church which he does not serve.[48]

Patrons of churches and also other persons in some regions were reported to be claiming so much of the revenues that even as little as but one-sixteenth remained for the clerics in charge of the church, with the result that in those regions almost no priest was found with the intellectual requirements demanded of his state. The Fourth Council of the Lateran (1215) severely forbade such abuses, and abrogated any custom to the contrary.[49] About two years later Richard Poore, Bishop of Sarum, in his constitution referred to this canon of the Council. To obviate fraud and simony he stated that he sometimes required that an oath should be taken before him by both parties to the effect that there were no illicit commitments or private agreements, and that the pension had not been nor would be increased amongst themselves beyond the original sum established by lawful authority.[50] Essentially the same legislation appeared in 1236 in the provincial constitution of St. Edmund of Canterbury.[51]

In the Provincial Council of Saumur (1253) a statute was directed against those prelates who overburdened the rectors by the imposition of new pensions, leaving an insufficient amount for the sustenance of the latter. Following the canon of the Fourth Lateran Council, the Archbishop of Tours with the advice of his colleagues, decreed that new pensions imposed without just and reasonable

[47] Or Celestine III (1159-1181), according to Compilatio II, cod. marburgensis, and Jaffé (1. ed.), n. 9052; but JL, n. 13986 ascribes the act to Alexander III.

[48] C. 6, X, *de clericis non residentibus*, III, 4.

[49] C. 32: *Ut patroni competentem portionem dimittant clericis*.—Mansi, XXII, 1019=c. 30, X, *de praebendis et dignitatibus*, III, 5.

[50] C. 46: *Ne pensio in ecclesiis detur alicui, sine assensu nostro*.—Mansi, XXII, 1122-1123.

[51] C. 28: *De nova pensione a praesentatis non praestanda*.—Mansi, XXIII, 424.

cause should be revoked, enjoining the ordinaries not to permit the aforesaid rectors to be burdened with such pensions in the future. Further, it was prescribed that, although the titulars were bound by oath to pay said pension, the pensioners were to be compelled by the ordinaries even under pain of censure to remit the oath.[52]

The Archbishop of Bordeaux convoked a synod at Cognac in 1260 wherein similar statutes were enacted against overburdening the churches with new pensions or increasing existing ones. Those which had been lawfully established were to continue, but if the revenues of the church had increased or decreased, the pensions ought rightfully to be augmented or diminished accordingly.[53]

Clement V (1305-1314) in the General Council of Vienne (1311-1312) declared that bishops and other prelates had been infringing on the rights of the churches of the monks, disposing of the fruits in such a way that not enough remained for their support. They had also frequently compelled the abbots and priors to assign perpetually or temporarily to their (the bishops') relatives goods of the monasteries or priories. The Supreme Pontiff decreed such concessions to be automatically null.[54]

Despite severe legislation, both general and particular, the abuse was so deeply rooted that by the fifteenth century the levying of new burdens, whether real or personal, on churches or ecclesiastical persons, was made a case reserved to the Pope.[55]

As stated in the definition, a clerical pension is conferred for a just cause. The causes may involve both public and private good. Thus in settlement of a litigation a pension was imposed, not indeed by the parties but by the judges delegated by the Pope, "*pro bono pacis et utilitatis.*"[56] The private good refers to the maintenance of a cleric who is not able to administer his benefice or otherwise participate in the active ministry, be it because of physical in-

[52] C. 13: *De pensionibus non imponendis.*—Guérin, II, 486; Mansi, XXIII, 813.

[53] C. 14: *Ne onera de novo ecclesiis imponantur.*—Guérin, II, 504; Mansi, XXIII, 1036.

[54] C. un., *de excessibus praelatorum*, V, 6, in Clem.

[55] C. 3, 5, *de poenitentiis et remissionibus*, V, 9, in Extravag. com.

[56] C. 21, X, *de praebendis et dignitatibus*, III, 5.

capacity through illness, disease, blindness, age, and the like, because of hostile expulsion from his benefice, because of legitimate resignation or even because of penal reasons. The motivating cause was the preservation of the dignity of the clerical state; poverty alone was sufficient cause for granting a pension. Alexander III (1159-1181) thus exhorted Thomas, Archbishop of Canterbury, to provide honorable but withal frugal support for a certain abbot.[57]

The amount of the pension was commonly expressed in a definite quantity or sum, as can be seen from many of the instances mentioned. It was held that bishops could not assign a certain quota (one-fourth, one-third, etc.), lest it appear to be division of a benefice, expressly forbidden by Alexander III in the Council of Tours (1163)[58] and by Innocent III, in the Fourth Council of the Lateran (1215).[59]

The time when pensions became due was frequently stated to the day in the decree of assignment. Payment was usually made in spring or autumn. Similarly, the particular standard of money was designated. A difficulty might arise with the fluctuation of currency. Pope Gregory IX (1227-1241) on one occasion decreed that payment was to be made in the former coin or its equivalent value according to the current standard.[60]

[57] Baronius, *Annales ecclesiastici, denuo excusi et ad nostra usque tempora perducti ab Augustino Theiner* (Barri-Ducis, 1864-1883), an. 1164, XIX, n. 41, p. 225: "Pauperibus Christi te duximus commendam, huic abbati pontiniacensi non educandum splendide, sed simpliciter, ut decet exulem et Christi athletam." Cf. Thomassinus, Pars III, lib. 2, c. 31, n. 5.

[58] C. 8, X, *de praebendis et dignitatibus*, III, 5.

[59] C. 28, X, *de praebendis et dignitatibus*, III, 5. Cf. also c. 2 and 20, *ibid.* Cf. Panormitanus, in c. 5, *de transactionibus*, I, 36, n. 2, citing a number of other authors.

[60] C. 26, X, *de censibus*, III, 39: "Cum canonis majoris ecclesiae quandam summam pecuniae ecclesiae tuae debitam aliquot annis persolveris, et iidem summam illam ex integro de meliori moneta exigant sibi solvi, tibi damus nostris literis in mandatis, ut canonicos ullos solutione prioris pecuniae, vel, si non sit in usu, aestimatione pensionis antiquae facias manere contentos." Cf. also c. 20, *ibid.* [Innocentius III (1198-1216), *Spoletano episcopo* (1200)]: "Solvendi sunt census ad antiquam monetam, in qua instituti fuerint, nisi sit in alterius monetae solutione praescriptum."

A pension is the right to receive the fruits of another benefice, but it does not necessarily contain an unlimited right to transfer such fruits. Such transaction would seem to be contrary to the purpose for which the pension was intended—the assuring of sufficient and becoming maintenance for a cleric—to say nothing of the dangers of fraud and illicit negotiating accompanying such an act. A council of Oxford in 1222 strictly forbade any abbot, prior, deacon, archdeacon, or other dignitary, and even subordinate clerics to sell pensions or fruits of their office, or to give them as security, or to alienate them in any manner whatever, contrary to the canons. The transfer was declared invalid, and the offender was to be deprived by his superior of the amount involved in the attempt, unless he recalled the transaction at his own expense within the time stipulated by the superior.[61]

The Holy See, by virtue of its supreme power could permit such transfer. By a decree of Paul II (1464-1471), however, it was forbidden not only to sell the pension but even to lend it beyond three years.[62]

Article 5. The Termination of Ecclesiastical Pensions

Obviously, a pension imposed for the life of the incumbent of the benefice or for the life of the pensioner ceased to exist absolutely with the death of the titular or of the pensioner respectively.

If a pension was assigned for a definite period, it would become extinct with the expiration of the period. Thus, a certain Berwardus, canon of the church of St. Peter of Strasbourg had been assigned a certain pension by the abbot and the community of the monastery of Maurus in the same diocese, until a benefice could be provided for him, with an annual income of ten marks or more. Litigation arose between the two parties, and it was defined by papal mandate that from the pension should be deducted the amount which the canon received from a smaller benefice which he was holding, and if his beneficial income increased, the pension should

[61] C. 36.—Mansi, XXII, 1161-1162.

[62] C. un., *de rebus ecclesiae non alienandis*, III, 4, in Extravag. com. Cf. also Navarrus, *De rebus ecclesiasticis*, consil. 11, passim.

be decreased accordingly, the abbot and the community being obliged to pay the balance. If the income ever became equal to the pension, the abbot and the community would be altogether free from paying the pension. Pope Innocent IV (1243-1254), mindful of the labors and the hardships of the canon, commanded that the deduction of the income of the smaller benefice then held by Berwardus should be tempered so as to leave an equitable balance which the abbot and his community should take care to pay in full each year until they had provided him with the larger benefice mentioned.[63]

Diminished income of a benefice was another cause for extinction or at least a reduction of pensions. Thus, a certain Benedictine abbey in Genoa, impoverished because of war conditions, was excused in 1248 by Innocent IV from henceforth paying pensions, which had been imposed by the authority of the Apostolic See, except when a special mandate would be presented.[64] On another occasion the same Pontiff reduced a pension in favor of a former bishop of Pécs, Hungary, by one half, because the income of the church had become attenuated and the Bishop was exceedingly burdened with financial obligations.[65]

In order to have a pension abrogated or reduced, it was for the beneficiary to prove that the revenues had been reduced beyond the point of his own fitting support.[66]

The rules of the Apostolic Chancery provided for a proportion between the pension and the income of benefices. It was required under pain of nullity that in every concession of a benefice the true value of the revenue be mentioned, and also whether the one receiv-

[63] "*Abbati de Villers, Cisterciencis ordinis, Metensis diocesis, Werico, et Johanni de Muceio, archdiacono Metensi.* Olim inter dilectos filios." (1248). —Berger, II, n. 4352, p. 46.

[64] "*Abbati et conventui monasterii Sancti Syri Januensis, ordinis sancti Benedicti.* Decet in gratia nos vobis."—Berger, I, n. 3700, p. 559. Cf. also, *idem*, "*Priori et conventui monasterii Sancti Oswaldi ordinis sancti Augustini, Eboracensis diocesis.* Cum sicut ex—si quis autem, etc." (1244).—Berger, I, n. 678, p. 115.

[65] "*Episcopo Quinqueecclesiensi.* Cum, sicut." (1253).—Berger, III, n. 6535, p. 220.

[66] Rebuffus, *De congrua*, n. 20, arguing from c. 9, D. I; *apud* Pallottini, "Pensio," n. 47.

ing the benefice retained others; then, when there was question of sustaining, annulling, or reducing a pension because of the condition of revenues of the benefice, it was necessary only to consult the beneficiary's statement of his income.[67] Increased income of a benefice could bring about an increase of the amount of the pension.[68]

Considered from the viewpoint of the cleric who received it, the pension could become extinct in various ways. Thus a pension was lost if the cleric passed to another state of life, as to military service[69] or the married state, just as a benefice was lost by such a transition.[70] Florianus, while differing from other authors in maintaining that a warning was necessary before one entering the military state could be deprived of his pension, held the common opinion that a pension was terminated by the very act of contracting marriage, inasmuch as the latter was an irrevocable act.[71]

Pensions were frequently lost by grave delinquencies. One such crime was the violation of the *privilegium canonis,* which was repeatedly censured during this period and sanctioned by severe penalties not excluding the privation of pensions.[72]

[67] *Regulae Cancellariae Apostolicae,* Reg. 55; cf. De Angelis, *Praelectiones,* Lib. III, tit. 12, n. 6.

[68] Council of Cognac (1260), c. 14.—Guérin, II, 504; Mansi, XXIII, 1036.

[69] Glossa in c. 17, X, *de clericis non residentibus,* III, 4, "redierint." Cf. also c. 6, C. XXIII, q. 8 (Council of Meaux, A. D. 845, c. 37.—Mansi, XIV, 827; *MGH, Legum,* sec. II: *Capitularia regum francorum,* II, 1, n. 293, p. 407); Rebuffus, *Praxis beneficiorum utilissima* (Venetiis, 1560), tit. *de tacita renunciatione,* in fine; Pallottini, "Pensio," n. 85.

[70] Glossa, *loc. cit.*: "Super hoc tamen distinguo, quia aut habet Ecclesia eum pro derelicto, aut non, si habet eum pro derelicto, puta quia contraxit Matrimonium, vel factus est Miles, etc., cum de hoc constitit, Episcopus statim potest Ecclesiam illam aliis conferre, etc., si vero non habet eum pro derelicto, monendus est."

[71] *Apud* Ioannem ab Imola, in c. 10 ["Ut consultationi"], X, *de clericis coniugatis,* III, 3, n. 4.—Pallottini, "Pensio," n. 81.

[72] Innocent IV (1243-1254): "*Electo Bobiensi et . . . abbati de Mezano, Placentine diocesis.* Superba insolentia . . . " (1251).—Berger, III, n. 5450, p. 3; c. 5, *de poenis,* V, 9, in VI° [Boniface VIII (1294-1303)]; c. 1, *de poenis,* V, 8, in Clem. [Clement V, in the Council of Vienne (1311-1312)]; c. un., *de poenis,* tit. XII, in Extravag. Ioann. XXII (1316-1324).

Chapter III

ECCLESIASTICAL PENSIONS FROM THE COUNCIL OF TRENT (1545-1563) TO THE PROMULGATION OF THE CODE OF CANON LAW

The institute of the ecclesiastical pension had its fullest development during the period of over three hundred years extending from the Council of Trent to the promulgation of the Code. The new epoch in the history of canonical science, beginning with the Council of Trent (1545-1563), witnessed new and more definite legislation on the matter of ecclesiastical pensions. Moralists and canonists studied the institution in great detail in the light of the *Corpus Iuris Canonici*, subsequent papal decrees, and curial practice.

Article 1. The Active Subject of Ecclesiastical Pensions

From the fact that the Supreme Pontiff had plenary power he was held empowered to confer not only temporary pensions but also perpetual ones.[1] Nor was it regarded as necessary that he express a canonical cause when he conferred a pension.[2] This power of the Holy See, it was declared, had always been used with care, lest the holder of the benefice be deprived of his fitting sustenance.[3]

Some of the older authors as Fagnanus,[4] Ventriglia,[5] and Bona-

[1] S. C. C., *Civitatis*, 18 dec. 1819, § Notissimae.—*Thesaurus Resolutionum Sacrae Congregationis Concilii* (Romae, 1718-1908), LXXIX, 348-349. Henceforth to be cited as *Thesaurus*. Leurenius, *Forum beneficiale sive quaestiones et responsa canonica* (Venetiis, 1742), pars III, q. 443. De Angelis, *Praelectiones*, Lib. III, tit. 12, n. 5.

[2] Fagnanus, in c. "Nisi essent" [21, X], *de praebendis et dignitatibus*, III, 5, nn. 6, 16. Reiffenstuel, Lib. III, tit. 12, n. 86, ubi "ex causa rationabili."

[3] S. C. C., *Ripana*, "Pensionis," 13 feb. 1819, § Quidquid.—*Thesaurus*, LXXIX, 51-52. *Idem*, *Civitatis*, 18 dec. 1819, § Notissimae.—*Thesaurus*, LXXIX, 349. *Idem*, *Arboren.*, 18 iun. 1831, § Attamen.—*Thesaurus*, XC, 175.

[4] In c. "Nisi," *de praebendis et dignitatibus*, n. 60-63, adducing declarations of the S. C. C. in n. 62.

[5] *Praxis rerum notabilium praesertim fori ecclesiastici* (Venetiis, 1694), Pars II, adnot. 11, § 1, n. 8. Henceforth cited as *Praxis fori*.

cina [6] were inclined to believe that the power of establishing a pension was reserved exclusively to the Holy See. Similarly, in a statute of the Provincial Synod of Aix (1585) it was decreed that all pensions reserved on benefices without the authority of the Holy See were unlawful and simoniacal, and altogether reprobated.[7] According to Fagnanus a pension imposed by an ordinary was actually imposed by the pope, and not merely confirmed by him.[8]

The opinion that bishops could reserve a pension for the life of the titular when there is a just cause was held by such authors as Garcias († after 1613),[9] Cardinal de Luca († 1683),[10] Laymann (†1635),[11] Tondutus (XVII century),[12] Suarez (†1617).[13] The opinion, therefore, with its basis in pre-Tridentine legislation, that

[6] *Opera omnia* (Venetiis, 1687), *De simonia*, disp. 1, q. 4, § 12, n. 8.

[7] Tit.: *Quae pertinent ad beneficiorum collationem, eorumque jurium et bonorum conservationem.*—Hardouin, X, 1574; Mansi, XXXIV B, 1000.

[8] In c. "Nisi," *de praebendis et dignitatibus*, n. 60. Thus also Ventriglia, *Praxis fori*, Pars II, adnot. 11, § 1, n. 8.

[9] *De beneficiis ecclesiasticis amplissimus et doctissimus tractatus* (Venetiis, 1618?), Pars I, c. 5, n. 295-296. Henceforth cited, *De beneficiis*.

[10] *Theatrum veritatis* (Coloniae Agrippinae, 1706), Tom. II, pars 2, *De pensionibus ecclesiasticis*, disc. 40, n. 2-3. Hereafter cited, *De pensionibus*.

[11] *Theologia moralis in V lib. partita* (Lutetiae Parisiorum, 1627), Lib. IV, tract. 2, c. 18, n. 3.

[12] *Tractatus de pensionibus ecclesiasticis* (Lugduni, 1661), c. 1, nn. 1, 6.

[13] *Opera omnia*, Lib. 4, *De simonia*, c. 52, n. 18. Cf. S. R. R., *Montis Falisci*, "Pensionis," 10 iun. 1630; *Regien.*, "Pensionis," 5 maii 1631,—Farinacius, *Sacrae Romanae Rotae decisionum* (Francofurti, 1623-1703), Pars V, tom. 1, decis. 386, n. 9-10; Pars VI, decis. 38, n. 10. Henceforth this collection will be cited as *Recent.* Cf. Ferraris, "Pensio," n. 16.

Cf. also S. C. C. *Ripana*, "Pensionis," 13 feb. 1819: " . . . Quidquid tamen sit de diversis Canonistarum Sententiis, quorum alii negant prorsus Praelatis inferioribus facultatem imponendi Pensiones, sed hoc jus ex laudabili Apostolicae Sedis usu Summo tantum Pontifici esse reservatum, ut sentiunt Fagn. in Cap. Nisi et sqq. *De Praebend. et dignit.*, Ventrigl. in *Praxi*, part. 2, annot. 1 [XI, § 1], n. 8. Paulut. *Jurisprud. Sacr.* lib. 6 tract. 10, cap. 9 et Bonacc. *Oper. Moral.* titul. de Simonia, Disput. I, quaest. 4, § 12, num. 8. Alii vero justa concurrente causa hanc facultatem etiam Episcopis tribuunt, ut Clericat., *de Pension.* disc. 1, Card. de Luca, *de Pens.* discur. 40, num. 41, Tondut. *eod. Tractat.* Cap. I, num. 5, Rigant, ad Regul. 24 Cancellar. § 5, n. 156."—*Thesaurus*, LXXIX, 52-53; Pallottini, "Pensio," n. 16-17. Cf. also Ferraris, "Pensio," n. 14-16.

finally came to be accepted as the more common one, was that bishops at the time of conferring a benefice by ordinary power could with the consent of the beneficiary, reserve pensions to last for his lifetime.[14] The canons against the diminishing of benefices, it was held, were not thereby violated, for this constituted a burden not on the benefice but on the incumbent. The general practice of bishops when granting benefices to assign pensions would seem to corroborate this opinion.[15]

Authors did not agree whether a bishop could by ordinary power reserve a relatively perpetual pension, i. e., one which would run for the lifetime of the pensioner, so that if the incumbent of the benefice died before the pensioner, the obligation to pay the pension would pass to the successor in the benefice.

The negative opinion was held by Fagnanus,[16] De Luca,[17] and several others.[18] Among the arguments advanced for this position there was the one based on the general rule prescribing that ecclesiastical benefices should be conferred without diminution, which would be violated if a pension were reserved on a benefice in such a manner that the obligation of paying it would pass to subsequent incumbents. It was argued that the reservation of a pension recorded in the classical chapter "*Nisi essent*" was imposed on the prior and not on the priorate. Again, a declaration of the Sacred Congregation of the Council was cited in support of the opinion that local ordinaries did not have power to reserve relatively perpetual pensions.[19] Reference was likewise made to c. 7, X, *de censibus*, III, 39 and c. 8, X, *de transactionibus*, I, 36, which, it was declared, forbade bishops from imposing new pensions on churches or increasing those already existing, without the authority of the Holy See.[20]

[14] Reiffenstuel, Lib. III, tit. 12, n. 89; tit. 39, n. 9; Hinschius, II, 414, nota 12.

[15] De Angelis, *Praelectiones*, Lib. III, tit. 12, n. 4.

[16] In c. "Nisi essent," *de praebendis et dignitatibus*, n. 40.

[17] *De pensionibus*, disc. 40, n. 5.

[18] Cf. Schmalzgrueber, *Jus ecclesiasticum universum* (Romae, 1843-45), Lib. III, tit. 12, n. 7, citing, e.g., Azor, Lessius, Sanchez, Van Espen, Clericatus, and Fatinelli. Cf. also Ferraris, "Pensio," n. 20.

[19] *Apud* Garcias, *De beneficiis*, Pars I, c. 5, n. 299.

[20] Cf. Schmalzgrueber, Lib. III, tit. 12, n. 7.

The opinion that bishops had competency to reserve relatively perpetual pensions, at least by virtue of custom, was defended by Gigas,[21] Garcias,[22] Leurenius,[23] and many others.[24] One of the arguments for this affirmative opinion was based on c. 5, X, *de transactionibus,* I, 36, which stated that a pension imposed by way of settlement, without episcopal authority, could not last beyond the lifetime of the one paying the pension. Hence, *e contra,* with the consent of the bishop, the pension could run beyond the lifetime of the beneficiary, and the bishop himself could then also reserve a pension in such a way that the obligation of paying it would pass to the successor in the benefice.[25] In reply to the arguments declaring the ordinary incompetent to reserve pensions for the lifetime of the pensioner, it was stated that the law directing that benefices should be conferred without diminution applied only when there was fraud, lack of a just cause, or a reservation in the bishop's own favor. The pension mentioned in *caput* "Nisi essent" was imposed not by the bishop but by the judges delegated by the Pope.[26] The declaration of the Congregation of the Council, it was explained, must be understood as referring to benefices reserved to the Holy See, over which the bishop has no authority to reserve pensions of any kind. It was also concluded that, inasmuch as the Sacred Congregation spoke in general terms, the pronouncement must be

[21] *Tractatus de pensionibus ecclesiasticis* (Venetiis, 1542?), q. 6, n. 4; q. 85, n. 11. Henceforth cited as *Tractatus de pensionibus.*

[22] *De beneficiis,* Pars I, c. 5, nn. 295, 339.

[23] *Forum beneficiale,* Pars III, q. 444.

[24] Cf. *apud* Schmalzgrueber, Lib. III, tit. 12, n. 8; Ferraris, "Pensio," n. 21.

[25] Cf. Ferraris, "Pensio," n. 21. Schmalzgrueber (Lib. III, tit. 12, n. 8) adds a confirmatory argument: "*Conf.* ex c. *audivimus* 3. *de collus. detegend.* ubi pensio post beneficiati obitum pensionario solvenda propter solam fraudem, in ea constituenda admissam, rejicitur: igitur aperte supponitur, eam, quae absque fraude, et interveniente episcopali authoritate, constituta est, solvendam esse."

[26] It was held that, although delegated by the Holy See, persons subordinate to the bishop could not reserve relatively perpetual pensions on benefices without the consent of the bishop, whose rights would otherwise be prejudiced; for, e.g., in the event that the beneficiary predeceased the pensioner, the bishop would not be able to confer the benefice save in a diminished condition because of the pension on it.—Schmalzgrueber, Lib. III, tit. 12, n. 9.

understood to mean that the bishop could not reserve a relatively perpetual pension without the presence of a just cause. The text of c. 7, X, *de censibus*, III, 39 must be viewed in the same light as the aforementioned declaration of the Congregation of the Council. C. 8, X, *de transactionibus*, I, 36 was not concerned with pensions to be paid from the income of a benefice, but with the permanent remission of the obligation of paying tithes, for which the authority of the Holy See was required in order that it would be valid.[27]

Legates *a latere* had the same power of reserving pensions as bishops. This is the conclusion of La-Croix (1652-1714), who points to Azor, Garcias, Leurenius, and others holding this opinion.[28]

The vicar of a bishop, however, could not impose pensions of his own authority; he had to have a special mandate.[29]

Other lesser prelates, and likewise parties to a compromise and judges, had to have the authority of the bishop, according to the teaching of Garcias, Leurenius, and others.[30]

Superiors of regulars could reserve pensions on benefices that were manual, movable and incorporated into their monasteries and administered by vicars of the religious institute. This opinion of Panormitanus in the former epoch[31] was embraced by Barbosa,[32] La-Croix[33] and many others.

The preceptor general of the military orders could impose pensions on the *commenda* pertaining to his institute.[34] Cardinal de Luca believed that the Magnus Magister of the Knights of Jerusalem could impose pensions even on dignities proper to the institute.[35]

27 Schmalzgrueber, Lib. III, tit. 12, n. 9. Cf. also Hinschius, II, 414; Ferraris, "Pensio," n. 21.

28 *Theologia moralis*, IV, n. 1123.

29 Hinschius, II, 414, 215, citing Barbosa, *Iuris ecclesiastici universi*, Lib. I, c. 15, n. 20. Also for this opinion: Garcias, Leurenius, and others; cf. La-Croix, *Theologia moralis*, IV, n. 1123.

30 La-Croix, *loc. cit.*

31 In c. "Nisi essent," *de praebendis et dignitatibus*, n. 12.

32 *Iuris ecclesiastici universi*, Lib. III, c. 11, n. 61.

33 *Theologia moralis*, IV, n. 1123.

34 Ferraris, "Pensio," n. 33; Barbosa, *Iuris ecclesiastici universi*, Lib. III, c. 11, n. 62.

35 *De pensionibus*, disc. 42. Cf. also Tondutus, *Tractatus de pensionibus*, c. 1, n. 22, 24.

Article 2. The Object of Ecclesiastical Pensions

Authors since the Council of Trent agreed that the object of a pension could be, at least as far as the power of the Roman Pontiff is concerned, any benefice whether burdened with the care of souls or not.[36]

The power of ordinaries in imposing pensions on benefices was considerably limited. They could not place any on consistorial abbeys,[37] nor on simple benefices whose revenue was less than 24 ducats *de camera*,[38] nor on canonries and dignities with incomes less than 100 ducats,[39] and even on those enjoying a greater income it was held that only the Pope is wont to levy pensions;[40] nor on the prebends of canons theologian, it being a privilege of such prebends to be exempt from paying pensions. The same can be said for preceptorial prebends.[41] Other abbeys and benefices, however, could become proper objects for the imposition of pensions within the power of the bishop to establish.[42]

Pensions could be imposed on cathedrals, but validly only as long as the annual revenues of the latter exceeded one thousand ducats. Parish churches likewise might be objects for the imposition of pensions, provided the yearly income of the latter was more than one hundred ducats.[43]

[36] Schmalzgrueber, *Jus ecclesiasticum universum*, Lib. III, tit. 12, n. 17. Henceforth cited as Schmalzgrueber. Leurenius, *Forum beneficiale*, pars III, c. 4, q. 464.

[37] Leurenius, *ibid.*, q. 469.

[38] Leurenius, *loc. cit.*; Ventriglia, *op. cit.*, pars II, adnot. 11, § 1, n. 39.

[39] Leurenius, *loc. cit.*; Ventriglia, *loc. cit.*

[40] Leurenius, *loc. cit.*; Ventriglia, *loc. cit.*

[41] Leurenius, *ibid.*, q. 471, citing Tondutus, *Quaestiones beneficiales*, pars II, c. 1, § 4, n. 51.

[42] Leurenius, *ibid.*, q. 472.

[43] Conc. Trid., Sess. XXIV, *de ref.*, c. 13: " . . . Ad haec in posterum omnes hae cathedrales ecclesiae, quarum reditus summam ducatorum mille, et parochiales, quae summam ducatorum centum secundum verum annuum valorem non excedunt, nullis pensionibus aut reservationibus fructuum graventur." Cf. Wernz, *Ius decretalium*, II, n. 321, Hinschius, II, 414; De Angelis, *Praelectiones*, Lib. III, tit. 12, n. 5; Pallottini, "Pensio," nn. 23, 37-38, 41-44.

The imposing of pensions on parishes was reserved absolutely to the Supreme Pontiff in the late seventeenth century. Pope Innocent XII (1691-1700) in the decree "*Cum velit,*" issued by the Apostolic Datary on November 11, 1692, forbade ordinaries and others who were empowered to confer parish churches, even those of lay patronage, from imposing pensions on them and from accepting resignations or exchanges with the reservation of a pension, even *alimentorum causa.*[44] This decree was confirmed and enlarged by Benedict XIII (1724-1730) in the constitution "*Quanta pastoribus*" of September 15, 1724.[45] The reason for limiting pensions on parishes was to eliminate abusive bidding for parishes, and more positively to assure an adequate maintenance for the pastor, and to permit him to aid his parishioners more effectually.[46]

Canonries and lesser benefices in collegiate chapters might become the objects of ecclesiastical pensions. When there was question of dignities in a chapter entrusted with the care of souls, the regulation of the Council of Trent was applied, so that such dignities could not be burdened with pensions except the annual income of the same exceeded one hundred ducats.[47] Seemingly, however, it was not the usual practice to reserve pensions on dignities or canonries even when the income exceeded one hundred ducats; and likewise simple benefices whose income was less than twenty-four ducats per year were not to be burdened with pensions, according to an extended application of the Tridentine ruling.[48]

[44] Text in Reiffenstuel, Lib. III, tit. 12, n. 100.

[45] Text in Ferraris, "Pensio," n. 28. Cf. also Leurenius, *Forum beneficiale*, Pars. III, q. 466-467; S. C. C., *Ripana*, 13 feb. 1819, § Certum.—*Thesaurus*, LXXIX, 51; Pallottini, "Pensio," n. 37.

[46] Benedict XIII, Const. "*Quanta pastoribus*," 15 sept. 1724, §§ 2-3.—Ferraris, "Pensio," n. 28. Cf. S. C. C., *Montisalti*, 5 dec. 1744.—Pallottini, "Ecclesia parochialis," § VIII, n. 127; "Pensio," n. 21. *Idem*, *Baren*., 30 iun. 1759.—*Thesaurus*, XXIII, 64; Pallottini, "Parochus," § IV, n. 57; "Pensio," n. 39. *Idem*, *Tyburtina*, 29 apr. 1854, § Praeterea.—*Thesaurus*, CXIII, 113-188.

[47] S. C. C., *Aquilana*, 19 iun. 1649; *Nullius*, 6 iul. 1657.—Pallottini, "Pensio," n. 44.

[48] Cf. Schmalzgrueber, Lib. III, tit. 12, n. 13; Vito, *Questioni canoniche* (Napoli: Raffaele Piccone, 1926-1930), IV, 149.

An instance in which a seminary was the object of spiritual ecclesiastical pensions appeared in the second decade of the last century. Pius VII (1800-1823) by a brief of June 16, 1818, granted permission to the bishop of Acquapendente to unite a certain parish church with a recently erected seminary, the latter to pay perpetually an annual amount to the pastor of the church for his proper mainenance. The ordinary was also granted the faculty to charge the seminary to pay temporarily a lesser annual amount to the pastor of another church.[49]

ARTICLE 3. THE PASSIVE SUBJECT OF ECCLESIASTICAL PENSIONS

There were instances of pensions in which not only physical persons but also moral persons were the recipients of ecclesiastical pensions. They were sometimes created in favor of poor parish churches,[50] by authority of the Holy See.

Again, seminaries were accorded pensions.[51] A bishop, however, had to have the authority of the Holy See in order to create a pension for the erection of a seminary, according to a decision of the Sacred Congregation of the Council.[52] In another case the same Congregation sustained a perpetual pension on a parish for the erection of a seminary.[53] It can be said that the reservation of a pension in favor of any moral person was beyond the ordinary competence of any prelate inferior to the Holy See.

To confer a pension on a lay person the Sovereign Pontiff alone was competent,[54] and he alone could permit such to retain it.[55]

[49] Cf. S. C. C., *Aquipendien.*, "Pensionis et subsidii," 18 sept. 1841.—Pallottini, "Pensio," n. 127.

[50] S. C. C., *Arboren.*, "Pensionis," 23 nov. 1816; *Romana*, "Pensionis," 21 iul. 1821; *Aquipendien.*, "Pensionis et subsidii," 18 sept. 1841.—Pallottini, "Pensio," nn. 19, 122, 127.

[51] Cf. S. C. C., *Eugubina*, "Pensionis," 15 ian., 26 nov. 1836.—Pallottini, "Aperitio oris," nn. 261, 267; "Pensio," n. 29. S. C. C., S. *Severini*, "Transactionis," 27 feb. 1836.—Pallottini, "Pensio," n. 62.

[52] *Maurianen.*, 14 feb. 1625.—Pallottini, "Pensio," n. 22.

[53] *Callien.*, 4 mart. 1651.—Pallottini, "Pensio," n. 40.

[54] Cf. S. R. R., *Aquilegien.*, "Fructuum castri S. Viti," 14 iun. 1599.—*Recent.*, pars IV, tom. 1, decis. 12, n. 3.

[55] Cf. S. R. R., *Ferrarien.*, "Pensionis," 14 iun. 1624.—*Recent.*, pars V, tom. 2, decis. 450, n. 25.

These grants to ecclesiastical moral persons and laymen, while they might be called ecclesiastical pensions in the sense that they were derived from goods of the Church, were not such in the proper sense. The true ecclesiastical pension could be held only by one who had been received into the ecclesiastical state by first tonsure. This was the teaching of Fagnanus (1598-1678),[56] based on the constitution of St. Pius V (1566-1572), "*Sacrosanctum*" of September 9, 1568 [57] and that of Sixtus V (1585-1590) published on the ninth of January, 1589, and beginning "*Cum sacrosanctum,*" [58] and the practice of the Curia.[59] Inasmuch as lay persons were incapable of obtaining ecclesiastical pensions, it was judged in one case that they were likewise incapable of receiving the income of a pension.[60]

With regard to age the Sacred Congregation of the Council declared that a pension could be received by a boy if he had reached the age of at least seven years, and if he had been admitted to tonsure.[61]

The person who was to receive the pension had to be determined exactly. When a bishop reserved a pension on the occasion of conferring a benefice, he must at that time expressly name the person for whom he was reserving the pension. Otherwise the reservation was invalid, and definitely forbidden as being included under cases

[56] In c. "Cum in cunctis" [7, X], *de electione et electi potestate*, I, 6.

[57] *Bullarum diplomatum et privilegiorum Sanctorum Romanorum Pontificum taurinensis editio, studio Al. Tomasetti et Card. Francisci Gaudé* (Augustae Taurinorum, 1857-1872), VII, n. 112, p. 709-713. Henceforth cited as *Bull. Rom. Taur.*

[58] *Bull. Rom. Taur.*, IX, n. 141, p. 66-69.

[59] E.g., S. R. R., *Ferrarien.*, "Pensionis," 14 iun. 1624.—*Recent.*, pars V, tom. 2, decis. 450, nn. 4, 20-21, 31, 34; *Albaricinen.*, "Pensionis," 15 mart. 1634.—*Recent.*, pars V, tom. 2, decis. 539, n. 6. S. C. C., *Caesanaten.*, "Pensionis," 26 feb. 1825, § Communis; *Derthonen.*, "Dispensationis," 22 maii 1841, § Ast.—Pallottini, "Pensio," nn. 72, 73. Cf. also De Luca, *De pensionibus*, disc. 2, n. 3; disc. 78, n. 11; Schmalzgrueber, Lib. III, tit. 12, n. 21.

[60] S. R. R., *Albaracinen.*, "Pensionis," 15 mart. 1634.—*Recent.*, pars V, tom. 2, decis. 539, nn. 17, 19.

[61] *Dubium*, ao. 1611; 24 mart. 1624; 24 maii 1624.—Pallottini, "Pensio," n. 74. Cf. Schmalzgrueber, Lib. III, tit. 12, n. 23.

of confidential simony, condemned by St. Pius V (1566-1572).[62] This was taught also by Fagnanus,[63] Tondutus,[64] and Garcias.[65]

Among the particular classes of clerics who were able to receive pensions mention must be made of cardinals. Pope Urban VIII (1623-1644) expressly refers to cardinals as recipients of pensions assigned by the Pope, in a declaration of the faculties which cardinals had in the matter of transferring and reserving new pensions on benefices held by them.[66]

The assistants to the cardinals during a conclave (*conclavistae*) were often accorded pensions for their services. Thus, Clement VIII (1592-1605) in the constitution "*Aequitati consentaneum,*" among other indults and privileges declared them qualified to receive pensions on any ecclesiastical benefice with or without care of souls.[67] The same privileges were given by the succeeding Popes, e. g., Paul V (1605-1621),[68] Gregory XV (1621-1623),[69] Urban VIII (1623-1644),[70] and most of the later Popes down to the nineteenth century.

Pope Pius X was the last Pope to grant pensions to conclavists.[71]

If the revenues of a see were too meagre, or if a bishop was im-

[62] Const. "*Intolerabilis multorum perversitas,*" 1 iun. 1569, § 3: "Itidem, si Ordinarius vel alius collator contulerit antehac, aut conferat in futurum beneficium ecclesiasticum, quovis modo vacans, ea conditione, tacita vel expressa, etc., ut pensionem illi, vel illis, quem, vel quos idem collator . . . scripto aut verbo iusserit seu significaverit, persolvat, . . . "'—*Bull. Rom. Taur.*, VII, n. 131, § 3, p. 755.

[63] In c. "Nisi essent," *de praebendis et dignitatibus,*" n. 36-37.

[64] *Tractatus de pensionibus*, c. 1, n. 16.

[65] *De beneficiis*, pars I, c. 5, n. 313-314. Cf. also Ferraris, "Pensio," appendix, 1, IV.

[66] "*Cum S. R. E., Cardinales, qui circa,*" 1 apr. 1631.—*Bull. Rom. Taur.*, XIV, n. 392, § 1, p. 210.

[67] 9 nov. 1592.—*Bull. Rom. Taur.*, IX, n. 45, § 9, p. 640-641.

[68] Bulla, "*Romanum decet Pontificem, ut erga,*" 31 iul. 1605.—*Bull. Rom. Taur.*, XI, n. 5, § 9, p. 209-210.

[69] Bulla, "*Romanus Pontifex,*" 15 mart. 1621.—*Bull. Rom. Taur.*, XII, n. 2, §§ 6, 12-13, p. 494-495.

[70] Bulla, "*Circumspecta,*" 6 aug. 1623.—*Bull. Rom. Taur.*, XIII, n. 1, §§ 12-13, p. 4-5.

[71] Motu propr., 19 kal. ian. 1904.—ASS, XXXVI (1903-1904), 584-586.

peded from taking possession, or from receiving the income, or if he resigned his see or was removed from it, one of the ways of providing for him was by conferring a pension on him, usually drawn from the revenues of his late see, except in the first case, in which the pension would be derived from another source.[72] Gregory XIII (1572-1585) is known to have granted a generous pension to a certain Bishop of Malvasia who had been driven into exile by the Turks.[73] During the last century Bishop Guglielmo Aretini-Sillani resigned his see of Terracina, Sezze and Piperno[74] and joined the Congregation of the Most Precious Blood. Pius IX (1846-1878) offered him a pension and his choice of a titular bishopric. The prelate, respectfully thanking the Pontiff, declared that it would not be necessary for him to have a pension in his life as a religious.[75]

Parish priests were for obvious reasons the most frequent recipients of pensions. They received pensions even while in active service when their parishes were too poor to provide decent maintenance. Thus, in a case already mentioned, a certain bishop of Acquapendente with permission of Pius VII (1800-1823) in 1818 reserved pensions on a seminary for two of the poorer parishes of his jurisdiction, one of which was conferred in perpetuity.[76] The more common instance in which pastors were recipients of pensions was that in which a pension was imposed on a parish in favor of its resigned pastor.[77]

Holders of benefices other than parochial ones could also resign and receive a portion of the fruits of their former benefices. Thus, a certain Conversi presented to Pius VII (1800-1823) the resignation of his canonry, reserving as pension a certain portion of the

[72] Tondutus, *Tractatus de pensionibus*, c. 74, n. 27.

[73] Moroni, *Dizionario di erudizione*, XXXII, 298.

[74] *Giornale di Roma*, (1854), n. 40, *apud* Moroni, *Dizionario*, LXXIV, 210-211.

[75] Moroni, *loc. cit.*

[76] S. C. C., *Aquipendien.*, "Pensionis et subsidii," 18 sept. 1841.—Pallottini, "Pensio," n. 127.

[77] E.g., S. C. C., *Sabinen.*, "Pensionis," 20 dec. 1856.—Pallottini, "Aperitio oris," n. 278-286.

prebendary income. The Pope accepted the resignation and reserved the pension for the retired canon.[78]

A certain professed member of a religious order was adjudged by the Rota as being capable of receiving a pension on a benefice of Regulars, notwithstanding the vow of poverty, and especially if this would serve to relieve the order from obligations with which it would otherwise be burdened. The pension was revocable at the will of the superior.[79] The Sacred Congregation of the Council in 1603 decreed that an annual pension of 60 *scuti* [*scudi*] should be paid to a certain cleric regular even after his profession. The reason for the grant was to enable the cleric to pay the debts left by his deceased father.[80]

The general rule, however, was that regulars could not receive pensions on secular ecclesiastical benefices, nor could they receive pensions on the benefices vacated by their profession.[81] Only by apostolic indult could they be authorized to retain the pension even after profession. All further impediments and incapacities that might arise from future profession were thereby removed, and the religious in virtue of the apostolic favor obtained capacity to receive a pension from a secular benefice. This was the common teaching.[82] Members of the Society of Jesus, after having taken the three vows, but before the fourth vow, could retain ecclesiastical pensions on secular benefices.[83] Similarly, members of the various military orders

[78] Cf. S. C. C., *Romana,* "Pensionis," 21 iul. 1821.—Pallottini, "Pensio," n. 122.

[79] S. R. R., *Troiana,* "Pensionis," 25 iun. 1610, coram Pirovana.—*Recent.*, pars II, decis. 302, n. 2-3.

[80] *Neapolitana,* 17 apr. 1603, ad c. 2, Sess. 25 de Regularibus posit. 129, p. 10.—Pallottini, "Pensio," n. 34.

[81] S. R. R., *Caesaraugustana,* "Pensionis," 31 ian. 1656.—*Recent.*, pars XII, decis. 121, n. 1: "pensio existinguitur." *De Luca, De beneficiis (Theatrum veritatis,* tom. I), disc. 64, nn. 3, 5-6; *De pensionibus,* disc. 44, n. 2; Leurenius, *Forum beneficiale,* III, q. 517.

[82] Ferraris, "Pensio," n. 52, pointing to commentaries on c. "Cum de beneficio," *de praebendis et dignitatibus,* III, 4, in VI°; S. R. R., *Caesaraugustana,* "Pensionis," 31 ian. 1656.—*Recent.*, pars XII, decis. 121, n. 2-3.

[83] De Luca, *De renuntiatione, (Theatrum veritatis,* Tom. V, part. 3), disc. 17, n. 7: ". . . iidem quodammodo retinent statum saecularem." Ventriglia, *Praxis fori,* tom. II, adnot. 11, § 3, n. 23. Cf. Ferraris, "Pensio," n. 53.

enjoyed a number of privileges in the matter of pensions.[84]

During the period of *ius novum* illegitimates had been ruled incapable of receiving ecclesiastical benefices.[85] The Council of Trent went further and expressly barred them from acquiring ecclesiastical pensions on benefices which their fathers were holding.[86] If, however, such an illegitimate son had been made a cleric after having obtained a dispensation, he was considered by that same fact capable of receiving a pension, no further dispensation being required.[87]

Some authors held that a person who was irregular could not obtain an ecclesiastical pension, which was said to be conferred *titulo clericali*.[88] It must be remembered, however, that the notion of irregularities was not always precisely circumscribed. The word was frequently used interchangeably with words signifying penalties, suspensions, ecclesiastical prohibitions. Nowhere in the Decretals can one find a special rubric *de irregularitatibus*. Many authors,

[84] Leurenius, *Forum beneficiale*, III, q. 517; Tondutus, *Tractatus de pensionibus*, c. 28, n. 31-33; c. 77, n. 29-40; Pallottini, "Pensio," n. 97-99; Ferraris, "Pensio," n. 45-50; Moroni, *Dizionario*, XXXVII, 177-178; LXX, 3-13.

[85] C. 3, C. XV, q. 8; c. 2, X, *de filiis presbyterorum ordinandis vel non*, I, 17, and nearly all the *capita* of this title; c. 1, *de filiis presbyterorum et aliis illegitime natis*, I, 11, in VI°.

[86] ". . . non liceat filiis clericorum, qui non ex legitimo nati sunt matrimonio, in ecclesiis, ubi eorum patres beneficium aliquod ecclesiasticum habent aut habuerunt . . . pensiones super fructibus beneficiorum, quae parentes eorum obtinent vel alias obtinuerunt, habere." Sess. XXV, *de ref.*, c. 15. Cf. also S. R. R., *Recent.*, pars II, decis. 549, n. 4; Ferraris, "Pensio," n. 42. This canon of the Council of Trent was incorporated into the statutes of the Provincial Council of Bordeaux (1583), approved by the Holy See. Besides the mere "*beneficium aliquod*" of Trent, this Provincial Council mentioned "*praebendam . . . vel officium aliquod ecclesiasticum.*" XVII.—Mansi, XXXIV, A, 766.

[87] Tondutus, *Tractatus de pensionibus*, c. 31, nn. 6, 7-9. S. R. R., *Veneta*, "Pensionis," 10 dec. 1572, coram Robusterio; *Caesaraugustana*, "Pensionis," 19 feb. 1595, coram Gypsio; *Melitensi*, 14 maii 1614, coram Buratto; cf. Ferraris, "Pensio," n. 55.

[88] E.g., Bonacina, *Opera omnia*, tract. de irregularitate, disp. 7, q. 1, § 4, n. 6; Garcias, *De beneficiis*, pars I, c. 5, n. 135; Tondutus, *Tractatus de pensionibus*, c. 73, *passim*; Barbosa, *Iuris ecclesiastici universi*, Lib. III, c. 11, n. 46, citing others. But cf. Schmalzgrueber, Lib. III, tit. 12, n. 24. Cf. also Ferraris, "Pensio," n. 57.

one of the greatest offenders being Maiolus,[89] failed to distinguish sufficiently between the generic notions of prohibitions, penalties, suspension and the specific notion of irregularity. They compiled lengthy lists of irregularities alleged to be expressed in the law. Even the more recent authors usually treated irregularities in connection with their discussion of censures.[90]

Heretics and their sons and nephews, as they were incapable of obtaining benefices,[91] were likewise, according to the common opinion, considered to be ineligible for pensions.[92]

Persons who joined the army or entered the married state were generally regarded as being essentially unqualified to receive pensions. This point will be resumed in the consideration of the extinction of pensions. The crime of voluntary homicide did not bring with it the incapacity of obtaining or retaining a pension, according to the Sacred Congregation of the Council in a reply of the seventeenth century.[93] A person who was excommunicated, suspended, or interdicted could not receive a pension until he had been absolved from the censure.[94]

[89] *De irregularitatibus, et aliis canonicis impedimentis* (Romae, 1575).

[90] Thus, e.g., F. Suarez,who rightly opposed the exaggeration of the number of canonical irregularities, treats the matter in his section on censures. *(Opera omnia*, tom. XXIII, *De censuris*, disp. XL-LI). Cf. Wernz-Vidal, *Ius canonicum*, IV, pars 2. (*De rebus*), n. 230; von Scherer, *Handbuch des Kirchenrechts* (Graz, 1886-1898), I, 337, not. 13-15.

[91] C. 2, *de haereticis*, V, 2, in VI°.

[92] Ferraris, "Pensio," n. 58, citing among others, Barbosa, *Iuris ecclesiastici universi*, Lib. III, c. 11, n. 43.

[93] *In dubium*, ao. 1618: "Non obstante ad hoc dispositione Concilii."—Pallottini, "Pensio," n. 14. Cf. also Schmalzgrueber, Lib. III, tit. 12, n. 25.

[94] Thus e.g., Leurenius, *Forum beneficiale*, pars 3, q. 624; La-Croix, *Theologia moralis*, IV, n. 1149; Schmalzgrueber, Lib. III, tit. 12, n. 22; Wernz, *Ius decretalium*, II, n. 321. But Tondutus wrote: "Suspensio autem est prohibitio officij, vel exercitij competentis alicui personae Ecclesiasticae, à jure vel ab homine facta. . . Et ideò Suspensio non nocet in adeptione beneficij, & multò minus pensionis, propter clausulam absolutionis quae in omnibus similibus concessionibus apponi solet, & apposita censetur."—*Tractatus de pensionibus*, c. 68, n. 2-3.

Article 4. Conditions for the Establishment of Ecclesiastical Pensions

A pension was a restriction of the beneficiary's right to a corresponding portion of his revenue from the benefice. Besides the creation of pensions by incompetent superiors, the conferring of them to canonically disqualified persons, and the simoniacal pacts that often accompanied their establishment, there was also the abuse of burdening the beneficiary to the extent that the revenue remaining for his own subsistence was insufficient. This was due to the multiplication of pensions without adequate cause.

Pope Paul III (1534-1549), who convoked the Council of Trent, was tireless in his efforts to uproot the numerous abuses that had grown up in the Church, greatly shaken by the Protestant revolt. Not the least of his energy was directed toward correcting the irregular practices in the matter of ecclesiastical pensions, particularly in their unwarranted multiplication.[95]

In the Council of Trent two canons proposing a limited reservation of pensions on cathedral and parish churches had been suggested in 1562 preliminary to the twenty-second session.[96] They were rejected by the Fathers, lest they give the impression of in any way

[95] Cf. Ehses, "Kirchliche Reformarbeiten unter Papst Paul III,"—*Römische Quartalschrift*, XV (1901), 158-174. *Consilium delectorum cardinalium Contareni, Sadoleti, etc., et aliorum praelatorum*—Mansi, Supplem. V, 539-548; Le Plat, *Monumentorum ad historiam concilii tridentini . . . amplissima collectio* (Lovanii, 1781-1787), II, 598, § 3; *Concilium Tridentinum, diariorum, actorum, epistularum, tractatuum; nova collectio edidit Societas Goerresiana* (Friburgi Brisgoviae: Herder, 1901-), IV, 27 adn. 2.

[96] "C. 3: Ecclesiae cathedrales, quarum fructuum verus valor quingentorum ducatorum auri de camera summam non excedit, pensionibus, etiam ex causa resignationis, minime graventur; quae vero (dictum valorem) excedunt, numquam ultra dimidiam fructuum neque etiam adeo gravari possint, ut saltem quingenti integri praelato non relinquantur.

"C. 4: Parochiales ecclesiae, quarum fructus quinquaginta ducatorum auri de camera [summam] non excedunt, pensionibus annuis, etiam ex causa resignationis, nullo modo graventur; quae vero excedunt, numquam, pensionibus et reservationibus fructuum ultra dimidiam posthac gravari possint, et semper ad minus quinquaginta ducati auri de camera rectori parochialis ecclesiae remaneant."—*Concilium Tridentinum, ed. Goerresiana*, VIII, 924.

approving or at least condoning the abuses connected with pensions.[97] After some revision, however, they were received into the thirteenth canon, *de Reformatione* of the twenty-fourth session, in 1563. The section was directed against excessive pensions on parishes and cathedrals, and provided that in future all cathedral churches whose revenue did not exceed one thousand ducats, and all parish churches whose revenue did not exceed a hundred ducats a year according to the current monetary evaluation, were not to be burdened with pensions or reservations of income.[98]

In order that this regulation of the Council might be duly observed, the obligation was stressed of declaring in the conferring of a benefice the financial status of the benefice, even of one not a cathedral or parish church.[99] In requesting and in conferring a pension mention was to be made whether the benefice was already burdened with a pension.[100] A petition directed to the Holy See for the reservation of an additional pension on a benefice already burdened was generally denied altogether or granted but rarely by the Pope.[101] The reservation of an additional pension on a benefice already burdened, if the presence of a prior pension was not revealed, was considered surreptitious, and declared null by the Rota in a number of cases.[102] This nullity was automatic, nor was there

[97] Cf. *ibid.*, pp. 928-942, "*Examinantur canones*"; IX, 1022, nota 2, and p. 1134.

[98] ". . . Ad haec in posterum omnes hae cathedrales ecclesiae, quarum reditus summam ducatorum mille, et parochiales, quae summam ducatorum centum secundum verum annuum valorem non excedunt, nullis pensionibus aut reservationibus fructuum graventur." Sess. XXIV, *de ref.*, c. 13.

[99] *Regulae Cancellariae Apostolicae*, Reg. 55; cf. De Angelis, *Praelectiones*, Lib. III, tit. 12, n. 6. Cf. supra, p. 38-39.

[100] S. R. R., *Cremonen.*, "Pensionis," 23 mart. 1615.—*Recent.*, pars II, decis. 566, n. 2; *Firmana*, "Pensionis," 8 mart. 1627.—*Recent.*, pars V, tom. I, decis. 46, n. 7.

[101] S. R. R., *Eugubina*, "Nullitatis Pensionis," 27 mart. 1669.—*Recent.*, pars XVI, decis. 69, n. 4. Cf. Ferraris, "Pensio," n. 106.

[102] E. g., *Cremonen.*, "Pensionis," 23 mart. 1617.—*Recent.*, pars II, decis. 666, n. 2; *Salutiarum*, "Pensionis," 22 iun. 1615.—*Recent.*, pars II, decis. 739, n. 1. Cf. also S. C. C., *S. Severini*, "Pensionis," 28 mart. 1835.—Pallottini, "Pensio," n. 61; S. C. C., *S. Severini*, "Transactionis," 30 ian. 1836.—Pallottini, "Pensio," n. 62.

any possibility that the second pension would become valid when the former one ceased, even though this second pension had been reserved *motu proprio.*[103] It was absolutely void.[104] By way of exception, however, the grant was sustained if the Pope was informed of the prior pension from other sources although nothing was expressed in the petition, or if notice of it was contained implicitly in the narrative portion of the rescript.[105]

The ordinary case of a pension was that in which it was granted to a retired holder of a benefice. The illicit practice of some beneficiaries who by private agreement resigned their benefices, but retained for themselves a pension on the fruits, never had the approval of ecclesiastical authority. St. Pius V (1566-1572) condemned such dealings and declared them null in the constitution "*Quanta Ecclesiae,*"[106] as did also Gregory XIII (1572-1585) in the constitution "*Humano vix iudicio,*"[107] and Benedict XIV (1740-1758) in the constitution "*In sublimi,*"[108] decreeing that the reservation of a pension following resignation of a benefice and a private agreement to terminate the pension by paying the resignor a determinate sum was simoniacal and utterly void. It may be noted that the older authors of the period considered in the present chapter, while admitting that such reservations in connection with the resignation of a benefice were contrary to the sacred canons, maintained that they could hardly be classed as simoniacal. They argued that the chapters

[103] S. R. R., *Regien.*, "Pensionis," 27 iun. 1636.—*Recent.*, pars VII, decis. 169, n. 1-3.

[104] S. R. R., *Regien.*, "Pensionis," 27 iun. 1636.—*Recent.*, pars VII, decis. 169, n. 1; *Melevitana*, "Pensionis," 18 mart. 1672.—*Recent.*, pars XVII, decis. 279, n. 15. Cf. also Garcias, *De beneficiis*, part. I, c. 5, n. 561; Ferraris, "Pensio," n. 107; Schmalzgrueber, Lib. III, tit. 12, n. 19.

[105] S. R. R., *Romana*, "Devolutionis domus," 16 maii 1660.—*Recent.*, pars XIII, decis. 227, n. 9; *Mediolanen.*, "Parochialis," 15 feb. 1664.—*Recent.*, pars XIV, decis. 139, n. 11. S. C. C., *Forolivien.*, 20 dec. 1851, § Nonnulla; *Verulana*, 14 maii 1831.—Pallottini, "Pensio," nn. 30, 31.

[106] Apr. 1, 1568.—*Codicis iuris canonici fontes cura Emi. Petri Gasparri editi* (Romae, *postea* Civitate Vaticana: Typis polyglottis vaticanis, 1923-1939), n. 125. Henceforth cited as *Fontes*.

[107] Jan. 5, 1584.—*Bull. Rom. Taur.*, VIII, 434-438.

[108] Aug. 29, 1741.—*Fontes*, n. 317.

of the Decretals usually cited against such practices[109] pertain only to benefices and not to pensions; for odious things should be restricted,[110] and, although pensions are said to be like benefices in some respects, the similarity, it seemed, could never be asserted in penal and odious matters like simony.[111]

In establishing a pension certain formalities were insisted upon. They consisted for the most part in the consent of the parties concerned. The Pope, of course, was held not to be bound to seek the consent of those interested; but papal reservations of pensions which did not expressly derogate the rights of the interested parties were considered surreptitious. It was maintained that he could reserve a pension on a benefice of *ius patronatus* even without the consent of the patron, as long as mention was made of the patron's right.[112] It was admitted that where there was question of royal patronage, the Pope is not wont to impose a pension on a benefice of this kind without the consent of such patron.[113] Prescinding from rights of royal patronage, the Sacred Congregation of the Council, pointing to Garcias[114] and Pitonius,[115] stated that the consent of the patron was not required; it sufficed that the Pope knew of the existence of the advowson, in order that thereby his intention of reserving a pension on the fruits of even a patronal benefice would be manifest.[116]

[109] C. 8, X, *de praebendis et dignitatibus*, III, 5; c. un., X, *ut ecclesiastica beneficia sine diminutione conferantur*, III, 12.

[110] Reg. 15, R. J., in VI°.

[111] Fagnanus, in c. "Ad audientiam," *de Rescriptis* [I, 3], n. 56. Tondutus (*Tractatus de pensionibus*, c. 26, n. 2-5) restricted the argument to the transfer of pensions, but not to the resignation of a benefice with reservation of a pension for one's self or for another (n. 5-7). For the absence of simony in resignation with reservation, cf. also Reiffenstuel, III, 5, n. 93; S. C. C., *Faventina*, "Pensionis," 17 dec. 1836, § Profecto. § Quod.—Pallottini, "Pensio," n. 5.

[112] De Luca, *De iure patronatus* (*Theatrum veritatis*, tom. II), disc. 66, n. 14. Tondutus, *Tractatus de pensionibus*, c. 25, n. 1-2.

[113] De Luca, *De iure patronatus*, disc. 66, n. 15; *idem*, *De pensionibus*, disc. 58, n. 3.

[114] *De beneficiis*, Pars I, c. 5, n. 361.

[115] *De Controversis patronorum nec non ab eis praesentatorum ad beneficia et cappellanias quascumque. . .* (Venetiis, 1733), alleg. 66, n. 1.

[116] *Verulana*, "Pensionis," 20 mart. 1830, § Notissima.—Pallottini, "Pensio," n. 24.

The Sacred Roman Rota resolved that knowledge is required because the Pope but rarely imposes pensions on such benefices.[117]

With regard to subordinate collators it was the practice of the Curia to insist that they obtain the consent of the patron not indeed for validity but for the security of the pension, lest the patron if later reduced to poverty should attack the pension.[118] The only time when his consent was not required was when he unreasonably refused to consent, while the good of the Church demanded it.[119] Hinschius suggested a special circumstance when the consent of the patron ought to be obtained, namely, when a pension was imposed before a new incumbent had been installed; for in this case the benefice became less desirable, and the patron was placed at a disadvantage in finding a candidate for presentation who would be willing to accept such an encumbered benefice. The only type of pension which would not touch the patron's interests was one imposed on an incumbent to last only as long as he remained in the benefice.[120] Aside from a special privilege or custom, the consent of the patron was probably not required for a pension on the beneficiary. If it were immoderate, the patron could ask that it be extinguished or at least reduced.[121]

It was taught that ordinaries had to obtain the consent of the chapter, inasmuch as the conferring of a pension was considered alienation in a broad sense.[122] Furthermore, the assent of the incumbent of the benefice to be burdened was required by law; for his right to the full enjoyment of the revenues could not be restricted against his will.[123] Tacit consent was regarded as sufficient, and this

[117] *Romana*, "Pensionis," 4 iul. 1601, *apud* Ventriglia, *Praxis fori*, Part. II, adnot. 11, § 1, n. 11.

[118] S. C. C., *Praenestina*, "Pensionis," 30 aug. 1845, § Reitellius; referring to decrees of the S. Congregation of March 6, 1595 and June 9, 1579.—Pallottini, "Pensio," n. 25. Lotterius, *De re beneficiaria* (Patavii, 1700), Lib. I, q. 35, n. 90-92.

[119] Garcias, *De beneficiis*, pars I, c. 5, n. 359-360.

[120] II, 414, note 3.

[121] Schmalzgrueber, Lib. III, tit. 12, n. 15. Cf. Ferraris, "Pensio," append. 1, III; St. Alphonsus, *Theologia moralis*, IV, n. 138, 3°.

[122] Schmalzgrueber, Lib. III, tit. 12, n. 12.

[123] Fagnanus, in c. "Nisi essent," *de praebendis et dignitatibus*, n. 22. Gar-

could be presumed by continued subsequent payments.[124] By way of exception the consent was not required in the case of a beneficiary who was incompetent to administer his office and who needed an adjutant.[125] If a pension was to be imposed on a vacant benefice, then the more common opinion was that a *defensor* had to be appointed, as was required for strict alienation of ecclesiastical property.[126]

Sanation or revalidation of the establishment of a pension was not to be granted without the consent of the titular, unless the Supreme Pontiff proceeded *motu proprio,* derogating the rules on consent.[127]

When an ordinary conferred a pension, it was held that he had to express a just cause for doing so. If the cause was not evident and capable of proof, the presumption was that the pension had been conferred by fraud.[128] The proofs, moreover, according to Cardinal de Luca were to be extrinsic; nor was the ordinary's own statement generally accepted, according to the rule: "*Ut prohibitus facere, dicatur etiam prohibitus confiteri, seu asserere.*"[129]

The final cause required at least implicitly in the establishment of every clerical pension was *alimentorum suppeditatio*—the provision for becoming subsistence. The motivating or impulsive causes,

cias, *De beneficiis,* pars I, c. 5, n. 320; Ventriglia, *Praxis fori,* tom. II, adnot. 11, § 1, n. 6.

124 Schmalzgrueber, Lib. III, tit. 12, n. 14.

125 Hinschius, II, 324.

126 Schmalzgrueber, Lib. III, tit. 12, n. 14; Pirhing, *Ius canonicum nova methodo explicatum* (Dilingae, 1722), Lib. III, tit. 12, n. 15. But Garcias (*De beneficjis,* pars I, c. 5, n. 320): ". . . existimo non requiri constituit [sic] eidem defensorem ad consentiendum pensioni praedictae." Fagnanus (in c. "Nisi," *de praebendis et dignitatibus,* n. 23) held that a bishop could not reserve a pension on a vacant benefice, as there was no rector to give consent, and that while a church was vacant the income could not be reduced. In n. 53 he cites a decision of the Rota to corroborate his opinion.

127 Amydenius, *Tractatus de officio et iurisdictione Datarii et de stylo Datariae* (Venetiis, 1653), Lib. I, c. 14, q. 7, n. 40-41. S. C. C., *Regien.,* "Pensionis," 17 sept. 1722, § Contulit.—Pallottini, "Pensio," n. 18.

128 Garcias, *De beneficiis,* pars I, c. 5, n. 322; Schmalzgrueber, Lib. III, tit. 12, n. 12.

129 *De pensionibus,* disc. 40, n. 4; Tondutus, *Tractatus de pensionibus,* c. 1, n. 19; S. R. R., *Comen.,* "Dismembrationis," 22 iun. 1648.—*Recent.,* pars X, decis. 24, n. 7.

according to Leurenius, could all be grouped under two main heads: 1) resignation, either pure and simple or as the result of litigation (*pro concordia*); 2) simple reservation.[130] Another slightly different division of the motivating causes was given by some of the older authors.[131] They were either burdensome (*onerosae*) or advantageous (*lucrativae*). Based on causes of the first class were pensions which resulted from the resignation of a benefice with reservation of a pension on it; pensions established to balance unequal income after exchange of benefices;[132] or, finally, pensions arising from a peaceful settlement of a law suit (*pro bono pacis*).[133] Among the advantageous motivating causes were: merit recognized by the Church; gratitude for service rendered; promotion of knowledge, by support of the learned or of clerics pursuing sacred sciences;[134] hospitality; reward and affection; uprightness of life; "*aliaque laudabilia.*"

With reference to the amount of the pension the Fourth Council of the Lateran (1215) had established a general rule that the pen-

[130] *Forum beneficiale*, Pars III, q. 438.

[131] *Idem, loc. cit.*, citing Castropolao, Azor, Parisius, Paulus Romanus and others. Cf. also Schmalzgrueber, Lib. III, tit. 12, n. 12.

[132] Cf. c. 6, X, *de rerum permutatione*, III, 19; Schmalzgrueber, Lib. III, tit. 12, n. 16.

D'Annibale (*Summula theologiae moralis* [5. ed., Romae, 1908], III, n. 73, nota 49) declared that a bishop is competent in a case of this kind, citing c. 26, X, *de praebendis et dignitatibus*, III, 5, Caccialup. *De pensionibus*, Quaes. XIII, 4. Thus also Barbosa, *Iuris ecclesiastici universi*, Lib. III, cap. 11, n. 58, pointing to others; Hinschius, II, 414; Ferraris, "Pensio," n. 24. But others, with cogent arguments held that no authority subordinate to the Pope could reserve a pension on a wealthier benefice to compensate for the lesser income of a benefice acquired in exchange of the former; cf. Schmalzgrueber, *loc. cit.*, et Lib. III, tit. XIX, nn. 56-50; De Angelis, *Praelectiones*, Lib. III, tit. 19, n. 3. Cf. also St. Alphonsus, *Theologia moralis*, III, n. 74.

[133] C. 21, X, *de praebendis et dignitatibus*, III, 5. In these cases the pension could not be established by agreement between the parties but only by the judge, properly delegated. Cf. Fagnanus, in *cit. c.*, n. 3 ff.

[134] S. R. R., *Albiganen.*, "Confidentiae," 6 mart. 1609.—*Recent.*, pars II, decis. 166, n. 4-5; in re poor nephew at study. De Luca, *De pensionibus*, disc. 40, n. 3. This type of support was more correctly called *pensio praestimonialis* or *praestimonium*: Reiffenstuel, Lib. III, tit. 5, n. 80; Phillips, *Kirchenrecht*, VII, 283.

sion was never to be so high as to deprive the incumbent of his sufficient and becoming maintenance.[135] The Council of Trent in 1563 laid down further restrictions for pensions on cathedrals with revenues of less than 1000 ducats and parish churches of less than 100 ducats per year.[136]

As in the earlier period, it was strongly urged that the amount of the pension be stated in a definite sum rather than in terms of a certain proportion of the income of the benefice.[137] It was held, moreover, that any pension in excess of the determined amount would be entirely void.[138] The S. Congregation of the Council resolved that a pension of an amount greater than half of the income could be imposed by the Pope, provided that the beneficiary consented thereto.[139] The benefice in such a case was usually one without the care of souls, for instance, a canonry.[140] As a general practice, however, the Sovereign Pontiff did not reserve pensions of over half the revenue of residential benefices.[141] It was held that normally a pension in excess of half the income of a residential benefice was invalid. Such a pension might be declared void even when the reservation had been granted by the Pope and it was subsequently proven that the consent of the beneficiary had not been knowingly and prudently given, or an insufficient balance remained to support the incumbent of the benefice.[142] The usual amount was not to exceed a third of the income.[143]

[135] C. 30, X, *de praebendis et dignitatibus*, III, 5. Cf. Hinschius, II, 414; Phillips, *Kirchenrecht*, VII, 308-309.

[136] Sess. XXIV, *de ref.*, c. 13, "Ad haec."

[137] Cf. Fagnanus, in c. "Nisi essent," *de praebendis et dignitatibus*, n. 37; De Luca, *De pensionibus*, disc. 40, n. 2; disc. 41, n. 12; Reiffenstuel, Lib. III, tit. 12, n. 98; Hinschius, II, 414; Phillips, *Kirchenrecht*, VII, 310. Cf. also S. R. R., *Recent.*, pars XIX, tom. 1, decis. 379, n. 11.

[138] La-Croix, *Theologia moralis*, IV, n. 1133.

[139] *Verulana*, "Pensionis," 14 maii 1833, § Peritiam.—Pallottini, "Pensio," n. 68.

[140] S. C. C., *Firmana*, "Concordiae," 21 nov. 1807, § Quamvis.—Pallottini, "Pensio," n. 67.

[141] S. R. R., *Recent.*, pars II, decis. 739, n. 2. Cf. also Pallottini, "Pensio," n. 67.

[142] Cf. S. R. R., *Beneventana*, "Pensionum," 28 iun. 1669; "Pensionis," 4 iul. 1670.—*Recent.*, pars XVI, decis. 157; decis. 342, n. 2, citing a constitution of Urban VIII (*Bull.* n. 69, § 2, tom. 1).

The pensioner had a right to the payment of a legitimately established pension. It was the common opinion that the beneficiary was obliged under pain of serious sin; for, in the document establishing the pension, payment was prescribed under pain of excommunication, which presupposed grave sin.[144] Moreover, by accepting a benefice on which there was a pension, the beneficiary was regarded as having made a contract with the pensioner.[145] The obligation of paying was an *onus reale* (at least for relatively or absolutely perpetual pensions), resting not so much on the person as on the benefice;[146] for by it there was created a kind of *hypotheca* (although not in the strict technical sense of mortgage) not on the church or benefice or its real estate, but on the fruits of the benefice.[147]

Sixtus V (1585-1590) provided that payment could not be withheld from those excused by him from wearing the clerical garb and tonsure, but he was referring to clerics whose annual pensions did not exceed sixty ducats *auri de camera*.[148]

Ordinarily the pension was to be paid by the actual incumbent of the benefice. Complications arose when a benefice became vacant

143 "Viget quidem in Dataria consuetudo non onerandi Beneficia residentialia ultra tertiam vel dimidiam partem ejus fructuum."—S. R. R., *Romana*, "Pensionis," 27 feb. 1761.—*Decisiones Sacrae Romanae Rotae coram . . . Bartholomaeo Olivatio* (Romae, 1784), tom. II, decis. 240, n. 10. Cf. Schmalzgrueber, Lib. III, tit. 12, n. 13.

144 Schmalzgrueber, Lib. III, tit. 12, n. 26, citing Leurenius, *Forum beneficiale*, Pars III, q. 544. Ojetti, *Synopsis rerum moralium et iuris pontificii* (ed. 3., Romae, 1909-1914), "Pensio," n. 3111, Vol. III, 2964.

145 S. R. R., *Recent.*, pars I, decis. 176, n. 1; pars III, decis. 110, n. 14. La-Croix, *Theologia moralis*, IV, n. 1159, citing many others.

146 S. R. R., *Recent.*, pars III, decis. 176, n. 3; pars XVI, decis. 23. S. C. C., Firmana, "*Capellaniae curatae*," 29 iul. 1837 § Hisce.—Pallottini, "Pensio," n. 100.

147 Ventriglia, *Praxis fori*, II, adnot. 11, § 2, n. 34; De Luca, *De pensionibus*, disc. 19, n. 5.

148 Const. "*Pastoralis*," 31 ian. 1589, §§ 1-3.—*Magnum Bullarium Romanum a beato Leone Magno usque ad S. D. N. Benedictum XIII*, ed. Laertius Cherubini, . . . Angelo Maria Cherubini, et al. (Luxemburgi, 1727), II, 712. Henceforth cited as *Magn. Bull. Rom.* Cf. S. C. C., *Caesenaten.*, "Pensionis," 16 apr. 1825.—Pallottini, "Pensio," n. 78. Fagnanus, in c. "Ad audientiam," *de rescriptis*, I, 3, n. 76; Ventriglia, *Praxis fori*, II, adnot. 11, § 3, n. 27.

on which there had been reserved a pension lasting beyond the life of the incumbent. If the pension was not paid by the beneficiary, then his heirs were bound. If they were unable, and the pensioner proved that he had used necessary diligence to obtain payment when it was due, then the successor in the benefice was bound to pay the portion of the pension unpaid by his predecessor, and could be sued by the pensioner.[149] The reason was that the obligation of paying the pension in instances of this kind seemed to be imposed not on the fruits of this or that particular year but on the income in general until the pension would be paid; and the Pope, it was explained in one case, seemed to have thus obliged the incumbent and his successors in the benefice. Hence, the latter were bound to meet the obligations of the past, not as their own debt but as that of the benefice.[150]

If the pensioner died before the payment of the pension became due, the beneficiary was bound to pay to his heirs an amount prorated on the income for the time while the pensioner was living and enjoyed the right to the pension.[151]

Article 5. Rights and Obligations of the Pensioner

Pope Leo X (1513-1521) in the Fifth Council of the Lateran (1512-1517) obligated those who had benefices to recite the divine office under pain of losing the fruits of their benefice.[152] St. Pius V (1566-1572) in the constitution "*Ex proximo,*" issued on September

[149] S. R. R., *Neritonensis,* "Pensionis," 10 iun. 1611.—*Recent.*, pars II, decis. 352, n. 2. Cf. Ferraris, "Pensio," n. 109 for additional cases. De Luca, *De pensionibus*, disc. 19, nn. 5, 14; disc. 31, n. 8; disc. 33, n. 4; disc. 87, nn. 2, 7; Ventriglia, *Praxis fori*, II, adnot. 11, § 2, n. 42.

In a case concerning a vacant canonry to which a pension was attached it was decided that the actual successor should make the payment rather than the canon who had an option on the prebend; S. C. C., *Signina*, "Optionis," 27 mart. 1858—Pallottini, "Optio," n. 54; "Pensio," n. 109-110.

[150] S. R. R., *Recent.*, pars XVI, decis. 231, n. 14.

[151] S. R. R., *Apud Coccin.*, decis. 327, n. 1; *apud Cavaler.* decis. 129.—cf. Ferraris, "Pensio," n. 110. Ventriglia, *Praxis fori*, II, adnot. 11, § 3, n. 7-8; De Luca, *De beneficiis*, disc. 81, n. 23; disc. 138, n. 10; *De pensionibus*, disc. 28, n. 3-4.

[152] Const. "*Supernae dispositionis,*" 5 maii 1514, § 38.—*Fontes*, n. 65.

20, 1571, explained this obligation in greater detail and imposed a corresponding obligation on all those receiving clerical pensions to recite the little office of the Blessed Virgin. Failure to observe this decree would result in the loss of a proportionate amount of the pension.[153] In 1583 the Provincial Council of Bordeaux, whose statutes were approved by the Holy See, repeated almost to the word the Pianine constitution, and further determined that if pensioned clerics contumaciously persisted in neglecting the little office, after an admonition they were to be deprived of the pension. By "omission of the office" as ground for deprivation was meant failure to say it at least twice during fifteen days unless legitimately excused because of some grave hindrance.[154]

Authors commonly taught that the pensioner satisfied his obligation if he recited the divine office and omitted the little office. Moreover, for a cleric in major orders or one having a benefice and a pension a recitation of the divine office alone sufficed, and the little office could be omitted.[155]

One whose pension was redeemed in full by authority of the Holy See was no longer obliged to recite the little office. This was not true, however, if without due authorization he accepted advance payment of the pension.[156]

The obligation of wearing clerical garb and tonsure was imposed by Sixtus V (1585-1590) on all those whose pension or pensions amounted to more than 60 ducats *auri de Camera*. Violation was punished with loss of the pension.[157] According to Pallottini, Bene-

[153] "§ 1 . . . At quicumque pensionem, fructus, aut alias res ecclesiasticas, ut clericus percipit, eum modo praedicto ad dicendum Officium parvum Beatae Mariae Virginis decernimus obligatum, et pensionum, fructuum, rerumque ipsarum amissione obnoxium."—*Bull. Rom. Taur.*, VII, n. 206, p. 942-943; *Fontes*, n. 140.

[154] III. *De ecclesiasticis precationibus*.—Mansi, XXXIV A, 749. Cf. Provincial Council of Aquileia (1596), XI: *De vita et honestate clericorum*.—Mansi, XXXIV B, 1398. Provincial Council of Avignon (1594), XXXIV; *De horis canonicis*, § 7.—Mansi, XXXIV B, 1351.

[155] Barbosa, *Iuris ecclesiastici universi*, Lib. III, c. 11, n. 12; Ventriglia, *Praxis fori*, II, adnot. 11, § 2, n. 86.

[156] La-Croix, *Theologia moralis*, IV, n. 1156.

[157] Const. "*Cum Sacrosanctum*," 9 ian. 1589.—*Magn. Bull. Rom.*, II, 713;

dict XIV (1740-1758) decreed that not only those whose pensions were less than 60 ducats *auri de Camera*, but also members of the pontifical family were excused from wearing the clerical habit and tonsure.[158]

Authors did not agree whether a pensioner had to give the superfluous income of his pension to pious causes as the beneficiary was bound to do. The greater weight of authority seemed to incline toward a negative opinion.[159]

Pensions were generally exempt from all taxes, tithes or similar burdens. The pensioner drawing on a prebend was not bound to contribute toward the distributions, this being the obligation of the titular.[160] In the document granting a pension it was usually stated that it should be paid *integre*—in its full amount, without any reductions.[161] Although ordinarily exempt from contributing to the support of the seminary—the Council of Trent did not include pensioners among those to be taxed[162]—extreme needs could justify the ordinary in taxing the pensioner, notwithstanding a custom of even 200 years favoring exemption, unless the right of exemption could be proven positively.[163] The Pope may have privileged the pension to be entirely free, immune, and exempt, freeing the pensioner from any obligation of assisting the benefice.[164] But unless so exempt by the Holy See, pensioners were held to be bound in extraordinary circumstances to contribute to the seminary in propor-

Bull. Rom. Taur., IX, 66-69; *Fontes*, n. 314. Const. "*Pastoralis*," 31 ian. 1589.—*Bull. Rom. Taur.*, IX, 69-71.

158 "Pensio," n. 77, pointing to S. C. C., *Melevitana*, 18 dec. 1762, § Altera.—*Thesaurus*, XXXI (1762), 272.

159 Cf. La-Croix, *Theologia moralis*, IV, n. 1157; St. Alphonsus Liguori, *Theologia moralis*, Lib. III, tract. 5, n. 491, quaer. 6; Ferraris, "Pensio," n. 140.

160 S. C. C., *Dubium* ad Sess. XXII, *de ref.*, c. 3, posit. 14.—Pallottini, "Pensio," n. 117.

161 De Angelis, *Praelectiones*, Lib. III, tit. 12, n. 6; Pyrrhus, *Praxis beneficiaria* (Venetiis, 1735), Lib. V, c. 7, n. 22.

162 Sess. XXIII, *de ref.*, c. 18.

163 Thus S. C. C., *Veliterna*, "Taxae Seminarii," 20 apr. 1771.—Pallottini, "Pensio," n. 113. Cf. also Ferraris, "Pensio," n. 130.

164 La-Croix, *Theologia moralis*, IV, n. 1158, citing Azor, Barbosa, Lotterius, Leurenius, *et al.*

tion to what the incumbents contributed.[165] Likewise, the pensioner was usually not obliged to contribute to the *mensa episcopalis,* for instance, toward the annual expenses for the cathedral preacher.[166] The pensioner was bound to contribute a prorated portion of his pension on a benefice toward the repairs of its church, just as the beneficiary was bound, unless the pension was imposed with the papal provision that it was to be free from all burdens.[167] The recipient of a pension was not included in the tax imposed by the *motu proprio* of Pius VII (1800-1823) issued on March 19, 1801.[168] He was bound, however, to pay tithes and other tributes to the civil government, unless specifically exempted.[169]

Only with permission of the Holy See was it allowed to transfer a pension either in whole or in part to another cleric.[170]

Popes Urban VIII (1623-1644)[171] and Innocent XI (1676-1689)[172] granted this faculty to cardinals.

The same faculty with certain restrictions as to the number of transfers permitted, the amount allowed to be transferred, and formalities to be observed at the time of executing the transfer (e. g., the required presence of a notary, witnesses) was granted to members of the papal household by a number of Popes, to mention only

[165] S. C. C., *Tridentina,* ao. 1595; *Lucana,* 5 iul. 1628; *Caven.,* 4 dec. 1638. —Pallottini, "Pensio," n. 114.

[166] S. C. C., *Nullius,* 29 maii 1649.—Pallottini, "Pensio," n. 116. Cf. S. C. C., *Calaritana,* 14 maii 1729.—Pallottini, "Pensio," n. 119.

[167] S. R. R., *Recent.,* pars IX, tom. 2, decis. 343, n. 32. S. C. C., *Civitatis,* "Plebis," 18 mart. 1628.—Pallottini, "Pensio," n. 115. Ventriglia, *Praxis fori,* II, adnot. 11, § 2, n. 1-3. Ferraris, "Pensio," n. 129-133. Hinschius, II, 416. Schmalzgrueber, Lib. III, tit. 12, n. 29.

[168] "Hoc enim vectigal impositum est super proprietate bonorum, et contribuere debent, qui ius habent super proprietate, et pensio imposita est super fructibus."—S. C. C., *Hortana,* "Congruae," 28 feb. 1807, § Hinc; Pallottini, "Parochus," § IV, n. 14; "Pensio," n. 118.

[169] S. R. R., *Recent.,* pars V, tom. 1, decis. 23, n. 31.

[170] Cf. Leurenius, *Forum beneficiale,* pars III, q. 607; Schmalzgrueber, Lib. III, tit. 12, n. 37; Hinschius, II, 416; Wernz, *Ius decretalium,* II, n. 321.

[171] Const. "*Cum S. R. E. Cardinales,*" 1 apr. 1631.—*Bull. Rom. Taur.,* XIV, n. 392.

[172] Const. "*Circumspecta,*" 7 feb. 1677—Text: Ferraris, "Pensio," nn. 79-80; De Luca, *De pensionibus,* appendix. Cf. Hinschius, I, 324.

Urban VIII (1623-1644), who permitted but one transfer;[173] Alexander VIII (1689-1691), permitting a transfer up to 300 ducats to be made before a notary and trustworthy witnesses;[174] Innocent XIII (1721-1724), with provisions similar to those of Alexander VIII;[175] and Pius VI (1775-1799), forbidding transfer of pensions drawn on cathedrals, monasteries, or other benefices in Rome and the Papal States, and permitting but one transfer of other pensions.[176]

Auditors of the Signatura were permitted by Clement XI (1700-1721) to transfer pensions up to an amount of 100 ducats.[177] Later the same Pontiff gave them the extended privilege of transferring pensions even after they had retired from active work, and up to the same amount.[178]

Pensions drawn on benefices held by cardinals were not to be transferred, according to the *bulla* of Urban VIII (1623-1644).[179] Likewise, the constitution of Innocent XI (1676-1689) was to be observed, in which it was decreed that only half of these pensions could be transferred by those who had an indult.[180]

Conclavists and dapifers, as they were generously given pensions, were also in most instances empowered to transfer them.[181]

In transferring a pension it was required to observe the solemnities

[173] Bulla "*Circumspecta*," 6 aug. 1623.—*Bull. Rom. Taur.*, XIII, n. 1; const. "*Inter gravissimas*," 8 mart. 1636.—*Bull. Rom. Taur.*, XIV, 522-524.

[174] Bulla VIII "*Venerabilibus fratribus*," 12 ian. 1690.—*Bull. Rom. Taur.*, XX, 23-33. Thus also Innocent XII (1691-1700), bulla "*Venerabilibus fratribus*," 27 nov. 1691.—*Bull. Rom. Taur.*, XX, 231-232.

[175] Const. IV, *Conceduntur privilegia familiaribus Sanctitatis Suae*, 26 maii 1721.—*Bull. Rom. Taur.*, XXI, 875.

[176] Ex Camera Apostolica, "*Ai venerabili fratelli*," 22 iun. 1775.—*Bullarii Romani continuatio* (Romae, 1835-1857), VIII, 106.

[177] Const. "*Romanus Pontifex*," 28 mart. 1701.—*Bull. Rom. Taur.*, XXI, 21-22.

[178] Const. "*Creditae nobis*," 12 aug. 1701.—*Bull. Rom. Taur.*, XXI, 38-40.

[179] "*Cum S. R. E. Cardinales*," 11 apr. 1631.—*Bull. Rom. Taur.*, XIV, 210.

[180] "*Circumspecta*," 7 feb. 1677.—Text: Ferraris, "Pensio," nn. 79-80.

[181] Urban VIII, const. "*Romanus Pontifex*," *Bull. Rom.*, tom. V, part. 5, p. 173. S. C. C., *Aesina*, "Pensionis," 13 maii 1702; *Faventina*, "Pensionis," 17 dec. 1836.—Pallottini, "Pensio," n. 11.

prescribed in the papal indult; otherwise the transfer was null;[182] but the faculty to transfer was not thereby lost.[183]

At the end of the last century Pope Leo XIII (1878-1903) revoked all papal concessions and abolished the rights of transferring pensions.[184]

Article 6. The Termination of Ecclesiastical Pensions

The income of a benefice might become so attenuated that it was insufficient becomingly to support the incumbent or to enable him to assist the poor, to practice hospitality towards travelers, to pay the episcopal taxes, and to meet other ordinary expenses. In such a case if there was a pension on a benefice it was reduced proportionately or at times completely extinguished.[185] The incumbent would not, however, be competent to reduce the pension of his own authority.[186]

In computing the reduction the basis was usually the average income of the benefice for a ten-year period.[187]

[182] Leurenius, *Forum beneficiale*, III, q. 660; La-Croix, *Theologia moralis*, IV, n. 1170; Tondutus, *Tractatus de pensionibus*, c. 28, nn. 19-33.

[183] Garcias, *De beneficiis*, I, c. 5, n. 249; Monacelli, *Formularium legale practicum fori ecclesiastici* (3. ed., Romae, 1844), II, tit. 14, formul. 6, n. 7.

[184] "Che sieno abrogati ed aboliti i privilegi dei quali, in virtù di pontificie concessioni, hanno fin qui usato i Cardinali di S. Romana Chiesa, i Conclavisti, altre persone o collegi di persone, di trasferire ad altri le pensioni ad esse conferite."—Dataria Ap., *Litterae Eminentissimi Cardinalis a Secretis Status, ad Emum Pro-Datarium quoad Beneficia et pensiones ecclesiasticas*, 24 maii 1899, 4°.—*Acta Sanctae Sedis* (Romae, 1865-1908), XXXIII (1900-1901), 122. Henceforth cited ASS. Cf. Ojetti, *Synopsis rerum moralium et iuris pontificii*, "Pensio," III, pp. 2965-2966, n. 3114.

[185] Garcias, *De beneficiis*, I, c. 5, n. 366. Schmalzgrueber, Lib. III, tit. 12, n. 13; De Angelis, *Praelectiones*, Lib. III, tit. 12, n. 7. S. R. R., *Recent.*, pars X, decis. 306, n. 22. S. C. C., *Ariminen.*, "Pensionis," 12 sept. 1829.—Pallottini, "Pensio," n. 45. S. C. Ep. et Reg., decr. "*Cum nuperrimis*," *De pensionibus ecclesiasticis pro rata portione imminuendis ob usurpationes et gravamina bonorum Ecclesiae in Italia existentium*, 20 ian. 1871.—ASS, VII (1872), 325-327; *idem*, *Quoad reductionem vel suppressionem pensionum*, 30 maii 1873.—ASS, *ibid.*, 328-336.

[186] S. C. C., *Mandelen.*, "Aperitionis oris et pensionis," 13 iun. 1885.—ASS, XVIII (1885), 200-203. Cf. Ojetti, *Synopsis*, "Pensio," III, p. 2964, n. 3111.

[187] S. C. C., *Reatina*, "Pensionis," 15 dec. 1804.—Pallottini, "Pensio," n.

Ventriglia maintained that in the case of diminished income the original amount assigned for the support of the beneficiary should be maintained; only the amount of the pension should be reduced.[188] This was indeed the necessary mode of computation for those benefices covered by the Tridentine canon,[189] and on which pensions were reserved with the clause, "*dummodo remaneant centum pro Rectore, mille pro Episcopo,*" respectively. If doubt persisted, the Apostolic Datary was to be consulted.[190]

The income of a benefice might have been impaired only for one or the other years because of invasion, poor crops, and the like. The Rota decided in one case that temporary diminution of the fruits did not excuse from paying the pension, since the prosperous years ought to compensate for the lean ones.[191] Clericatus (1633-1717) objected to this principle of compensation for three reasons: first, the fruits of a benefice are intended to serve as means of subsistence from year to year; secondly, a pension is a part of the fruits of each year; thirdly, a pension, being assigned for sustenance, ought to be regulated according to the current food supply.[192]

The acceptance of a benefice on which a pension was reserved, together with the statement that the income of the benefice was able to meet this obligation, cast the burden of contrary proof on the beneficiary, if he later sought to have the pension reduced or deleted.[193]

58; *Ripana,* "Pensionis," 13 feb. 1819, § Contra.—Pallottini, "Pensio," n. 54; *Firmana,* "Pensionis," 17 mart. 1827, 20 sept. 1828.—Pallottini, "Aperitio oris," nn. 247-252, "Pensio," n. 49; *Civitatis Castellanae,* "Pensionis," 12 sept. 1807, § Quatenus.—Pallottini, "Pensio," n. 65.

188 *Praxis fori,* II, adnot. 11, § 3, n. 12-13.

189 Sess. XXIV, *de ref.,* c. 13.

190 Cf. S. C. C., *Reatina,* "Pensionis," 15 dec. 1804.—Pallottini, "Pensio," n. 58. Cf. also S. C. Ep. et Reg., "*Cum nuperrimis,*" 28 ian. 1871, conclusiones, V.—ASS, VII, (1872), 327.

191 *Divers.,* pars I, decis. 757, n. 3.—Ferraris, "Pensio," append. n. 14.

192 *Tractatus de pensionibus,* discord. 2, n. 6 sq., *apud* Ferraris, "Pensio," append. n. 14.

193 S. R. R., *Recent.,* pars XVI, decis. 120, nn. 5, 65. S. C. C., *Forosempronien.,* "Pensionis," 23 iun. 1821, § Iusta.—Pallottini, "Pensio," n. 52; cf. also *ibid.,* nn. 47-49. Lotterius, *De re beneficiaria,* Lib. I, q. 38, n. 45; q. 42, n. 60. Garcias, *De beneficiis,* Lib. I, c. 5, n. 424.

It was generally forbidden to sell a pension or to redeem it by advance payments, although some authors drew fine distinctions between various kinds of pensions, and between the sale of the pension as such or only of its fruits.[194] Pope Pius V (1566-1572) decreed that any sale or redemption of a pension without permission of the Holy See was simoniacal and null.[195] By the eighteenth century there had arisen a widespread practice by which some beneficiaries, who with apostolic permission resigned their benefices and reserved a pension on them, agreed privately with the one in whose favor the resignation was made that the pension could be redeemed by anticipated payments. Whereupon Pope Benedict XIV (1740-1758) by apostolic constitution decreed that any petition for the reservation of a pension after resignation of a benefice, if colored with such private agreements, was surreptitious, simoniacal and invalid; further, that any redemption of a pension within six months after taking possession of the benefice, even in the absence of any previous pact, was likewise null.[196]

Authors commonly found nothing intrinsically reprehensible in loaning the fruits of a pension or the use thereof. They maintained, however, that it could not be done for more than three years without permission of the Holy See.[197]

The question whether a pension could become extinct by a long period of non-payment was studied by civilists, canonists, and theologians. They applied the general principle that thirty years were required to prescribe against annual payments, but then not the entire debt was extinguished, but only the amount due for one year. Hence, payment could always be demanded for the other twenty-nine years.[198]

194 Barbosa, *Iuris ecclesiastici universi*, Lib. III, c. 11, nn. 19-25. Cf. also Ferraris, "Pensio," nn. 100-101.

195 Const. "*Ex proximo*," 20 sept. 1571.—*Fontes*, n. 140.

196 Const. "*In sublimi*," 29 aug. 1741.—*Fontes*, n. 317.

197 C. un., *de rebus ecclesiae non alienandis*, III, 4, in Extravag. com.; Garcias, *De beneficiis*, Pars II, c. 1, n. 37; Ventriglia, *Praxis fori*, Tom. II, adnot. 11, § 3, n. 42; De Angelis, *Praelectiones*, Lib. III, tit. 12, n. 7, 10°.

198 " . . . quot sunt anni tot requiruntur praescriptiones, quarum unaquaeque incipiat à singulis annis." S. R. R., *Recent.*, pars XVII, decis. 330, n. 20; cf. also n. 19. Cf. Gigas, *Tractatus de pensionibus ecclesiasticis*, q. 83, n.

Failure to demand payment of the pension sometimes furnished a presumption for its nullity or extinction, according to the axiom that when the pensioner could act but neglected to do so, the pension is presumed to be extinct.[199] There were decisions rendered by the Rota where the cessation of pensions was admitted after ten [200] and even five years of non-payment.[201]

Ought a pension cease if the poverty of the pensioner ceased? Cardinal de Luca, although he had admittedly been unable to find any authority, was inclined to hold the affirmative as more probable, at least for pensions imposed by ordinaries.[202] The opinion seemed to be borne out by analogy in a Rota case,[203] quoted by the same author. It was decided that a pension imposed on certain benefices to support a newly established college was to cease after provision had been made for its proper maintenance from other sources, the reason being the cessation of the final cause of the pension.

The pension is extinguished if the pensioner is promoted to the benefice on which he had been drawing the pension, just as usufruct becomes extinct with the acquisition of dominion over the object whose fruits were enjoyed.[204]

A pension was not extinguished by the fact that the recipient

9-11; De Luca, *De pensionibus*, disc. 67, n. 6; Clericatus, *De pensionibus*, discord. 18, nn. 17-18. Ferraris, "Pensio," append., n. 18.

199 Clericatus, *De pensionibus*, discord. 18, n. 7, although in n. 13 he holds the contrary opinion; cf. Ferraris, "Pensio," append., n. 19.

200 Coram Priolo, decis. 266, n. 22; *Melevitana*, "Pensionis," (1669).—*Recent.*, pars XVI, decis. 152, in fin.; Ferraris, "Pensio," append., n. 19. But in S. R. R., *Melevitana*, "Pensionis," (1672), (*Recent.*, pars XVII, decis. 279, n. 3), it was resolved that a ten-year lapse alone was not sufficient to establish a presumption in petitory action.

201 Coram Boratto, decis. 591, n. 9.—Ferraris, "Pensio," append., n. 19.

202 *De pensionibus*, decis. 40, n. 6. He based his argument on the rule, "Cessante causa cessat effectus." Cf. c. 7, C. I, q. 1; c. 11, X, *de renunciatione*, I, 9, *glossa* in v. "Cessante."; c. 60, X, *de appellationibus, recusationibus et relationibus*, II, 28.

203 *Melevitan.*, "Contributionis," 21 apr. 1660, coram Cerro; cf. De Luca, *De pensionibus*, disc. 77, n. 2; *De beneficiis*, disc. 88; Ferraris, "Pensio," append., n. 25.

204 De Angelis, *Praelectiones*, Lib. III, tit. 12, n. 7, 4°; Tondutus, *Tractatus de pensionibus*, c. 74, n. 9-12, invoking Roman law.

was elevated to the papacy. Lotterius not only proves this opinion in law, but also adduces cases where it was carried out in practice.[205]

It had been held that promotion to the cardinalate likewise did not necessarily bring about the extinction of any pensions previously held.[206] Indeed, a pension conferred in favor of a cardinal continued even after he abdicated or resigned from the cardinalate.[207]

By promotion to the episcopate pensions were deemed extinguished not, it is true, by common law,[208] but by the *stylus Curiae* based on a certain decree of Julius II (1503-1513) and approved by Clement VII (1523-1534).[209] Not only did the pensions cease, but any former indult to transfer such pensions failed likewise.[210] If it was intended that the bishop retain his pension, the clause "*cum retentione compatibilium*" was included in the letter of appointment;[211] and although the bishop-elect was permitted to "obtain, retain, receive, and freely dispose of pensions," it was the prevalent opinion that this concession could not be extended to the transfer of pensions, in the sense of a transfer of the right itself.[212]

The extinction touched only those promoted to a residential bish-

[205] *De re beneficiaria*, Lib. I, q. 41, n. 1 sq. Thus also Ventriglia, *Praxis fori*, Tom. II, adnot. 11, § 3, n. 26. *Contra*, La-Croix, IV, n. 1177, with a number of others. Cf. also Ferraris, "Pensio," n. 71.

[206] De Luca, *De pensionibus*, disc. 75, nn. 4-5, 9; La-Croix, *Theologia moralis*, IV, n. 1177.

[207] De Luca, *De beneficiis*, disc. 2, n. 3; *De pensionibus*, disc. 2, n. 4.

In the footnote to canon 235 of the Gasparri edition of the *Codex iuris canonici*, the constitutions "*Sanctissimus*," of Sixtus V and "*Decet Romanum Pontificem*," of Urban VIII, cited as the *fontes* of the canon make no express mention of loss of pensions. Said documents are concerned in the main with incompatible offices and dignities.

[208] C. 7, X, *de electione et electi potestate*, I, 6 mentions only benefices.

[209] Const. "*Cum dudum*," 19 apr. 1524.—*Bull. Rom. Taur.*, VI, 67-69. Cf. Schmalzgrueber, Lib. III, tit. 12, n. 42.

[210] S. R. R., *Tricaricen.*, "Pensionis," 8 iun. 1735, § 4, coram Crescent.; *Imolen.*, "Pensionis," 21 iun. 1748, § 7, coram Vicecomit.—Ferraris, "Pensio," nn. 146, 148. *Recent.*, pars II, decis. 143, n. 1.

[211] Schmalzgrueber, Lib. III, tit. 12, n. 42.

[212] S. R. R., *Tricaricen.*, "Pensionis," 8 iun. 1735, § 4, coram Crescent.—Ferraris, "Pensio," n. 148. *Recent.*, pars II, decis. 143, n. 1. Barbosa, *Iuris ecclesiastici universi*, Lib. III, c. 11, n. 38.

opric, and became effective only after their consecration and installation,[213] with the exception of suburbicarian cardinalatial bishoprics, which were exempted in virtue of a decision rendered by a special congregation appointed by Alexander VII (1655-1667).[214] A further exception was the case of bishops *in partibus infidelium*, or titular bishops, as they had neither possession of nor income from their titular sees, but only the name and the dignity.[215]

Pope Leo XIII, considering on the one hand the diminished number of benefices, and on the other hand desiring to assist priests in poverty, laid down severe restrictions with regard to the retention of pensions by those promoted to higher dignities or offices. He decreed that on the day of their promotion all cardinals, residential bishops, nuncios, secretaries of the Sacred Congregations of Bishops and Regulars, of the Council, and of the Propagation of the Faith, assessors of the Holy Office, and majordomos of His Holiness, would lose all pensions which they may have.[216]

As benefices became vacant by religious profession,[217] so it was commonly held that pensions likewise became extinguished.[218] Religious profession included those professed in a military order, but only if they were true religious, like the Teutonic Knights and the Knights Templar.[219] Jesuits who had taken only the simple vows binding for two years, could retain pensions just as they could retain other goods.[220]

[213] De Luca, *De pensionibus*, disc. 43, n. 2; Ventriglia, *Praxis fori*, Tom. II, adnot. 11, § 8, n. 32; De Angelis, *Praelectiones*, Lib. III, tit. 12, n. 7, 5°.

[214] Schmalzgrueber, Lib. III, tit. 12, n. 42.

[215] De Luca, *De pensionibus*, disc. 43, n. 3; disc. 58, n. 11; disc. 75, n. 2; Schmalzgrueber, Lib. III, tit. 12, n. 42.

[216] Dataria Ap., *Litterae Eminentissimi Cardinalis a Secretis Status, ad Emum Pro-Datarium quoad Beneficia et pensiones ecclesiasticas*, 24 maii 1899, 1°.—ASS, XXXIII (1900-1901), 121.

[217] C. 4, *de regularibus et transeuntibus ad religionem*, III, 14, in VI° referring to solemn profession, since religious congregations appeared after the XVI century; cf. Wernz-Vidal, *Ius canonicum*, III *(De religiosis)*, n. 37.

[218] Barbosa, *Iuris ecclesiastici universi*, Lib. III, c. 11, n. 39. S. R. R., *Recent.*, pars IV, tom. 1, decis. 246, nn. 2, 6; pars XII, decis. 121, n. 1. Cf. Ferraris, "Pensio," n. 51-52.

[219] Leurenius, *Forum beneficiale*, Pars III, q. 648, n. 2.

[220] Schmalzgrueber, Lib. III, tit. 12, n. 43.

Clerics who contracted marriage could not retain pensions. It mattered not whether the marriage was valid or invalid; for the will to act is manifest even from an invalid act.[221] If, however, the marriage was invalid for lack of consent, the pension was not lost.[222] For clerics in minor orders, who were free to contract marriage, the pension became extinct *ipso iure* in virtue of tacit resignation.[223] For a cleric in major orders, all maintained that the pension was extinguished by way of penalty, but there was difference of opinion whether the penalty had to be inflicted by judicial declaration or whether privation was automatic.[224] A pension lost by contracting marriage was irrevocably lost, so that it did not revive in case the marriage was dissolved when the wife, before consummation of the marriage, made solemn religious profession.[225] The Pope alone could permit a cleric who had entered the married state to retain his pension.[226] Such indult had to be received before the marriage consent was given; there could be no question of a sanation, since the pension became extinct *ipso facto* even though the marriage was contracted in the sincere belief that the privilege had been dispatched.[227] A dispensation to retain a pension had to be interpreted strictly; it could not be effective if a further cause for terminating a pension was present.[228]

[221] "Voluntas recedendi ab Ecclesiasticae castitatis observatione probatur etiam actu nullo." Tondutus, *Tractatus de pensionibus*, c. 75, n. 25.

[222] Barbosa, *Iuris ecclesiastici universi*, Lib. III, c. 11, n. 30. S. R. R., decis. 30, n. 12-13, et addit. n. 54, coram Ansaldo; S. C. C., *Regien.*, "Pensionis," 17 sept. 1722, § Praemisso.—Pallottini, "Pensio," n. 81.

[223] Tondutus, *Tractatus de pensionibus*, c. 75, n. 3.

[224] Tondutus, *ibid.*, n. 43; Barbosa, *Iuris ecclesiastici universi*, Lib. III, c. 11, n. 30.

[225] Conc. Trid., Sess. XXIV, *de matrimonio*, c. 6. Barbosa, *Iuris ecclesiastici universi*, Lib. III, c. 11, n. 30 S. R. R., coram Ansaldo, decis. 30, n. 12-13, et addit. n. 54; S. C. C., *Regien.*, "Pensionis," 17 sept. 1722, § Praemisso.—Pallottini, "Pensio," nn. 81, 95.

[226] S. R. R., *Recent.*, Pars V, tom. 1, decis. 50, n. 10. S. C. C., *Nullius Foropompilii*, 21 aug. 1819, § Nec.—Pallottini, "Pensio," n. 80; *Praenestina*, "Pensionis," 2 mart. 1844, 30 aug. 1845, 2 maii 1846.—Pallottini, "Bigamus," nn. 41-50.

[227] S. C. C., *Regien.*, "Pensionis," 17 sept. 1722.—Pallottini, "Pensio," n. 95.

[228] Monacelli, *Formularium*, II, tit. 14, formul. 7, n. 11.

Failure to dress as a cleric could effect the extinction of a pension. Pope Sixtus V (1585-1590) decreed that those who failed to wear the tonsure and clerical garb would automatically without further admonition lose their pensions, unless it was a pension specifically exempt from such obligation.[229] Twenty-one days later another constitution was promulgated in which it was decreed that a pension of more than 60 *scuti de camera* ceased automatically, without any previous admonition, citation, or judicial decree, if the pensioner failed to wear the clerical habit and tonsure.[230]

Entrance into the ranks of the secular army constituted a specific cause for extinction of pensions. Thus, a certain cleric (in minor orders) who had permission to receive a pension by an ample dispensation excusing him from wearing the required clerical dress, and also allowing him to contract marriage, or to become professed in some military order approved by the Holy See, nevertheless could not extend the privilege to his membership in the secular army.[231] A specific dispensation had to be obtained, nor were sanations readily granted.[232] Such extinction was not automatic, but followed only upon an unheeded warning.[233] The extinction took effect even if the person before having engaged in actual battle withdrew from the army and returned to his former state.[234]

Members of the various military orders usually enjoyed a number

[229] Const. "*Cum Sacrosanctam*," 9 ian. 1589, § 2.—*Bull. Rom. Taur.*, IX, n. 141, p. 66-69; *Fontes*, n. 167.

[230] Const. "*Pastoralis est curae*," 31 ian. 1589.—*Bull. Rom. Taur.*, IX, 69-71. This constitution apparently excused those whose pension was less than the amount specified; Hinschius, II, 416, note 10. Cf. also De Luca, *De pensionibus*, disc. 48, n. 7; Ventriglia, *Praxis fori*, II, adnot. 11, § 3, n. 28; Schmalzgrueber, Lib. III, tit. 12, nn. 28, 45.

[231] S. C. C., *Nicien.*, 19 dec. 1648.—Pallottini, "Pensio," n. 87; *Ulixbonen.*, "Orientalis pensionis," 23 nov. 1737.—Pallottini, "Pensio," n. 90.

[232] Ferraris, "Pensio," n. 143.

[233] Schmalzgrueber, Lib. III, tit. 12, n. 43, § 5; but cf. S. R. R., *Perusina*, "Pensionis," 11 maii 1716, coram Herrera; *Recent.*, pars XVI, decis. 279, n. 3 sq.; *Romana*, "Pensionis," 8 iun. 1685, coram Rondinino, cited as precedents in S. C. C., *Romana*, "Indulti," 20 dec. 1721, involving a light armed papal guard.—Pallottini, "Pensio," n. 93.

[234] S. C. C., *Nicien.*, 19 dec. 1648, *apud* Moriacelli, *Formularium*, II, tit. 14, formul. 7, n. 11. Cf. also De Luca, *De pensionibus*, disc. 46, n. 3.

of generous papal privileges in the matter of retaining pensions, even if married or dispensed from wearing clerical garb.[235]

That irregularity renders a person not only incapable of obtaining a pension but also of retaining it was the teaching of Barbosa,[236] Ventriglia,[237] and many others.[238] But Cardinal de Luca held an apparently less common opinion that neither voluntary homicide nor any other crime, no matter what the degree of irregularity arising therefrom, caused the loss of a pension.[239] Fagnanus is of the same opinion, adducing a conclusion of the Sacred Congregation of the Council of July 11, 1577 under Gregory XIII (1572-1585) and another of August 8 of the same year, *de mente Sanctissimi,* that a cleric and his co-operator in voluntary homicide could receive and retain pensions without previous dispensation from this irregularity, notwithstanding the restriction imposed by the seventh chapter of the fourteenth session of the Council of Trent on the reservation of cases, which, it was declared, applied to prospective beneficiaries, but not pensioners.[240]

The commission of serious crimes punishable by loss of office wrought also the extinction of pensions, by reason of the crime.[241] Among the crimes producing this effect were mentioned specifically heresy, *laesae maiestatis aut Sedis Apostolicae,* striking a cardinal or a bishop if, in the latter case, he was the ordinary in whose diocese the pension was had.[242]

[235] Barbosa, *Iuris ecclesiastici universi,* Lib. III, c. 11, n. 32-34.

[236] *Ibid.,* n. 21.

[237] *Praxis fori,* Tom. II, adnot. 11, § 1, n. 20.

[238] Cf. Ferraris, "Pensio," n. 57.

[239] *De pensionibus,* disc. 47, n. 11, citing in corroboration, S. R. R., *Perusina,* 29 ian. 1663, coram Cerro. But S. R. R., *Recent.,* Pars IX, tom. 1, decis. 1, annot. n. 6-9, resolved that a pension is lost by qualified homicide although not *ipso iure.*

[240] In c. "Audientiam" [31, X], *de rescriptis,* I, 3, nn. 133-134; thus also Leurenius, *Forum beneficiale,* Pars III, q. 640. Cf. Schmalzgrueber, Lib. III, tit. 12, n. 24; Ferraris, "Pensio," n. 57. V. *supra,* concerning the confused teaching of the nature and number of canonical irregularities, p. 52-53.

[241] Barbosa, *Iuris ecclesiastici universi,* Lib. III, c. 8, n. 64; Hinschius, II, 417, n. 10; Wernz, *Ius decretalium,* II, n. 321. S. C. C., "Caducitatis a pensione," 4 mart. 1876.—ASS, IX (1876), 376-381.

[242] Schmalzgrueber, Lib. III, tit. 12, n. 45, § 9. It would seem that volun-

An excommunicated incumbent was not permitted to receive the fruits of his benefice; analogously a pension was suspended for the duration of the censure.[243]

tary homicide, one of the capital crimes of the early Church, also wrought the privation of pensions by way of penalty notwithstanding the exception noted in regard to irregularities.

[243] Suarez, *De censuris*, disp. 13, sect. 1, n. 10. Barbosa, *Iuris ecclesiastici universi*, Lib. III, c. 11, n. 47.

PART THREE

COMMENTARY

The ecclesiastical pension is treated in the Code of canon law in the third book, part 5, on benefices and other non-collegiate ecclesiastical institutes, title xxv, on benefices, chapter two, on the union, transfer, division, dismemberment, conversion, and suppression of benefices, canon 1429:

> § 1. Beneficiis quibuslibet nequeunt Ordinarii locorum pensiones perpetuas aut temporarias imponere quae ad vitam pensionarii durent, sed possunt, dum beneficium conferunt, ex iusta causa in ipso collationis actu exprimenda, eisdem imponere pensiones temporarias, quae durent ad vitam beneficiarii, salva huic congrua portione.
>
> § 2. Beneficiis autem paroecialibus non possunt, nisi in commodum parochi vel vicarii eiusdem paroeciae a munere abeuntis, imponere pensiones, quae tamen ne excedant tertiam partem reditus paroeciae, quibusvis deductis expensis et incertis reditibus.
>
> § 3. Pensiones beneficiis sive a Romano Pontifice sive ab aliis collatoribus impositae, cessant morte pensionarii, qui tamen nequit eas alienare, nisi id expresse concessum sit.[1]

Chapter IV

THE ACTIVE SUBJECT OF ECCLESIASTICAL PENSIONS

Article 1. The Holy See

From the moment he accepts his election the Supreme Pontiff, by virtue of his sovereignty over the Church as vicar of her Founder,[1]

[1] *Codex iuris canonici, Pii X Pontificis Maximi iussu digestus, Benedicti Papae XV auctoritate promulgatus, praefatione fontium annotatione et indice analytico-alphabetico ab Emo Petro Card. Gasparri auctus* (Romae: Typis Polyglottis Vaticanis, 1917, reimpressio 1934), pp. 492-493.

[1] Cf. canons 218, 219.

has the power to reserve pensions on any and all benefices and for the benefit of any persons he deems worthy. Pensions on consistorial benefices are reserved through the Sacred Consistorial Congregation, while those on other reserved benefices are arranged through the Apostolic Datary.[2] Others inferior to the Pope can act only within the limits established by law.

Article 2. Local Ordinaries

The right to reserve ecclesiastical pensions is conferred by the Code upon local ordinaries.[3] Besides the Roman Pontiff, the following, unless expressly excepted, are considered local ordinaries for their respective territories: the residential bishop, the abbot or prelate *nullius,* and their vicars general; the administrator apostolic; the vicar and prefect apostolic. In case the see is vacant (or its ordinary is impeded from the exercise of jurisdiction),[4] those are ordinaries who succeed by prescription of law (e. g., the cathedral, abbatial, or prelatial chapter, diocesan consultors, the vicar general *sede impedita,* the senior in the territory, or the senior priest) or by approved particular constitutions (e. g., in an abbacy or prelacy *nullius*).[5] The following are not *per se* included in the term "ordinary": cardinals, legates, patriarchs, metropolitans, primates, titular bishops, coadiutor and auxiliary bishops, abbots without territory, superiors of missions not erected into prefectures or vicariates apostolic, prelates, vicars forane, pastors, or officials and vice-officials of ecclesiastical courts.[6]

[2] Canons 248, 261. Cf. Blat, *Commentarium,* III, part. II-VI *(De rebus),* n. 336.

[3] " . . . Ordinarii locorum . . ." Canon 1429, § 1.

[4] Blat, *Commentarium,* II, pars I *(De personis),* n. 147.

[5] Canon 198, §§ 1, 2. Cf. Wernz-Vidal, *Ius canonicum,* II *(De personis),* n. 367; Vermeersch-Creusen, *Epitome iuris canonici,* (5, 6. ed., Romae: H. Dessain, 1934-37), I, n. 317.

[6] Cf. Coronata, *Institutiones iuris canonici,* (1., 2. ed., Taurini: Marietti, 1933-1939), n. 280; Ayrinhac, *General Legislation in the New Code of Canon Law* (New York: Longmans, Green and co., 1933), p. 357. Re incompetency of judge, cf. S. R. R., *Vercellen.,* "Pensionis," 18 dec. 1928.—*S. Romanae Rotae Decisiones seu Sententiae quae . . . prodierunt anno 1909-* (Romae: Typis Vaticanis, 1912-), XX (1928), 492-498. Henceforth cited as *Decisiones.*

a) Sede plena

According to law, pensions on non-parochial benefices are to be reserved at the time of the conferring of the benefice upon a new incumbent,[7] and pensions on parochial benefices in behalf of a retiring pastor or vicar are to be reserved by the ordinary receiving the resignation from the parochial benefice.[8] Consequently only such ordinaries are empowered to reserve pensions as are capable of conferring benefices[9] or of accepting resignations.[10] In particular, then, such ordinaries are, besides the Roman Pontiff for the universal Church, 1) residential bishops after having taken canonical possession of their sees,[11] in view of the fact that they enjoy a presumption of law[12] favoring their competence to confer vacant benefices in their territories; 2) abbots and prelates *nullius*, after having taken canonical possession of their abbacies or prelacies,[13] because they enjoy the same powers in this respect as residential bishops;[14] 3) administrators apostolic (unless their letters of appointment expressly provide otherwise) if permanently appointed, because in that case they, too, have the same powers as residential bishops;[15] but not if temporarily appointed, because then they have only the powers of a vicar capitular;[16] 4) vicars and prefects apostolic, because in virtue of faculties from the Sacred Congregation of the Propagation of the Faith, they are explicitly empowered to assign a relatively perpetual

[7] ". . . dum beneficium conferunt . . ." Canon 1429, § 1. Cf. Blat, *Commentarium*, III, part. II-VI (*De rebus*), n. 336: "in ipso conferendi actu."

[8] Cf. canons 2154; 2161, § 2.

[9] Canon 1432. Cf. D'Angelo, *Tasse e pensioni*, p. 121, nota 1.

[10] Cf. canons 1484, 2147-2161.

[11] Canons 335, § 1; 334, § 2.

[12] ". . . intentionem in iure fundatam..."—Canon 1432, § 1. Cf. Coronata, *Institutiones*, II, n. 990, citing Reiffenstuel, Lib. III, tit. 5, n. 177; Vermeersch-Creusen, *Epitome*, II, n. 763; Blat, *Commentarium*, III, part. II-VI (*De rebus*), n. 341.

[13] Canon 322, § 1.

[14] Canon 323, § 1.

[15] Canons 314; 315, § 1.

[16] Canon 315, § 2. Cf. McDonough, *Apostolic Administrators*, The Catholic University of America Canon Law Studies, n. 139 (Washington, D. C.: The Catholic University of America Press, 1941), pp. 145-149.

pension to a quasi-pastor, to a missionary, and to a vicar of either, who would be compelled to resign for reasons of health or advanced age after he has served the quasi-parish or the mission for a period either continued or interrupted amounting to ten years;[17] 5) the vicar general of a residential bishop, abbot or prelate *nullius*, who, however, requires a special mandate, in order to confer a benefice and consequently to reserve a pension.[18]

b) Sede vacante

The time-honored principle discountenancing changes while a see is vacant has been canonized by the Code.[19] The rights of the future incumbent and the common good of ecclesiastical society demand this precaution for stability. Exception is made only when it will be for the better observance of external ecclesiastical order, and particularly when the spiritual needs of the members of the society would otherwise be exposed to disproportionate inconvenience and hardship.

The see of a residential bishop or of an abbot or prelate *nullius* becomes vacant by death, resignation, transfer, or deprivation.[20] Unless the diocese is under an administrator apostolic, whose jurisdiction does not cease with the death of the bishop,[21] or unless there is some other provision of the Holy See, the government of the see passes into the hands of the cathedral, abbatial or prelatial chapter, or the board of diocesan consultors in dioceses in which no chapter has been established. Within eight days of notification of the vacancy the cathedral chapter or board of consultors must depute a vicar capitular or diocesan administrator by canonical election,[22]

[17] Reproduced in Vermeersch-Creusen, *Epitome*, I, p. 645, n. 45; Coronata, *Institutiones*, V, p. 294, n. 26; p. 298, n. 25; p. 303, n. 34; p. 309, n. 34; p. 316, n. 45; p. 323, n. 45. The same faculty appears in each formula. Cf. Vromant, *De bonis Ecclesiae temporalibus* (Louvain: Editions du Museum Lessianum, 1927), pp. 117-119.

[18] Canon 1432, § 2.

[19] "Sede vacante nihil innovetur."—Canon 436.

[20] Canon 430.

[21] Cf. canon 318, § 1.

[22] Thus, Wernz-Vidal [*Ius canonicum*, II (*De personis*), n. 709, b] although the Code refers to canons 160-182 which include postulation. It

which does not require confirmation.[23] If they fail to do so, the metropolitan or, if the vacancy occurs in the metropolitan see, the senior suffragan appoints the vicar capitular or diocesan administrator. If the chapter of an abbacy or prelacy *nullius* fails to elect its vicar capitular, the appointment, unless the constitutions provide otherwise, devolves upon the neighboring metropolitan previously elected once and for all as extra-provincial ordinary according to canon 285.[24]

The vicar capitular or diocesan administrator has no power whatever to confer non-parochial benefices of free appointment,[25] and hence also no power to reserve pensions on the same.[26] With reference to parochial benefices the vicar capitular or administrator can confirm an election or accept a presentation for a vacant parish and grant canonical institution to candidates thus elected or presented, but he cannot confer a parochial benefice of free appointment unless the see has been vacant for a year.[27] He could then also reserve pensions on these parochial benefices.

seems that postulation, at least practically, does not enter into the matter of deputing a vicar capitular; for the postulation is to be sent to the superior who is empowered to confirm the election (c. 181, § 1); but confirmation is not required here (c. 438); and furthermore very likely the only superior to whom the postulation could be presented would be the Holy See, but the appointment of the vicar capitular must be made in at least eight days unless it could be proven that there was a just hindrance. (c. 181, §§ 1-2.)

23 Canon 438.

24 Canon 432.

25 Canon 1432, §2. Benefices of free appointment are conferred by exclusive right of the local ordinary (cf. canon 152). They are distinguished from benefices of necessary appointment because of vested rights following upon election or postulation on the part of a collegiate body, upon presentation or nomination on the part of a patron or other privileged person, or because of a mandate from an ecclesiastical superior. Cf. canons 147-182; 1431-1447; 1448-1472; Wernz-Vidal, *Ius canonicum*, II (*De personis*), n. 182, III.

26 If the see is vacant for a long time the Holy Father may and perhaps ought to be petitioned for the faculty permitting the temporary incumbent to confer such benefices. Cf. Wernz-Vidal, *ibidem*, n. 710, c, 5. A footnote (20) cites an instance in which a vicar capitular had an apostolic indult to this effect; reported in *Archiv für katholisches Kirchenrecht*, XXIII (1870), 135-136. Henceforth cited as *AKKR*.

27 Canons 1432, § 2; 455, § 2, 2°-3°.

A temporary apostolic administrator, who might be appointed by the Holy See to take charge of a vacant see, by common law has only the powers of a vicar capitular or diocesan administrator.[28]

It may also happen that in some places by special provision of the Holy See the archbishop or another bishop designates the administrator for the vacant diocese. The latter has precisely the same powers as the vicar capitular.[29]

If the diocese becomes vacant because of transfer, the bishop from the day he receives authentic notification of his transfer until he takes canonical possession of his new see, continues to rule his former see, but again only with the powers of a vicar capitular or diocesan administrator.[30]

The cathedral chapter or the board of diocesan consultors ruling the diocese in a body before they have deputed a vicar capitular or administrator within the eight days granted by law is obviously without power to confer benefices of free appointment regardless of whether they are parochial or non-parochial. On the other hand, since either body temporarily governs the diocese according to law, and is, therefore, similar in the enjoyment of jurisdiction to local ordinaries, there seems to be no reason for denying it the powers given to vicars capitular "or another one who rules the diocese" qualifying it to confirm elections, accept presentations and to grant canonical institution in office.[31] Practical considerations of prudence may counsel otherwise in particular circumstances.

c) Sede impedita

Besides the complete vacancy just considered, situations may arise wherein the ordinary is impeded from ruling his diocese even by letter, because of captivity, relegation, exile, or inability through serious physical or mental infirmity. In such cases, unless the Holy See provides otherwise, the diocese is ruled either by the vicar general

[28] Canon 315, § 2.

[29] Canon 431, § 2.

[30] Canon 430, § 3, 1°.

[31] Canon 455, § 2, 2°-3°. Cf. also Maroto, "De iuribus capituli cathedralis in casu sedis impeditae,"—*Apollinaris,* II (1929), 213-214.

or by one or more clerics delegated by the bishop to succeed one another.[32]

Common law entrusts the government of the diocese to the vicar general without expressing any restrictions.[33] Whereas in a vacancy the ordinary loses his title to the see, in a see temporarily deprived of its incumbent the ordinary, while retaining his title, is hindered from carrying out the functions of his office, and the vicar general retains the powers which he had while his ordinary was free to act.[34]

As has been noted, the vicar general must have a special mandate to confer benefices, and consequently to reserve pensions. The more common opinion holds that those acts for which the vicar general requires a special mandate of the bishop are within the vicar general's ordinary jurisdiction, so that the giving of the mandate merely releases a restriction placed there by the law.[35] The purpose of requiring the special mandate is to place the more important acts of jurisdiction exclusively in the hands of one person. During a quasi-

[32] Canon 429, §§ 1-2.

[33] ". . . dioecesis regimen . . . penes Episcopi Vicarium Generalem vel alium virum ecclesiasticum ab Episcopo delegatum esto."—Canon 429, § 1.

[34] Cf. canons 371; 430, § 3, 1°.

[35] Thus Wernz-Vidal (*Ius canonicum*, II [*De personis*], n. 640), Maroto (*Institutiones iuris canonici* [Matriti: Editorial del Corazón de Maria, 1919], I, n. 699, 9), Stutz ("Der Geist des Codex iuris canonici,"—*Kirchenrechtliche Abhandlungen*, XCII-XCIII [1918], p. 325-327), Coronata (*Institutiones*, I, n. 421), Blat (*Commentarium*, II [*De personis*], n. 402), Ayrinhac (*Constitution of the Church* [New York: Longmans, Green and co., 1930], p. 213), Von Kienitz (*Generalvikar und Offizial* [Freiburg im Breisgau: Herder, 1931], p. 97-98), Creusen (Vermeersch-Creusen, *Epitome* [2. ed., 1923, I, n. 436, 3; 6. ed., 1937, I, n. 479, 3]—although in 4. ed., 1924, I, n. 436, 3 he favored the opposite opinion), Haring (*Grundzuege des katholischen Kirchenrechtes* [3. ed.,Graz: Ulrich Moser, 1924], 294, Note 5). The opposite opinion, that the vicar general has only delegated jurisdiction in executing acts with a special mandate, is held by Hilling (*Das Personenrecht des Codex Iuris Canonici* [Paderborn: Schöningh, 1924], p. 183; "Die Iurisdiktion des Generalvikars,"—*AKKR*, CIV [1924], 199-205), Toso ("Summa de officio ac potestate vicarii generalis,"—*Jus Pontificium*, VII [1927], 143-144), Chelodi (*Ius de Personis* [2. ed., Tridenti: Libr. Edit. Tridentinum, 1927] p. 330), and Kearney (*The principles of delegation*, The Catholic University of America Canon Law Studies, n. 55 [Washington, D. C.: The Catholic University of America, 1929], pp. 72-74).

vacancy the bishop is prevented from giving the mandate. Would it have to be concluded that unless the bishop gave the special mandate before the vacancy, the vicar general was utterly incapable of conferring benefices or reserving pensions in virtue of his ordinary power? Would he have no more power than a vicar capitular, who can confer parishes of free appointment only after the lapse of a year? [36] Blat believes that during a quasi-vacancy the vicar general has only the powers of canon 455, § 2.[37] It seems, however, that, unless the Holy See makes other arrangements upon being informed of the quasi-vacancy, it can be assumed that it tacitly approves the vicar general and warrants the exercise of all his ordinary powers.[38]

The second paragraph of canon 455 describes the powers of the vicar capitular and other analogously situated rulers of the see, such as the provicar in vicariates apostolic,[39] the temporary administrator apostolic,[40] and the cathedral chapter [41] or the board of diocesan consultors.[42] Coronata,[43] differing from Ferreris [44] and Schäfer,[45] believes that the "other ruler of the see" in this second paragraph does not mean the vicar general or the ecclesiastics whose rights are determined according to canon 429, §§ 1-2; for the third paragraph

[36] Canons 429, § 3; 455, § 2; 1432, § 2.

[37] *Commentarium*, II (*De personis*), n. 503.

[38] On the other hand, granting though not conceding, that the special mandate of a bishop confers only delegated powers, and that the vicar general confers benefices only by delegated power, it does not seem unreasonable that if no such special power had been delegated to him by the bishop before he became impeded, this power would be delegated to him by common law when it places him in charge of the quasi-vacant diocese (Cf. canons 200, § 1 and 429, § 1), and by the Holy See in not making other arrangements.

[39] Canon 309.

[40] Canon 315, § 2.

[41] Canon 435.

[42] Canon 427.

[43] *Institutiones*, I, n. 472, 3°, a, and notes 5, 9, p. 572, citing Augustine (*A Commentary on the New Code of Canon Law* [3.-5. ed., St. Louis: Herder, 1925-1938], II, 525).

[44] *Institutiones canonicae* (2. ed., Barcinone: Subirana, 1920), I, n. 738, II.

[45] *Die Kirchenämter, II, Pfarrer und Pfarrvikare* (Muenster i. W.: Aschendorff, 1922), p. 16.

of the same canon (455) declares that the vicar general can do none of these things without a special mandate, safeguarding the prescription of canon 429, § 1, providing for the see temporarily deprived of its incumbent, the entire government of which devolves upon him.[46]

The conclusion, therefore, seems to be that during a quasi-vacancy the vicar general can, without a special mandate, confirm an election or accept a presentation to a vacant parish and grant canonical institution to the elected or presented candidate, reserving pensions on them if circumstances warrant. He can also "according to a convincing opinion of canonists" confer parishes of free appointment, even before the diocese has been deprived of its incumbent for a year,[47] and hence, can also reserve pensions on them. In speaking of the vicar capitular's power of conferring benefices, the lawgiver distinguishes between parochial and other perpetual benefices of free appointment, stating that the vicar capitular cannot confer parochial benefices except during a vacancy or quasi-vacancy and then only after a year, and that he is utterly incapable of conferring the other perpetual benefices. The vicar general, on the other hand, in normal times requires a special mandate to confer any kind of benefice whatever, no distinction being made.[48] Hence, during a quasi-vacancy when the vicar general can confer a parochial benefice without a special mandate and even before a year's quasi-vacancy, it would seem that he can confer also non-parochial benefices under

[46] Cf. Vermeersch-Creusen, *Epitome*, I, n. 541, 2-3;Augustine, *Canonical and Civil Status of Catholic Parishes*, p. 210.

[47] Jaeger, *The Administration of vacant and quasi-vacant dioceses in the United States*, (The Catholic University of American Canon Law Studies, n. 81, Washington, D. C.: The Catholic University of America, 1932), p. 215. "Ob erst, wenn die Behinderung ein Jahr lang gedauert hat? Nach dem Wortlaut von can. 455 § 2 und 3 müsste man das annehmen. Jedoch der Grundsatz des can. 436, dass sede vacante nihil innovetur, und die Ausnahme davon, die bisher nach Jahresfrist oder nach längerer Dauer der Stuhlerledigung auf Grund ausserordentlicher päpstlicher Vollmachten (vgl. Archiv für katholisches Kirchenrecht XXIII 1870 S. 135 f.) eintrat, in Zukunft aber von Gesetzes wegen eintreten soll, kommt bei behindertem Stuhl nicht in Betracht."—Stutz, *Der Geist des Codex iuris canonici*, p. 311, footnote 5. Cf. also Sipos, *Enchiridion*, p. 285.

[48] Canon 1432, § 2.

the same circumstances. He can then also reserve pensions on them.

At all times, however, the vicar general in administering the impeded diocese is to be mindful of the admonition not to use his powers contrary to the mind and will of his bishop.[49]

Only after the vicar general or the last special episcopal delegate has been similarly impeded is the cathedral chapter or board of consultors authorized to elect its vicar or diocesan administrator. The latter will rule the diocese with the powers of vicar capitular as already outlined,[50] and with the same restrictions as regards the imposing of pensions.

The law distinguishes between a quasi-vacancy due to physical impediments and one due to the canonical impediments of excommunication, interdict, and suspension. In the case of canonical impediments the metropolitan, or the senior suffragan, or the canonically selected extra-provincial metropolitan,[51] respectively, must have immediate recourse to the Holy See in order that it, and no one else, may provide.[52] The vicar general has no authority; for his jurisdiction is suspended when the jurisdiction of his bishop is suspended.[53] Lest the diocese be left for any length of time without any ruler whatever, it seems that until the Holy See makes some provision, the government of the diocese should devolve upon the cathedral chapter and the vicar capitular or the board of diocesan consultors and the diocesan administrator, according to the general procedure and limitations outlined in the Code.[54]

The Holy Father sometimes, for weighty and special reasons, entrusts the government of a canonically erected diocese to an administrator apostolic.[55] If the jurisdiction of the apostolic administrator should become impeded or come to an end (e. g., by death, lapse of time), the Holy See is to be advised immediately. Meanwhile, if the see is vacant or the bishop is without full use of his

[49] Canon 369, § 2.
[50] Canon 429, § 3.
[51] Cf. canon 285.
[52] Canon 429, § 5.
[53] Canon 371; cf. Vermeersch-Creusen, *Epitome*, I, n. 483.
[54] Cf. canons 429, § 3; 431 ff.; 455, § 2; 1432, § 2.
[55] Cf. canon 312.

faculties, the usual procedure for quasi-vacant or vacant sees set down in canons 429 ff. is to be observed. Otherwise the bishop reassumes temporary control unless the Apostolic See would have made some other previous arrangement.[56]

In mission countries vicars and prefects apostolic, as soon as they enter their territory, are directed, unless the Holy See has appointed a coadjutor with right of succession, to appoint a pro-vicar or a pro-prefect. When a vacancy or quasi-vacancy occurs in a vicariate or prefecture apostolic (in which there is no coadjutor with right of succession), the full government of the territory passes to the pro-vicar or pro-prefect, and remains with him until the Holy See makes other arrangements. Having assumed the rule of the vicariate or prefecture, the pro-vicar or pro-prefect without delay is to appoint a cleric as his successor. If it should happen that no one had been deputed as successor by the vicar or prefect or by the pro-vicar or pro-prefect, or they become similarly impeded, then he who is present in the territory for the longest time, reckoned from the time he presented his letters of appointment, assumes government as a delegate of the Holy See. In case of equality on this score, seniority in the priesthood determines who will rule.[57]

The apostolic faculty of assigning pensions passes to him who succeeds the vicar or prefect apostolic if the vicariate or prefecture should become vacant or quasi-vacant.[58]

The law of the Code recognizes no vicar general properly so called in a vicariate or prefecture apostolic. Pope Benedict XV, however, authorized the ordinaries of these territories to appoint vicars delegate (*vicarii delegati*), with such competence as is given in canons 66 and 368 to vicars general.[59] If the vicar delegate and pro-vicar or pro-perfect are different persons, it is possible that a conflict may arise with regard to their prerogatives of succession. The solution given by Creusen [60] is that in a vacancy the pro-vicar or pro-

[56] Canon 317.

[57] Canon 309.

[58] Cf. Vermeersch, "Commentaria de formulis facultatum quas S. Congr. de Propaganda Fide concedere solet,"—*Periodica,* XI (1922), p. (73).

[59] S. C. de Prop. Fide, epistola, 8 dec. 1919.—AAS, XII (1920), 120.

[60] Vermeersch-Creusen, *Epitome,* I, n. 429, 3.

prefect would succeed; for the latter has vicarious powers, while the vicar delegate more probably has only delegated powers.[61] In defect of all of the three appointed administrators (coadjutor with right of succession, pro-vicar or pro-prefect, the latter's designated successor) the vicar delegate could succeed prior to the senior missioner; for the vicar delegate can in this case be considered as elected by the vicar or prefect to take up the government. This would not be true, however, if the power delegated to the vicar had expired either by reason of particular law [62] or the mode of concession.[63]

In cases of quasi-vacancy, on the other hand, it would seem that the vicar delegate, who practically has the jurisdiction of a vicar general [64] can and ought to assume government, without acting contrary to canon 309, § 2, since the Code did not consider the nomination of a vicar delegate; indeed, the matter was settled only after the promulgation of the Code.[65]

The apostolic faculty of assigning pensions granted to vicars or prefects apostolic passes to the ordinaries who lawfully succeed them. Therefore, in a vacancy the pro-vicar or pro-prefect, the vicar delegate (except for particular restrictions), and the senior priest, in the order named, enjoy the faculty. When the see is quasi-vacant the vicar delegate seems to have first right of succession.[66]

[61] Cf. Vromant, *Facultates Apostolicae, supplementum* (Louvain: Museum Lessianum, 1930), p. 3; Von Kienitz, *Generalvikar und Offizial*, pp. 81-82.

[62] E. g., I Council of China, n. 77: "Sede vacante, iurisdictio Vicarii Delegati exspirat, et totum regimen assumit Pro-vicarius vel Pro-praefectus Apostolicus, nisi S. Sedes aliter providerit."—Vromant, *Facultates*, p. 3.

[63] Cf. canon 207.

[64] ". .. cui practice concessa sit jurisdictio in spiritualibus et temporalibus, qua ex Codice I. C. uti potest Vicarius Generalis in dioecesi."—S. C. de Prop. Fide, epistola, 8 dec. 1919.—*AAS*, XII (1920), 120.

[65] Vermeersch-Creusen, *Epitome*, I, n. 429, 3. Cf. Winslow, *Vicars and Prefects Apostolic* (Maryknoll, N. Y.: Catholic Foreign Mission Society of America, Inc., 1924), p. 68-69.

[66] Canon 310, § 2. Cf. Vermeersch, "Commentaria de formulis facultatum quas S. Congr. de Propaganda Fide concedere solet,"—*Periodica*, XI (1922), (73).

ARTICLE 3. CARDINALS IN THEIR OWN TITLES AND DEACONRIES

Although not included in the term "local ordinary," [67] authorized by canon 1429 to impose pensions, cardinal priests and cardinal deacons, after having taken canonical possession of their titular churches or deaconries are legally presumed as competent to confer benefices in them and consequently also to reserve pensions on these benefices.[68] But they are entitled to this right only if they are true and actual residents in the Roman Curia.[69] The conferring of dignities in a chapter even of their titular churches is, however, reserved to the Holy See.[70] Cardinal bishops, ruling over the suburbicarian sees, are true bishops of their dioceses and have the same powers as other residential bishops.[71]

[67] Cf. canon 198.

[68] Canons 1432, § 1; 240, § 2.

[69] Wernz-Vidal, *Ius Canonicum*, II, n. 243.

[70] Canon 396, § 1.

[71] Canons 231, § 1; 240, § 1.

Chapter V

THE OBJECT OF ECCLESIASTICAL PENSIONS

The Code of canon law especially mentions benefices as the proper objects on which pensions may be reserved. A distinction is made between parochial benefices and all other benefices.[1]

Among the canons introducing the law on ecclesiastical benefices there is one giving a list of the juridical entities which are called benefices.[2] A review of these benefices in the light of legislation on pensions will disclose on which of them specifically the various local ordinaries are competent to reserve pensions.

Article 1. The Competence of the Holy See

Consistorial benefices, as the name implies, are such as are conferred in the Sacred Consistorial Congregation, of which the Pope is prefect. The usual benefices conferred in consistory are the benefices of bishops and of apostolic administrators.[3] If there should be question of reserving pensions on benefices of this kind, the same congregation alone will be competent.

Besides strictly consistorial benefices there are others which are conferred by the Holy See. Among these may be mentioned the benefices (if there actually are such in a particular territory) of vicars and prefects apostolic. These are conferred by the Pope through the Sacred Congregation for the Propagation of the Faith.[4] The installation of abbots and prelates *nullius* is likewise exclusively in the hands of the Supreme Pontiff.[5] By devolution the ordinary's right to confer a benefice within his competency passes to the Apostolic See for this one time, if after six months of certain

[1] Canon 1429, § 1: "Beneficiis quibuslibet. . ." § 2: "Beneficiis autem paroecialibus. . ." Cf. S. C. C., Dioecesis N., "Renuntiationis paroeciae," 11 nov. 1922.—*AAS*, XV (1923), 454-456, especially 455.

[2] Canon 1411.

[3] Canons 248, § 2; 312; 329, § 2.

[4] Canons 293; 252.

[5] Canon 320, § 1.

knowledge of its vacancy he fails to make an appointment thereto, unless, in the case of a parochial benefice, circumstances arising from the locality or the persons involved make it appear more advisable in the prudent judgment of the ordinary to postpone it.[6] If the ordinary failed to make the appointment not because of negligence but because of absolute want of subjects, the ordinary's right does not pass by devolution to the Holy See.[7] The same law of devolution obtains with regard to benefices which a cardinal priest or deacon neglects to confer within the same period in his titular church.[8]

Among other non-consistorial benefices, the conferring of which is reserved to the Apostolic See, are all dignities in cathedral and collegiate chapters.[9] Similarly reserved are all benefices, including those with the care of souls, which have become vacant by the death, the promotion, the resignation, or the transfer of cardinals, legates of the Roman Pontiff, major officials of the Roman Congregations, Tribunals, and Offices, and members of the papal household even if only honorary. Other benefices, although established outside of the diocese of Rome, which become vacant by the death of the incumbent while he is in the eternal city also become reserved to the Holy See. The only penal reservation retained in the Code is the one on benefices which have been conferred invalidly because of simony. They are reserved specially and only for the one time.[10] Another type of special reservation concerns benefices on which the Roman Pontiff has "placed hands" either directly or through a delegate, in one of the following ways: by declaring the election to a benefice to be null; by forbidding the election; by accepting the resignation of the benefice; by promoting and transferring the incumbent, or depriving him of office; by giving the benefice *in commendam*. It is to be noted that an express statement is required

[6] Canons 1432, § 3; 155; 458.

[7] C. P. I., 24 nov. 1920.—AAS, XII (1920), 577.

[8] Blat, *Commentarium*, Lib. III, part. II-VI (*De rebus*), n. 341, p. 471.

[9] Canon 396, § 1.

[10] Wernz-Vidal, *Ius canonicum*, II (*De personis*), n. 231, 4, a.

before a temporary benefice or one of lay or mixed patronage can be considered as reserved to the Holy See.[11]

All non-consistorial benefices which are withdrawn from the competency of subordinate ordinaries are conferred by the Holy See through the Apostolic Datary, which is also expressly authorized to look after the pensions (either temporary or perpetual) which the Supreme Pontiff may have imposed in the conferring of such benefices.[12]

All other vacant benefices can be conferred by superiors subordinate to the Supreme Pontiff, and they can also reserve pensions on such benefices observing the other prescriptions and requirements of the law.

Article 2. The Competence of the Local Ordinary

Benefices which local ordinaries are empowered to confer and upon which the law permits them to reserve pensions are usually capitular and parochial benefices, provided, of course, they have not been reserved to the Holy See.

The benefices existing in a cathedral or collegiate chapter are known as dignities and canonries. There may also be inferior benefices, but these do not belong to the chapter in the strict sense except by apostolic indult or immemorial custom.[13] With the excep-

[11] Canon 1435, §§ 1-2.

[12] Canon 261, confirming Pius X, const. "Sapienti Consilio," 29 iun. 1908, § III, n. 2°, 1-2.—*ASS*, XLI (1908), 437; *AAS*, I (1909), 16; *Fontes*, n. 682. "Ordo servandus in S. Congregationibus, Tribunalibus, Officiis Romanae Curiae," 29 sept. 1908, Pars II, Normae peculiares, cap. IX, art. II, n. 5°. —*ASS*, XLI (1908), 741; *AAS*, I (1909), 104. Cf. Cappello, *De Curia Romana iuxta reformationem a Pio X sapientissime inductam* (Romae, 1911-1912), I, 467. Cf. also Dataria Apostolica, "Normae servandae ab Ordinariis in impetranda ab Apostolica Sede collatione beneficiorum," 11 nov. 1930.—*AAS*, *XXII* (1930), 525-526.

Apostolic Delegates have the faculty: "3. Conferendi personis idoneis ea beneficia de quibus in canone 1435, § 1, 1° et 3°, servatis regulis ab Apostolica Dataria datis vel dandis."—*Periodica*, XII (1923), (72). Cf. also Anon., "Papal Reservation of Appointment to Parishes"; "Domestic Prelates and Reservation of their Beneficies,"—*AER*, LXXXIX (1933), 432-434; 627.

[13] Canon 393, § 2. Cf. C. P. I., 24 nov. 1920, *De canonicis*, II.—*AAS*,

tion of dignities, all other canonries and benefices, unless reserved, are conferred by the bishop after consulting the chapter. Contrary customs and privileges are no longer recognized by the law, although contrary conditions in the law of foundation are sustained.[14] Hence, the bishop at the time of conferring a canonry or a lesser benefice can also reserve a pension on the same, and if the law of foundation would be contrary to such reservation, it would have to be clearly demonstrated, for the right of the bishop enjoys the favor of the law.[15]

The reservation of pensions on parochial benefices is dealt with separately in the second paragraph of canon 1429. The right to appoint and install parish priests belongs to the local ordinary. Contrary custom is reprobated, but a legitimate privilege of electing or presenting a candidate must be respected.[16] Consequently, even though the chapter or a religious institute or a patron has the right to elect or present its candidate, the actual installation pertains to the local ordinary, who can also reserve a pension on such a benefice.

Quasi-parishes and missions in vicariates or prefectures apostolic can be burdened with pensions according to the express declaration of the faculty given by the Sacred Congregation for the Propagation of the Faith.[17] Quasi-parishes and missions are very probably not synonymous. *Formula III maior*, number 37,[18] distinguishes a

XII (1920), 573. *Periodica*, X (1922), 253. Wernz-Vidal, *Ius canonicum*, II (*De personis*), n. 665; Vermeersch-Creusen, *Epitome*, I, n. 502.

According to the different ways in which such beneficiaries assist the canons they are known by various names, such as *mansionarii, assissii, quartenarii, quarantisti, tertianarii, hebdomadarii, choristae, matricularii, habituati*. Cf. Maupied, *Juris canonici universi . . . compendium* (Paris, 1863), I, 898-899; Barbosa, *Tractatus de canonicis et dignitatibus* (Lugduni, 1658), cap. IV, n. 36-45; Calamita, *I Capitoli canonicali nel Codice del diritto canonico* (Napoli: Gennaro Tavassi, 1923), p. 29.

14 Canon 403.

15 Canon 1432, § 1.

16 Canon 455, § 1.

17 "Assignandi pensiones quasi-parochis vel missionariis . . . solvendas annuatim a successore. . ."—*Formula III maior*, n. 45.—Coronata, *Institutiones*, V, 323. The same faculty appears in all the other *formulae*.

18 *Apud* Coronata, *Institutiones*, V, p. 322.

mission from a quasi-parish in the same manner as a parish properly so-called is distinguished from a quasi-parish. Moreover, as a parish and quasi-parish are distinct entities under the new law,[19] thus also a quasi-parish and a mission do not appear to be identical in the faculties. A mission seems to be a portion of a vicariate or prefecture apostolic not yet canonically erected into a quasi-parish by the assignment to it of its own rector.[20] While it is true that only one moral person (the vicariate or prefecture) holds ecclesiastical goods, there may nevertheless be various donations which by the will of the benefactors are not to be applied to the vicariate in general but to a definite work or section of the territory. The faculty for pensions on missions refers precisely to such property, as well as other revenues, e. g., stole fees, in a specified section not yet canonically erected into a quasi-parish. The faculty for a pension on a quasi-parish refers, of course, to the same type of property.[21]

The law permits that a parochial vicarship be duly erected as a canonical benefice.[22] If such is the case, a pension can be reserved on it, although, of course, only for the retiring vicar.[23]

Competent ecclesiastical authority can establish an office for the celebration of Mass, and for the performance of other sacred functions in a certain chapel or church, and join thereto the right to receive an income from goods designated by a founder for this purpose. Such an institution is regarded as an ecclesiastical chaplaincy and is a true and proper benefice.[24] The reservation of a pension on such a chaplaincy would not be contrary to the law.

[19] Cf. canon 216.

[20] Cf. canon 216, § 3.

[21] Blat, *Commentarium*, II (*De personis*), n. 170, p. 192; Vromant, *De bonis Ecclesiae temporalibus*, p. 117, note 2. But Vermeersch ["Commentaria de formulis facultatum"—*Periodica*, XI (1922), (106) d]: "*Missio* autem hic est idem quod quasi-paroeciae."

[22] Cf. canon 477, § 2. ". . . ut v. gr. accidit in coadiutoribus beneficiatis coronae Aragonis." Ferreris, *Institutiones canonicae*, I, n. 772, I.

[23] Canon 1429, § 2.

[24] Canons 1409; 1412, 2°. Pistocchi, *De re beneficiali iuxta canones Codicis iuris canonici* (Taurini: Marietti, 1928), p. 33. ". . . Cappellania est intelligenda verum beneficium: a) si fundator hoc expresse declaraverit, vel Episcopo ius erectionis tribuerit; b) si statuerit bona esse administranda ab

There are certain institutes which may indeed resemble benefices in certain aspects, but which are nevertheless not recognized as such in law;[25] and consequently there can be no possibility of reserving an ecclesiastical pension on them in accordance with canon 1429. Thus, there can be no pensions on parochial vicarships not erected in perpetuity, or on lay chaplaincies, i. e., chaplaincies not erected by competent ecclesiastical authority, or on coadjutorships either with or without succession, since they are by their nature temporary. There can likewise be no reservation of a pension on a pension, and much less on a temporary *commenda,* e. g., on the income of one entrusted with the administration of a vacant church or benefice.[26]

Authors add to this list of the Code the *praestimonium* or portion drawn from ecclesiastical goods for the maintenance especially of clerics engaged in studies. In order that the *praestimonium* may be a benefice, it is required that it be joined to a sacred office and established in perpetuity as a juridic entity by competent ecclesiastical authority with a right in the payee to the revenues flowing from the endowment joined to the office.[27] This is generally not the case; for one or more of the requisite elements will usually be wanting.[28] Hence, pensions can usually not be reserved on the *praestimonium.* Practically, clerical aid available in a subsidy of this kind would hardly ever be so abundant as to offer maintenance for an additional ecclesiastic.

ipso cappellaniae titulari; c) si erecta fuerit in titulum conferendum a legitimo Superiore ecclesiastico clerico idoneo, ad celebrandum."—Cocchi, *Commentarium in Codicem iuris canonici ad usum scholarum* (3-5. ed., Taurinorum Augustae: Marietti, 1931-1940), VI, n. 84, p. 195.

[25] Canon 1412.

[26] Cf. Pistocchi, *De re beneficiali,* p. 37; Cocchi, *Commentarium,* VI, n. 84, *e*), p. 196; Ayrinhac, *Administrative Legislation in the New Code of Canon Law* (New York: Longmans, Green and Co., 1930), p. 315.

[27] Canon 1409.

[28] Reiffenstuel, Lib. III, tit. 5, nn. 80-83; Wernz, *Ius decretalium,* II, n. 240, II, Scholion; Vermeersch-Creusen, *Epitome,* II, n. 745; Prümmer, *Manuale iuris canonici* (6. ed., Friburgi-Brisgoviae: Herder & Co., 1933), p. 508; Coronata, *Institutiones,* II, p. 359, n. 973, 6°.

CHAPTER VI

THE PASSIVE SUBJECT OF ECCLESIASTICAL PENSIONS

ARTICLE 1. MORAL PERSONS

In the consideration of the law prior to the Code instances were cited to show that at times pensions were reserved in favor of moral persons, such as poor parish churches or seminaries. Such pensions, however, were reserved by the Holy See either directly or through special delegation granted to the local ordinary. Reservations of this kind have always been regarded as extraordinary. Such pensions are an excessive burden. From the standpoint of the recipient of the pension they are absolutely perpetual, for moral persons by their nature are perpetual.[1] As in pre-Code law, under the present discipline the necessary conclusion is that the Supreme Pontiff alone is competent. Contemporary canon law does not explicitly consider the question, but implicitly such pensions are utterly excluded; for local ordinaries are expressly forbidden to reserve pensions on non-parochial benefices to last for the life of the subject receiving the pension. They may establish only a pension coterminous with the beneficiary's incumbency, excepting the pensions on a parochial benefice, allowed solely for the retiring pastor or vicar, which may be established to last for the life of these retired clerics.[2]

ARTICLE 2. PHYSICAL PERSONS

a) Laymen

The Code contemplates only physical persons as the recipients of ecclesiastical pensions. Lay persons, however, are ineligible. The

[1] Cf. canon 102.

[2] Canon 1429, §§ 1, 2; S. C. C., *Dioecesis N.*, "Renuntiationis paroeciae," 11 nov. 1922.—*AAS*, XV (1923), 454. Cf. Vito (*Questioni canoniche*, II, 107-114), discussing a case in which the ordinary burdened a parochial benefice with the obligation to pay 1,700 lire to the cathedral chapter for an undetermined time. He concludes (p. 110-113) that the obligation cannot be sustained even as the extraordinary subsidy or tax of canon 1505.

latter can hold certain positions which may be called offices in a broad sense, though predominantly of a temporal rather than spiritual nature, such as are held by a sexton, a sacristan, an organist, a chanter, the employees of the Vatican State,[3] for which they may receive so-called temporal pensions upon disability or retirement in consideration for services rendered; but such "pensions" are not strictly ecclesiastical pensions (*pensiones ecclesiasticae*): they are better called church pensions (*pensiones in Ecclesia*). The same must be said of those pensions which have been reserved for a patron and for his successors in the advowson, established at the time of the foundation of the benefice.[4] Such a pension is now valid only if it was established prior to the Code; for the present common law no longer admits the establishment of any right of patronage.[5] Consequently, to establish a pension for a patron as such would seem now to require the special intervention of the Holy See.

The question is not pertinent in the United States. Although the Spanish kings had received from Pope Julius II (1503-1513) the rights of patronage over all parishes in the Spanish possessions,[6] these rights ceased when the territory came under the jurisdiction of the United States government.[7] The First Provincial Council of Baltimore in 1829 explicitly declared that no right of patronage of whatever kind, as recognized by the sacred canons, can be validly asserted "in this province," [8] which comprised the twenty-eight states

[3] Cf. Pius XI, motu propr. "*De pensionibus ordinandis,*" 31 dec. 1937—AAS, XXX (1938), 33-50.

[4] Cf. canon 1455, 2°; S. C. C., *Resolutio*, "Gerunden.," 13 iul. 1918.—AAS, XI (1919), 80; Blat, *Commentarium*, III, part. II-VI (*De rebus*), n. 367, p. 501; Wernz-Vidal, *Ius canonicum*, II (*De personis*), n. 307.

[5] Canon 1450, § 1.

[6] Bulla, "*Universalis ecclesiae regimini,*" 28 iul. 1508. Cf. Guilday, *A History of the Councils of Baltimore* (New York, The MacMillan Company, 1932), p. 25.

[7] Cf. Ayrinhac, *Administrative Legislation in the New Code of Canon Law*, p. 348.

[8] N. 6.—*Concilia provincialia, Baltimori habita ab anno 1829 usque ad annum 1849* (2. ed., Baltimori, 1851), p. 75. In the instruction of the S. C. de Prop. Fide which accompanied the decree of approval it was suggested that the word "*hactenus*" be added. (*Ibid.*, p. 66.)

and territories constituting the Union at that time;[9] and all doubt as to the future is removed by the express prohibition of the Code.[10]

b) Clerics

The fundamental requirement demanded of the recipient of an ecclesiastical pension is that he be in the clerical state,[11] to which he is introduced with the reception of first tonsure.[12] The former requirement of a minimum age of seven years for tonsure no longer obtains except by obvious implication; for tonsure in the present law is not to be conferred until the candidate has begun his course in theology.[13]

Priesthood is required implicitly in one who receives a pension on a parochial benefice; for such may be reserved only for the retiring pastor or a vicar of the same parish; but the prospective pensioner in this instance must have been ordained to the priesthood even before he could have been validly appointed to the benefice or office, respectively.[14]

Cardinals are provided for according to their princely dignity. The Code expressly declares that upon their elevation to the purple they lose such pensions as they may have had, unless there are other provisions by the Holy See for particular cases.[15]

As in former times, situations are not impossible in which a residential bishop might be hindered from taking possession of his see

[9] Guilday, *A History of the Councils of Baltimore*, p. 86.

[10] Canon 1450, § 1.

[11] "Soli clerici possunt . . . pensiones ecclesiasticas obtinere." Canon 118.

[12] Canon 108, § 1.

[13] Canon 976, § 1.

[14] Canon 154: "Officia quae curam animarum sive in foro externo sive in interno secumferunt, clericis nondum sacerdotio initiatis conferri valide nequeunt."

Canon 451, § 1: "Parochus est sacerdos vel persona moralis cui paroecia collata est in titulum cum cura animarum sub Ordinarii loci auctoritate exercenda."

Canon 453, § 1: "Ut quis in parochum valide assumatur debet esse in Sacro presbyteratus ordine constitutus."

[15] Canon 235. Cf. Prümmer, *Manuale iuris canonici*, Q. 97, n. 5, p. 134. V. *infra*, on the extinction of pensions, p. 163.

or from receiving the revenue thereof, either in its entirety or in an amount adequate for his support; or the revenue of the episcopal manse in certain poverty-stricken regions might be so meagre as to prove inadequate for a decent livelihood. A clerical pension could be one of the ways of securing fitting maintenance for him. Again, he may have been expelled from his diocese by civil authority or removed by ecclesiastical authority, or he may have resigned. In these cases a pension could be reserved for him on his former manse, if that is possible, or on some other benefice by the Holy See, or probably even on a non-parochial benefice by a competent local ordinary. If on the former, the pension could last for the life of the episcopal pensioner, analogously to the pension for a retiring parish priest.[16]

Titular bishops, inasmuch as they do not take possession of their dioceses,[17] acquire none of the rights to the revenue of the see that residential bishops enjoy.[18] The dignity is honorary and is generally conferred upon ecclesiastics who serve the Church in such capacities as vicars apostolic, apostolic delegates, members of the Roman Congregations and Offices, auxiliaries or coadjutors of residential bishops or sees, and rectors of institutes of graduate studies, seminaries, or colleges.[19] Their sustenance is usually provided for by the income derived from the revenue of their benefice or office distinct from the episcopal dignity. If, however, this should not be sufficient, and particularly if they should be compelled to retire from office because of infirmity, then a fitting mode of providing for them might be by an ecclesiastical pension.

The more usual subjects of pensions and those whom the legislator has most in mind are clerics in orders inferior to the episcopacy. Thus, the canons of a chapter together with the incumbents of the other benefices annexed to the chapter, parish priests (both

[16] Canon 1429, § 2.

[17] Canon 348.

[18] Canon 349, § 2, 1°.

[19] Chelodi, *Ius de personis*, n. 187; Coronata, *Institutiones*, I, n. 402; Ayrinhac, *Constitution of the Church*, n. 148 (p. 183); *Annuario Pontificio*, published annually (Città del Vaticano, Tipografia poliglotta Vaticana), e.g., 1940, "Arcivescovati e Vescovati titolari," pp. 301-526.

pastors and vicars), chaplains,—in short, all clerics who for some reason are without the ordinary income of a benefice or even of an office— may for just cause be given a pension, provided that the other conditions of law are fulfilled with regard to the benefice to be burdened, and provided the cleric's own status, worthiness, and needs are of such a nature as to advise or warrant this manner of clerical support to safeguard the dignity of the clerical state.

If the actual income of a benefice should not be sufficient for the beneficiary, he could be given a pension on a non-parochial benefice to complement the inadequate revenue of his own benefice. It would seem, however, that investigation should first be made as to the possibility of transferring the cleric to another benefice or office whose revenue will be sufficient for his needs (it being generally admitted that no universal standard can be established absolutely as the minimum sufficient for livelihood), or of uniting the benefice with another one. If the revenues are so diminished that not even the most frugal incumbent can subsist on them, the benefice ought to be suppressed.

The levying of a pension on any benefice is always a restriction on, or a diminution of, the benefice, although the Code permits it for a just cause;[20] for "they that *serve* the altar, partake with the altar," and "they who *preach* the gospel should live by the gospel."[21] Hence, while a cleric is capable of serving in a benefice or office, he ought not shift the burden of his own support on another. Those holding offices or benefices who are guilty of grave neglect of their duties are probably disqualified for ecclesiastical pensions, as will be pointed out.

Pensions on parochial benefices may be reserved when those who have given their services to the parish go out of office. A person is said to go out of office (*a munere abire*) as a consequence of removal,[22] transfer,[23] resignation duly accepted,[24] or exchange.[25] Nega-

[20] "Beneficia ecclesiastica sine deminutione conferantur, salvo praescripto can. 1429, §§ 1, 2." Canon 1440. The pension is the exception and not the rule.

[21] I Cor. IX, 13-14.

[22] *Codex Iuris Canonici*, Lib. IV, tit. XXVII, *De modo procedendi in*

tively, a person may be said to go out of office if he is not penally deprived of the care of souls by way of a condemnatory judicial sentence of an ecclesiastical judge,[26] or by means of a particular administrative decree of the competent ecclesiastical superior.[27]

In the light of canon 1488, which establishes certain negative conditions for the exchange of benefices, it would seem that the exchange of benefices is not a valid cause for ordinaries subordinate to the Holy See to reserve pensions.[28] While canon 1440 forbids the conferring of benefices with diminution of the same, by way of explicit exception it permits the reservation of temporary pensions and pensions for pastors and vicars going out of office; but canon 1488, § 1 expressly forbids any compensation in the temporalities of exchanged unequal benefices by way of reserving some of the income of the more lucrative benefice for the incumbent of the other. It would seem, therefore, that the exception of canon 1440 cannot be applied here. The Holy See could, of course, permit an exception to the common law, but it is not wont to do so.[29]

Pistocchi [30] in explaining canon 1488 points out that the reserva-

remotione parochorum inamovibilium, can. 2147-2156; tit. XXVIII, *De modo procedendi in remotione parochorum amovibilium*, can. 2157-2161.

[23] Lib. IV, tit. XXIX, *De modo procedendi in translatione parochorum*, canons 2162-2167; canons 193-194.

[24] Canons 1484-1486.

[25] Canons 1487-1488.

[26] "Abire quis dicitur, qui non in poenam e cura animarum post sententiam in criminali foro emissam expellatur. Propterea qui per remedium remotionis, tit. XXVII n. VIII, translationis, XXIX, ob dimissionem a Praelato acceptatam, VI, permutatione, VI, beneficium paroeciale seu curam relinquit, intelligitur hoc loco."—Pistocchi, *De re beneficiali*, pp. 148-149.

[27] Cf. Meier, *Penal administrative procedure against negligent pastors*, The Catholic University of America Canon Law Studies, n. 140 (Washington, D. C.: The Catholic University of America Press, 1941), pp. 90-93.

[28] "Si beneficia permutanda inaequalia sint, nequeunt compensari reservatione fructuum aut praestatione pecuniae seu cuiusque rei pretio aestimabilis." —Canon 1488, § 1.

[29] Cf. Wernz-Vidal, *Ius canonicum*, II (*De personis*), n. 340; Vermeersch-Creusen, *Epitome*, II, n. 811; Coronata, *Institutiones*, II, p. 427, n. 1022; Blat, *Commentarium*, III, part. II-VI (*De rebus*), n. 404.

[30] *De re beneficiali*, pp. 499-500. But cf. above, note 26.

tion of the income of exchanged benefices by way of compensation would be dismemberment of the property of a benefice while leaving the spiritual rights and obligations intact, this being reserved to the Holy See by canons 1421-1422.

In spite of this objection the contrary view seems tenable. Of a number of authors consulted, none specifically mentions ecclesiastical pensions as being comprehended in the phrase *reservatio fructuum*. C. 5, X, *de rerum permutatione*, III, 19, cited as the source of canon 1488, § 1, forbade arbitrary exchanges agreed to privately between the beneficiaries, but not exchanges approved by the bishop.[31] Under the present legislation the ordinary is permitted to accept the resignation of a benefice and to reserve a pension on the benefice in behalf of the retiring cleric[32] without violating the prohibition of canon 1486 forbidding the acceptance of a resignation with a condition affecting the income;[33] but an exchange of benefices, according to a common opinion, contains at least implicitly two resignations and two new appointments.[34] Therefore, it does not seem repugnant that the ordinary, when he implicitly accepts the resignation by granting his consent to the exchange, can also reserve a pension on the benefice provided there is a just cause for doing so,[35] and provided compensation is not made because of inequality arising out of spiritual elements, e. g., greater dignity or jurisdiction pertaining to the one benefice.[36]

[31] Cf. Wernz-Vidal, *Ius canonicum*, II (*De personis*), n. 334.

[32] C. P. I., 20 maii 1923, ad 8.—*AAS*, XVI (1924), 116.

[33] Cf. *Jus Pontificium*, IV (1924), 114-115.

[34] Cf. e. g., Coronata, *Institutiones*, II, pp. 424-427, nn. 1021-1022; Wernz-Vidal, *loc. cit.*

[35] "Caeterum praedictis non obstantibus potest authoritate Episcopi constitui pensio solvenda illi, qui permutando pinguius Beneficium dimittit, non quidem pro conpensatione excessus, ob rationem jam dictam, sed ob aliam causam justam & rationabilem, v. g. quia fit commutatio ob bonum commune, aut bonum pacis privatae, aut quia pensionem praetendens est infirmus, vel aetate decrepitus."—Reiffenstuel, Lib. III, tit. 19, n. 33, citing Barbosa in c. 6, X, *de rerum permutatione*, III, 19, n. 3, Navarrus, *De simonia*, consil. 43, n. 3, Engel, *in hoc titulo*, and others.

[36] Cf. St. Alphonsus, *Theologia moralis*, III, n. 76. He admitted the affirmative opinion as probable, but preferred the negative opinion as being more probable. On the conflicting teaching of the pre-Code authors, cf. *supra*, p. 60.

As recipients of parochial pensions mention is made first of all of retiring pastors.[37] The Code,[38] in outlining the processes of removal from office primarily because the pastor's ministry, even though through no fault of his own, is injurious to souls or at least ineffective for the salvation of souls,[39] expressly declares that the removed pastor can be given a pension; but the facts and circumstances must be weighed, and if he is capable he should rather be transferred to another parish or assigned to another office or benefice.[40] If, however, a pastor is removed by one of the penal administrative processes because of non-residence, concubinage, or neglect in fulfilling his parochial obligations,[41] he can hardly claim to be worthy of an ecclesiastical pension. Removals of this kind have the character of a vindicative penalty: to confer pensions on the delinquents would be tantamount to setting a premium on remissness in fulfilling the duties of an office or benefice and even of one's state.[42] Non-resident or negligent pastors are to be punished to the extent of privation of income and even of the benefice itself.[43] It would be absurd under these circumstances to establish a pension for a recalcitrant cleric. When clerics disregard the admonition and precept of their ordinary and continue to keep under their roof or associate with women of suspicious character, the legal presumption of concubinage arises against them.[44] If the clerics neither obey the precept, nor reply (or fail to give legitimately acceptable excuses),[45] the

[37] Canon 1429, § 2: "Beneficiis autem paroecialibus non possunt [Ordinarii locorum], nisi in commodum parochi . . . a munere abeuntis, imponere pensiones . . . "

[38] Lib. IV, tit. XXVII, XXVIII.

[39] Canon 2147, § 1.

[40] Canons 2154, § 1; 2161, § 2, referring to canon 2154, § 1.

[41] Lib. IV, tit. XXX, *De modo procedendi contra clericos non residentes*, can. 2168-2175; tit. XXXI, *De modo procedendi contra clericos concubinarios*, can. 2176-2181; tit. XXXII, *De modo procedendi contra parochum in adimplendis paroecialibus officiis negligentem*, can. 2182-2185.

[42] D. (50. 17) 134: "Nemo ex suo delicto meliorem suam conditionem facere potest". C. 7, X, *de iudiciis*, II, 1: "Ne ex sua malitia commodum reportet"; also in c. 9, X, *de dolo et contumacia*, II, 14.

[43] Canons 2172-2174; 2184-2185.

[44] Canon 133, §§ 1, 4.

[45] Canons 2178-2181.

ordinary, after having ascertained that they could have obeyed or given an answer, is directed by law to suspend them *a divinis*.[46] One of the effects of any suspension is the incapacity to obtain ecclesiastical pensions.[47] In the cases of non-residence and grave negligence in parochial duties, the legislator makes no mention of pensions, and in the case of clerics living in concubinage he indirectly outlaws pensions.

The parochial vicar is declared to be similarly eligible for a pension on the parish when he goes out of office.[48]

The Code does not specify which vicars are meant. The term would seem to include not only perpetual vicars in charge of parishes united fully with a moral body (*vicarii curati seu perpetui*),[49] vicars econome or administrators of a vacant parish (*vicarii oeconomi*),[50] substitute vicars (*vicarii substituti*),[51] and parochial adjutants (*vicarii adiutores*),[52] but also parochial curates or assistants (*vicarii cooperatores*).[53] In positing the capacity of a retiring parochial assistant to obtain a pension, canonists argue that, the text of the canon being general, there is no sufficient reason for excluding them; that there is question here of a benefit granted by law, which is to be extended;[54] and that parochial assistants no less than pastors can become physically incapacitated and reduced to circumstances in which it becomes impossible or at least inexpedient to provide for them in any other way than by a pension to be reserved on the parish in which they discharged their ministry.[55]

[46] Canon 2177, 1°.

[47] Canon 2283, referring to canon 2265, § 1, 2°.

[48] Canon 1429, § 2: "Beneficiis autem paroecialibus non possunt [Ordinarii locorum], nisi in commodum parochi vel vicarii eiusdem paroeciae a munere abeuntis, imponere pensiones . . . "

[49] Canon 471.

[50] Canons 472-473.

[51] Canon 474.

[52] Canon 475.

[53] Canon 476.

[54] " . . . favores convenit ampliari."—Reg. 15, R. J., in VI°.

[55] E. Suarez, "De pensionibus beneficiis paroecialibus imponendis,"—*Angelicum*, VI (1929), 224. D'Angelo, "De pensione super beneficio paroeciali,"—*Apollinaris*, II (1929), 320.

Since, then, *even*[56] parochial assistants are capable of obtaining pensions on the parishes which they are leaving canonically, *a fortiori* the other vicars ought to be able to obtain similar pensions under like circumstances.[57]

The law, moreover, considers those parochial vicars who are appointed with full parochial powers as equivalent pastors with all the parochial rights and obligations of pastors.[58] Besides the perpetual vicars of parishes fully united to a moral person,[59] these are parochial administrators,[60] vicars substitute,[61] and parochial adjutants if they take the place of the pastor in all things,[62] but generally not the parochial assistants.[63]

Since, then, he who shares in the burdens should also have a proportionate share in the advantages of an office, all of the first four classes of vicars have from this standpoint an even stronger claim to receiving a pension than the mere parochial assistant. The arguments that were given to establish the capacity of the latter for pensions are applicable equally well to the case of any of the other vicars.

When a parochial vicarship has been erected into a benefice,[64] it would seem that pensions on such a benefice can be reserved only

[56] De Meester, *Juris canonici et juris canonico-civilis compendium* (nova ed., Brugis: Desclée, 1921-1928), III, n. 1411, nota 1, p. 339; Coronata, *Institutiones*, n. 985, b, Vol. II, 381.

[57] Cf. Fanfani, *De iure parochorum* (ed. 2., revisa atque notabiliter aucta, Taurini-Romae: Marietti, 1936), n. 196, B, p. 214: " 'vicarii paroeciae' sine addito, possunt esse tam vicarii *coadiutores* tam *cooperatores*." Vermeersch-Creusen, *Epitome*, II, n. 759, 2: "Vicarii, sine addito, possunt esse tam vicarii quasi-parochi quam cooperatores." Cocchi, *Commentarium*, VI, n. 108, *b)*, p. 232 : " . . . vicarii (*tum* ad instar quasi-parochi, *tum* cooperatoris) . . . "

[58] Canon 451, § 2, 2°.

[59] Canon 471.

[60] Canons 472-473.

[61] Canon 474.

[62] Canon 475.

[63] Wernz-Vidal, *Ius canonicum*, II (*De personis*), n. 719; Vermeersch-Creusen, *Epitome*, II, nn. 516; 518; 519, 3; 522; Blat, *Commentarium*, II (*De personis*), nn. 521; 523; 524; 525; 526, § 6; Coronata, *Institutiones*, n. 467, 2°, b, Vol. I, 565.

[64] Cf. canon 477, § 2.

in favor of the retiring vicar, to the exclusion of the pastor. While he is indeed subject to the pastor in the discharge of his office, in the administration of his beneficed vicarship he is independent. If there is question of removal, the same process of law as outlined in the case of pastors is to be followed, although an additional cause has been placed in the law for the removal of the vicar: serious insubordination to the pastor in the exercise of his functions.[65]

In the United States a kind of provision for the decent support of incapacitated clerics is to some extent effected by various kinds of clerical aid societies.

It is true that the Third Plenary Council of Baltimore mentions such a mode of support for ecclesiastics.[66] It must be remembered, however, that this legislation was enacted at a time when it was commonly believed even by the bishops of the country that there were no canonically erected parishes in the country and consequently no parochial benefices on which pensions might be reserved.[67] Archbishop Leonard Neale, the successor to Archbishop Carroll, stated categorically that "In the diocese of Baltimore . . . there are no parishes established here, no benefices conferred . . ."[68]

The acts and decrees of the American synods and councils including those of the Third Plenary Council of Baltimore furnish additional evidence that the prevailing opinion affirmed the non-existence of benefices. The Holy See had been urging the establishment of the system of cathedral chapters as being more in accord with canon law. During the preliminary meetings for the Third Plenary Council in November and December, 1883, there was a temporary deadlock on this question between the American representatives and the S. Congregation for the Propagation of the Faith. By way of compromise the system of diocesan consultors was ad-

[65] Canon 477, § 2.

[66] *Acta et Decreta Concilii Plenarii Baltimorensis III, A.D. MDCCCLXXXIV* (Baltimorae, 1886), n. 71.

[67] Cf. Augustine, *The Canonical and Civil Status of Catholic Parishes in the United States*, pp. 49-52.

[68] To Rev. James Lucas, Georgetown, March 6, 1816.—Shea, *A History of the Catholic Church within the Limits of the United States* (New York, 1886-1892), III, 27. Cf. also *ibid.*, II, 260.

mitted,[69] and appropriate legislation was enacted, embraced in five statutes. The introductory paragraph expresses the strong desire that chapters according to canonical provisions might be established, but contends that conditions of the dioceses at the time did not permit this. Hence the system of diocesan consultors was established until other provisions would be made.[70]

In treating of the care of souls the Council carefully explained that circumstances did not yet warrant the establishing of parishes in the strict sense of the sacred canons and in particular according to the decrees of the Council of Trent. In each diocese certain missions, based on a proportionate relation to the total number in the diocese, were to be selected as a kind of parish (*paroeciarum instar*). A permanently installed or irremovable missionary rector (*rector missionarius*) was to be placed in charge.[71]

From these brief considerations it can be seen that the Fathers for the time contemplated no institution approaching that of a canonical benefice.

The Council's provision for infirm and aged priests can be justly appreciated only when viewed in this light. In the third section of the chapter on diocesan clergy the Fathers established a mode of taking care of their diocesan clergy whose strength had been spent in the service of the faithful. A diocesan fund administered by a committee of priests under the chairmanship of the bishop was to be established. The capital was to be derived from a tax imposed on each parish, or, if this should be too burdensome, from an annual contribution from the diocesan clergy levied in proportion to their salaries. As an alternative the Council provided for a mutual aid society among the priests, again under the presidency of the bishop, and which every priest belonging to the diocese was to be urged to join.[72]

[69] Guilday, *A History of the Councils of Baltimore (1791-1884)*, pp. 230-231.

[70] *Acta et Decreta Concilii Plenarii Baltimorensis III*, Cap. II (nn. 17-22).

[71] *Ibid.*, n. 33.

[72] *Acta et Decreta Concilii Plenarii Baltimorensis III*, n. 71. This enactment of the Council of Baltimore has not been abrogated by the Code; it belongs to the class of particular legislation *praeter Codicem*. Cf. Barrett, A *compara-*

In dealing with irremovable rectors who had resigned freely or who had been removed, the Council[73] mentioned that provision should be made for them by means of a "*pensio,*" but it does not explain the juridical nature of this grant. Possibly it referred to the subsidy derived from the diocesan fund to be established for the support of incapacitated priests. It can hardly be regarded as an ecclesiastical pension in the strict sense, depending usually on an ecclesiastical benefice, since the ecclesiastical benefice was not acknowledged in the Council's legislation.

The special legislation that was enacted by the Third Plenary Council of Baltimore was not in any way a defiance of the general law of the Church: it was recognized to be a temporary expedient to meet in the best way possible the peculiar needs and circumstances of the youthful Church in America. The Fathers of Baltimore desired nothing more than conformity with the universal legislation of the Church—"wise laws, based upon the experience of centuries, and representing the perfection of Church organization." This is the desire that has been handed down by them in their "Pastoral Letter of the Archbishops and Bishops of the United States Assembled in the Third Plenary Council of Baltimore, to the Clergy and Laity of their Charge":

> It is obvious that in countries like our own, where from rudimentary beginnings our organization is only gradually advancing towards perfection, the full application of these laws is impracticable; but in proportion as they become practicable, it is our desire, not less than that of the Holy See, that they should go into effect. For we have the fullest confidence in the wisdom with which the Church devised these laws, and we heartily rejoice at every approach towards perfect organization in the portion of the vineyard over which we have jurisdiction.[74]

tive study of the Councils of Baltimore and the Code of canon law, The Catholic University of America Canon Law Studies, n. 83 (Washington, D. C.: The Catholic University of America, 1932), Chap. III, tit. 4; "Conciliar Laws Abrogated and not Abrogated by the Code,"—*The Jurist,*. II (1942), 63.

[73] N. 38, VII.

[74] *Acta et Decreta Concilii Plenarii Baltimorensis III,* pp. lxxx-lxxxi.

Some authors have attempted to show that at least in some particular instances there were parishes and benefices in the earlier days of the Church in America, and that a denial is "canonically speaking, not quite logical."[75] The negative opinion, however, was the one generally accepted as applying to the period in which the Church in the United States was subject to the Sacred Congregation for the Propagation of the Faith.[76] As to the status of parishes afterwards, even in the period following the promulgation of the Code, doubts continued to persist, and the question was not settled until 1922, when Archbishop Bonzano,Apostolic Delegate, addressed a letter to the bishops of the United States, in which he related the response he had received from Cardinal Gasparri, President of the Pontifical Commission for the Authentic Interpretation of the Canons of the Code. Summarizing the reply from Rome, the Most Reverend Delegate concluded:

> It is evident from this official answer that all the parishes of the United States having the three necessary qualifications, viz., (1) a resident pastor; (2) endowment (resources or revenue according to the provisions of canons 1410 or 1415, § 3); and (3) boundaries, are not only parishes in the strict canonical sense, but are also ecclesiastical benefices.[77]

The ardent wish of the Fathers of Baltimore has been fulfilled to the extent that there are now parochial benefices in our country. Consequently pensions on parochial benefices are no longer juridically impossible, and, if it be permitted to add, the writer has been informed of cases where such exist.

In mission countries quasi-pastors or missioners, who because of infirmity resign the quasi-parishes or missions which they have held

[75] Augustine, *Canonical and Civil Status of Catholic Parishes*, p. 49-52. Cf. Golden, *Parochial benefices in the new Code*, The Catholic University of America Canon Law Studies, n. 10 (Washington: The Catholic University of America, 1921), chapter IX.

[76] Cf. Pius X, const. "*Sapienti consilio*," 29 iun. 1908, § 1, n. 6°, 2—*AAS*, I (1909), 12.

[77] 10 Nov., 1922.—Bouscaren, *The Canon Law Digest* (Milwaukee: Bruce Publishing company, 1934), I, 151.

for ten years or more, may be given a pension drawn from their former quasi-parish or mission, in virtue of the faculty granted to the ordinaries by the Sacred Congregation for the Propagation of the Faith.[78] Viewed in the light of canon 1429, § 2, to which it bears some similarity, the faculty ought to be extended to include not only the titular of the quasi-parish or the mission, but also the vicar or assistant as qualified to receive a pension, provided that the other conditions are verified and especially resignation is caused by infirmity ensuing after ten years of service. The law does not distinguish; and where the reason is the same, the application of the law ought to be the same.[79]

Scholion. The effects of canonical irregularity on the capacity to acquire ecclesiastical pensions

The common, although not universal, teaching prior to the Code was that persons who were canonically irregular could not lawfully obtain ecclesiastical pensions.[80] It remains true according to the present law that irregularity affects primarily and directly the reception and exercise of the power of orders;[81] but that secondarily and indirectly it affects the cleric's capacity of obtaining a benefice

[78] Facultas I minor, n. 26; I major, n. 25; II minor, n. 34; II major, n. 34; III minor, n. 45; III major, n. 45.—Coronata, *Institutiones*, V, 294, 298, 303, 309, 316, 325.

[79] "Ubi eadem est ratio, eadem debet esse iuris dispositio."—Reiffenstuel, Lib. I, tit. II, n. 504-508. Cf. Vromant, *De bonis Ecclesiae*, p. 118.

[80] Cf. Ferraris, "Pensio," nn. 57-58. It is probable that the authors had in mind irregularities known before first tonsure, or those resulting from grave crimes. It must also be noted that prior to the Code's exposition of the law on irregularities and its restriction to one precise concept, the term was used somewhat loosely even to denote suspension, penalties, and ecclesiastical prohibitions or impediments. Cf. Wernz-Vidal, *Ius canonicum*, IV, pars I (*De rebus*), n. 230.

"Codex in hoc articulo [II. *De irregularitatibus aliisque impedimentis*, can. 983-991] totam de integro ordinat legis materiam quoad irregularitates. Ideo priores leges abrogantur . . . " Claeys-Bouuaert-Simenon, *Manuale juris canonici* (Gandae et Leodii: apud auctores, 1930-1931), II, 175. Cf. De Meester, *Juris canonici et juris canonico-civilis compendium*, III, n. 1918, p. 296.

[81] Canon 968.

at least lawfully.[82] For, inasmuch as a benefice consists of two elements,—a sacred office and the right to receive the fruits of the annexed endowment—[83] if an irregular cleric may not exercise the order demanded by the sacred office, then neither may he obtain the benefice.[84] It seems, however, that this cannot be extended to ecclesiastical pensions. Authors generally agree that at least in odious matters pensions cannot be likened to benefices, and irregularities are odious. Moreover, when pensions are granted to disabled clerics there is no question from a positive standpoint of the contemporary exercise of orders or discharge of an office by a correlative obligation; negatively the disability may even be a factor in favor of awarding a pension.

It is evident, of course, that an irregular candidate for first tonsure is excluded from lawfully obtaining an ecclesiastical pension for the reason that he is excluded from the clerical state.

What is to be said about irregularities incurred or discovered after the reception of tonsure or orders? Ruling this case, there is, besides the principle that the highest reverence for the sacrament must be preserved by debarring from it those whom the Church deems unfit, the other principle that respectable maintenance must be provided for clerics in keeping with their state. In accordance with the latter it would seem that irregularity subsequent to ordination is not sufficient cause for depriving a cleric of decent livelihood. In reconciling this conflict of principles, several procedures are conceivable. A dispensation from the irregularity might be obtained, if that is possible and feasible. If a dispensation from the particular irregularity in question would result only in disgrace to the clerical state, steps might have to be taken to have the cleric laicized. There is, however, the possibility that a dispensation on the one hand might jeopardize the reverence due the clerical state,

[82] Cf. canon 991, § 3. Cappello, *Tractatus canonico-moralis de sacramentis*, II, pars 3 (*De sacra ordinatione*), n. 444. Wernz-Vidal (*Ius canonicum*, II [*De personis*], n. 199; IV, pars 1 [*De rebus*], n. 234) believe it more probable that validity is involved; but cf. Cappello, *ibid.*, n. 422, § 5.

[83] Canon 1409.

[84] "Cum quid prohibetur, prohibentur omnia quae sequuntur ex illo." Reg. 39, R. J., in VI°.

and on the other hand reduction to the lay state might be unwarranted, as in the case of grave physical or mental disability.[85] In the case of such unfortunate clerics, if in the judgment of the ordinary they cannot be permitted further to exercise the orders they have received, one mode of providing for their decent support would be by pension.

It would seem, therefore, that irregularity as such and in itself does not prevent a cleric from receiving ecclesiastical pensions. It will be recalled that many of the irregularities are at the same time delicts which carry with them the inability to obtain pensions, and hence disqualify indirectly. This is also implied by the Code when in speaking of the effects of the vindicative penalty of infamy of law it states: "A person who has incurred infamy of law is *not only irregular . . . but in addition* he is incapacitated from obtaining ecclesiastical . . . pensions."[86]

The question of illegitimacy and its effects on the capacity to acquire clerical pensions was much discussed prior to the promulgation of the Code. The law today lists illegitimacy as the first of the irregularities *ex defectu*,[87] and the question of illegitimacy and the lawfulness of receiving a pension must consequently be decided according to what has just been said about irregularities in general.

[85] Canon 984, 2°, 3°.

[86] Canon 2294, § 1. Woywod, *A Practical Commentary on the Code of Canon Law* (4 rev. ed., New York: Joseph F. Wagner, 1932), II, pp. 457-458, n. 2135. Italics inserted.

[87] Canon 984, 1°.

Chapter VII

PERSONS WHO CANNOT ENJOY ECCLESIASTICAL PENSIONS

Article 1. Members of Religious Institutes

Offhand, it is almost paradoxical to conceive of a religious as the recipient of a pension. A religious by his very profession obtains the right to be supported by the institute, whose corresponding duty it is to care for the bodily as well as the spiritual needs of its members.[1] The religious on their part are directed by the Code carefully to observe the common life even in the matter of food, dress, and furniture.[2]

A religious who has made simple profession of either perpetual or temporary vows retains title to his property (*dominium radicale*) and also the capacity to acquire additional property, unless the constitutions of the institute provide otherwise;[3] but the administration of such property is to be entrusted to a person of his choice and he must dispose of its use and usufruct, although he is free in determining the end to which the use or usufruct is to be applied, unless the constitutions provide otherwise.[4] The law adds, however, that whatever a religious in simple vows acquires, not by way of patrimony, but through his own industry or in behalf of his institute accrues to the institute.[5] Consequently it seems that a religious in simple vows may not lawfully acquire the right to an ecclesiastical pension for himself, with the exception, somewhat

[1] Cf. Schaefer, *De religiosis ad normam Codicis iuris canonici* (3. ed., Roma: S. A. L. E. R., Rappresentante della casa editrice Herder, 1940), n. 267, 10, p. 584.

[2] Canon 594, § 1.

[3] Canon 580, § 1.

[4] Canon 569, §§ 1, 2; C. P. I., 16 oct. 1919, n. 9.—*AAS*, XI (1919), 478. Cf. Blat, *Commentarium*, II (*De religiosis*), nn. 403, 405; Larraona, "De paupertate simplici,"—*Commentarium pro Religiosis* (Romae, 1920-), I (1920), 338. Hereafter this periodical will be cited *CpR*.

[5] Canon 580, § 2.

rare, of a purely gratuitous pension or one given to him as a private person; but even here he must cede its administration, income, and use, as prescribed for other property of which he retains ownership.[6]

A religious in solemn vows, on the other hand, unless he has a special indult of the Holy See,[7] cedes all his property and income of every kind, present and future to the Order, province, or house, according to the constitutions. If the Order is one that is incapable of holding possession, all property taken in its name is acquired by the Holy See.[8] It is clear, therefore, that according to common law and prescinding from particular indults, a solemnly professed religious cannot validly acquire the right of pension for himself.[9]

There is, however, nothing in the common law to prevent a religious from becoming the recipient of a pension either civil[10] or ecclesiastical, if circumstances warrant. The Code does not prohibit a religious from receiving goods, but it clearly directs what is to be done with goods once they have been received, and prescribes definitely in whom the title is to be vested.[11]

Sometimes parochial benefices are entrusted to members of an institute either as pastor or as vicar.[12] With regard to the revenues

[6] Cf. canons 569, § 2; 579; 580.

[7] It will be recalled that in pre-Code law an apostolic indult was expressly required in order that a regular might be enabled to receive a pension on a secular benefice. Cf. Ferraris, "Pensio," nn. 51-53. *V. supra*, p. 51.

[8] Canon 582. Among the Orders incapable of possessing are the Friars Minor, the Capuchins, the Discalced Carmelites, and the professed members or formed coadjutors of the Society of Jesus. Cf. Wernz-Vidal, *Ius canonicum*, III (*De religiosis*), n. 342, and nota 29, pp. 337-339.

[9] Cf. canons 579; 581; 582. " . . . ius ad bona temporalia [professus sollemniter] sibi acquirere nequit." Vermeersch-Creusen, *Epitome*, I, n. 736, 6.

[10] Cf. S. C. de Rel., "Circa pecunias religiosis obvenientes occasione servitii militaris praestiti tempore belli," n. V.—*AAS*, XIV (1922), 196. Schaefer, *De religiosis*, n. 332, p. 691. Goyeneche, "Annotationes, V,"—*CpR*, IV (1923), 37-38; *idem*, "Consultatio: Praemium bellicum quod redeuntibus e militia nunc obvenit, religiosi simpliciter professi acquirunt sibi ad normam can. 580 § 1, vel potius religioni ad normam eiusdem can. 580 § 2,"—*CpR*, I (1920), 340-343. Cf. also *Jus Pontificium*, I-II (1921-1922), 60.

[11] Canons 580, 582.

[12] Canons 626; 630-631; 471-477.

the law states that whatever comes to the religious in behalf of the parish over which he has charge accrues to said parish; the rest he acquires after the manner of other religious.[13] Among the latter, authors enumerate Mass stipends, stole fees, revenues from the endowment of the benefice, salaries, and subsidies from the State.[14] Here also, it seems, must be included ecclesiastical pensions, if any are given to the religious pastors or vicars. They would accrue to the institute.

A distinction must be noted between parishes which are fully incorporated into a religious institute [15] and other parishes. In the former instance it would be pointless for a religious institute, which must provide for its members, to reserve a pension on its own parish in favor of its own member, to be paid by the succeeding pastor, who as a religious acquires the income from the benefice for the selfsame institute.

In some parts of America as well as elsewhere a religious is sometimes appointed to a secular parish temporarily or provisionally, because of a lack of diocesan priests.[16] According to the general wording of canon 1429, § 2 there seems to be no fundamental inconsistency involved in awarding a pension to a religious pastor or vicar upon his retiring from a secular parish. Furthermore, in mission territories quasi-parishes or missions are frequently in charge of religious. There seems to be no reason for construing the general wording of the apostolic faculty on pensions to exclude religious, who retire for a just cause from the service of a quasi-parish or a mission.[17] Yet, there is a kind of incongruity between the religious life and the holding of benefices;[18] and the solicitude of the

[13] Canon 630, § 3.

[14] Fanfani, *De iure parochorum*, n. 426, b, p. 452. Schaefer, *De religiosis*, n. 501, b, nota 72, p. 905.

[15] Canon 1425, § 2.

[16] Schaefer, *De religiosis*, n. 500, p. 904. Goyeneche, *CpR*, XVI (1935), 434.

[17] Cf. Vromant, *De bonis Ecclesiae*, p. 119.

[18] "Exclusa autem fundatione et incorporatione revera dicendum est notionem plenam beneficii proprie dicti minus aptari religiosis praesertim ratione voti obedientiae et paupertatis."—Coronata, *Institutiones*, I, p. 838, n. 633,

legislator about keeping secular and religious benefices distinct[19] would seem to indicate some reluctance also in the matter of reserving pensions on secular benefices in behalf of religious. The conferring of a pension would not, however, be against the law, if based on good reasons, such as acknowledgment of outstanding services rendered, recognition for unusual difficulties emerging from the assignment, compensation for injuries to health suffered while in the service of the parish, or indirect assistance to a religious institute, province, or house.

Scholion. Quasi-Religious

A word remains to be said about quasi-religious. Clerics living in a society without public vows, as required in order that one may be considered a religious, are capable of receiving pensions, subject, however, to such restrictions as the constitutions and rules of their respective societies may impose.[20]

Article 2. Those Guilty of Crime

There are a number of crimes which prohibit and even disqualify the offender from receiving ecclesiastical pensions. In general, every

nota 6. Cf. Haring, *Grundzuege des katholischen Kirchenrechtes*, pp. 812-813.

[19] E. g., Canon 1411, 2°: " . . . omnia autem beneficia, erecta extra ecclesias vel domus religiosorum, in dubio saecularia esse praesumuntur."

Canon 1422: ". . . beneficii religiosi translatio, divisio et dismembratio quaelibet uni Sedi Apostolicae reservantur."

Canon 1423, § 2: "Nequeunt vero [Ordinarii locorum] paroeciam unire . . . cum monasteriis, ecclesiis religiosorum . . . "

Canon 1425, § 1: "Si a Sede Apostolica paroecia domui religiosae uniatur *ad temporalia tantum* quod attinet, domus religiosa particeps fit solummodo fructuum paroeciae, et Superior religiosus sacerdotem e clero saeculari in eadem instituendum, assignata congrua portione, Ordinario loci praesentare debet."

Canon 1427, § 5: "Divisa paroecia quae ad aliquam religionem iure spectat, vicaria perpetua aut paroecia noviter erecta non est religiosa."

Canon 1430, § 1: ". . . beneficia religiosa [ab Ordinariis] in saecularia [converti nequeunt], nec saecularia in religiosa."

Canon 1442: "Beneficia saecularia nonnisi clericis e clero saeculari conferenda sunt; religiosa sodalibus illius religionis, ad quam beneficia pertinent."

[20] Cf. canon 676, § 3.

excommunication forbids the lawful obtaining of ecclesiastical pensions. If the person excommunicated is *vitandus* or if a declaratory or condemnatory sentence has been rendered, the pension would, moreover, be conferred invalidly.[21] In the case of those who usurp or convert to their own use property or rights belonging to the Roman Church, the specially reserved automatic excommunication does not render the criminal *vitandus*. Nevertheless, the canon expressly states that if he is a cleric he is to be declared *incapable* of obtaining pensions.[22]

Personal interdict [23] and suspension [24] produce the same effects as excommunication in the matter of obtaining pensions.

Infamy of law, one of the canonical irregularities *ex defectu,*[25] as a vindicative penalty expressly renders the subject incapable of obtaining pensions.[26]

In enumerating the effects of infamy of fact the law makes no mention of a prohibition against the acquiring of pensions.[27] Inasmuch as persons infamous by fact are under a simple impediment preventing the reception of orders,[28] infamy of fact antecedent to first tonsure indirectly makes one ineligible for a clerical pension. When, however, infamy of fact is incurred subsequent to entrance into the clerical state, while there is no intention of minimizing its force as a vindicative penalty, nevertheless to infer that one of its effects is a general prohibition against the receiving of pensions appears unjustified; for when speaking of infamy of law, the legis-

[21] Canon 2265, § 1, 2°; § 2.

[22] Canon 2345. This is the only specific delict for which the penalty of incapacity to receive a pension is expressly stated in this third part of the fifth book, "De poenis in singula delicta."

[23] Canon 2275, 3°.

[24] Canon 2283.

[25] Canon 984, 4°.

[26] Canon 2294, § 1: "Qui infamia iuris laborat, non solum est irregularis ad normam can. 984, n. 5, sed insuper est inhabilis ad obtinenda[s] . . . pensiones . . . " This disability would arise even prior to sentence if the penalty is incurred *ipso facto;* cf. canons 2314, § 1, 3°; 2320; 2328; 2343, § 1, 2°, § 2, 2°; 2351, § 2.

[27] Canon 2294, § 2.

[28] Canon 987, 7°.

lator expressly mentions as an effect the inability of the delinquent to acquire pensions—not so when speaking of infamy of fact. And in penal matters the more favorable interpretation ought to be applied.[29]

By deposition a cleric is rendered incapable of obtaining ecclesiastical pensions.[30] Because of the severity of the measure the legislator hastens to add that this vindicative penalty cannot be inflicted except in cases expressed in the law.[31]

Article 3. Laicized Clerics

If a cleric who has been deposed and deprived of the ecclesiastical garb continues for a year to give scandal, he can be degraded. Besides this added penalty for contumacy, there are other crimes expressly sanctioned with the same penalty of degradation. By degradation a cleric is reduced to the lay state.[32] As a layman he is incapable of acquiring clerical pensions.

Besides degradation the Code outlines other ways in which clerics are reduced to the lay state.[33] By returning to the lay state, clerics automatically lose all offices, benefices, clerical rights and privileges.[34] There is no longer the same responsibility on the part of the Church to provide proper maintenance for them as there was while they were members of the clerical state. Having resumed their place in the ranks of the laity, they have no capacity to receive ecclesiastical pensions by any claim greater than that of other members of the laity, the common law stating explicitly that only members of the clerical state can be recipients of ecclesiastical pensions.[35]

[29] Canon 2219, § 1.

[30] Canon 2303, § 1.

[31] Canon 2303, § 3. The cases expressed in the law are such that the reception of pensions is already forbidden by reason of previously incurred or inflicted censures or infamy; e. g., canons 2314; 2320, 2°; 2322; 2328; 2350, § 1; 2354, § 2; 2359, § 2; 2379; 2394, 2°; 2401.

[32] Canon 2305, §§ 1-2. It will be recalled that trials for delicts involving deposition or degradation are reserved to a tribunal of five judges;— canon 1576, § 1, 2°.

[33] Lib. II, pars II, tit. VI, *De reductione clericorum ad statum laicalem*, canons 211-214.

[34] Canon 213, § 1.

[35] Canon 118.

CHAPTER VIII

CONDITIONS FOR THE ESTABLISHMENT OF ECCLESIASTICAL PENSIONS

The active and passive subjects and the object of ecclesiastical pensions having been considered, the present chapter will be concerned with questions pertaining to the actual reservation of a pension and with problems that can arise while the pension is in existence.

ARTICLE 1. THE TIME OF RESERVING THE PENSION

Before the promulgation of the Code it was commonly held that pensions could be reserved on a benefice even while it was without an incumbent, but not while a benefice was occupied and against the will of the incumbent, whose acquired right would otherwise be violated through a reduction of the income of his benefice.[1] Wernz pointed out that the law may make exceptions, as when it would become necessary to appoint an assistant to a disabled beneficiary.[2]

In the present law it is expressly stated that local ordinaries can reserve ecclesiastical pensions on non-parochial benefices " when they confer the benefice." [3]

[1] St. Thomas, *Summa theologica*, II-II, q. 100, art. 4, ad 3; Pistocchi, *De re beneficiali*, p. 140; Garcias, *De beneficiis*, pars I, c. 5, n. 320; Schmalzgrueber, Lib. III, tit. 12, n. 14; De Angelis, *Praelectiones*, Lib. III, tit. 12, n. 4; Wernz, *Ius decretalium*, II, n. 321. Cf. S. R. R., *Vercellen.*, "Pensionis," 18 dec. 1928, n. 4.—S. R. R. *Decisiones*, XX (1928), 494.

[2] ". . . nisi agatur de casu a iure excepto, quo v. g. beneficiato inhabili constituendus esset coadiutor."—*Ius decretalium*, II, n. 321.

[3] ". . . dum beneficium conferunt . . ."—Canon 1429, § 1. Cf. S. C. C., *Dioecesis N.*, "Renuntiationis paroeciae," 11 nov. 1922—AAS, XV (1923), 454. Wernz-Vidal, *Ius canonicum, II* (*De personis*), n. 180, b. Cf. also Pitocchi on this paragraph (*De re beneficiali*, p. 143): ". . . nulla item [est concessio] quae ab eodem [Ordinario] concedatur ex fructibus beneficii vacantis, *dum vacat*, eam alteri (etsi non sibi) reservando, quia tunc nullus est qui pro beneficio *actione iuridica* potiatur et consentire queat, et insuper non liceat (salvo privilegio) vacantis beneficii vel ecclesiae fructus minuere (Videas in textu capp. citt. *De praeb. et dign.*—*De his quae fiunt a Prael.*—*De excessibus Praelat.*, passim) "

The second paragraph of canon 1429 deals exclusively with pensions on parochial benefices.[4] The time when such pensions can be reserved is not explicitly stated. It would seem that such pensions could be reserved not only at the time of conferring the parochial benefice, but also before a new appointment takes place.[5]

When a pension is reserved for a pastor who has been removed by administrative process,[6] circumstances may be such as to demand that the reservation of a pension should become effective even before the new successor has been appointed. The ordinary is urged by the general law itself to make new provision for the removed pastor in the very decree of removal or as soon as possible thereafter,[7] that is, as a rule at least within a month,[8] whereas the appointment to the vacated parish may lawfully take place under ordinary circum-

It may be noted that such pensions are temporary pensions and give rise to personal obligations by directly burdening the beneficiary, whose actual incumbency is therefore obviously presupposed; cf. Wernz-Vidal, *op. cit.*, n. 180, a.

[4] "Beneficiis autem paroecialibus . . . " Cf. S. C. C., *Resolutio*, 11 nov. 1922—*loc. cit.*

[5] The rubric of c. un., X, *ut ecclesiastica beneficia sine diminutiòne conferantur*, III, 12, forms the general rule of canon 1440, but from it ecclesiastical pensions are expressly excepted. Consequently, at the time of conferring benefices there is permitted no diminution of any kind with the exception of ecclesiastical pensions; but it does not seem that one must conclude from this rule that the reservation of pensions is permitted only at the time of the conferring of benefices. Canon 1440 re-states former law, and hence is to be interpreted, according to canon 6, 2°, "ex veteris iuris auctoritate, atque ideo ex receptis apud probatos auctores interpretationibus." Cf. Blat, *Commentarium*, III, part. II-VI (*De rebus*), n. 349. Ecclesiastical pensions were treated by pre-Code authors in connection with their commentary on the aforementioned title of the Decretals. The present law on ecclesiastical pensions is found specifically in canon 1429, as referred to by canon 1440.

[6] Canons 2147-2161.

[7] Canon 2155. E. Suarez (*De remotione parochorum* [Romae: Angelicum, 1931], n. 76, p. 89) aptly points out that "Amoto parocho" of canon 2154, § 1 is dative and not ablative absolute, and consequently the law does not demand that the removal should be completed before the determination of provision is to be made.

[8] Suarez, *De remotione parochorum*, n. 83, p. 89. Noval, *De processibus*, II, 519. Coronata, *Institutiones*, III, n. 1594, p. 520.

stances at any time within the succeeding six months, or it may even be postponed for a longer period if a reasonable cause warrants postponement.[9] Cocchi repeats the former law, arguing that if a pension is to be reserved on a vacant benefice, a competent advocate must be appointed.[10]

The rule prohibiting the reservation of pensions while the benefice is occupied, if extended to parochial benefices, may be faced with a practical difficulty when there is question of assigning a pension for a retiring substitute (*vicarius substitutus*), administrator (*vicarius coadiutor*), or assistant (*vicarius cooperator*). The fact of their retiring does not effect a vacancy of the benefice, excepting, of course, the somewhat rare case when the assistantship is itself a benefice.[11] Unless the pastor retires at the same time, the benefice remains occupied. Does this mean that no pension can be reserved for the vicar until his pastor also goes out of office? Canon 1429, § 2 does not expressly mention any time within which the pension is to be reserved, and on the other hand the legislator's purpose in permitting ordinaries to reserve parochial pensions for retiring vicars is to provide them with respectable maintenance at the time they have need of it. Hence, it seems the pension for retiring vicars imposed on a parochial benefice may be lawfully reserved even when the benefice is not vacant and outside the time of conferring the benefice. Assuming that the parish is in good financial state, any objections thereto on the part of the pastor are unreasonable in law; for the law assures him the usufruct of the revenues to the amount required for his decent maintenance, but it also obliges him to distribute the superfluous income to the poor or to devote it to other pious causes.[12] And who could have a worthier claim than a former assistant who is in need of provision for decent maintenance? Moreover, the law of pensions safeguards the prior right of the beneficiary to fitting livelihood, for the pen-

[9] Canons 458; 155. C. P. I., 24 nov. 1920—*AAS*, XII (1920), 577.

[10] *Commentarium*, VI, n. 106, p. 230. *V. supra*, p. 59.

[11] Cf. canon 477, § 2.

[12] Canon 1473.

sion may never exceed one-third of the parish revenues after all expenses and uncertain income have been deducted.[13]

Article 2. Just Cause

When the ordinary reserves a pension it is required that there be a just cause for doing so,[14] to be determined according to the judgment of the ordinary.[15]

Since a pension for the life of the pensioner involves some change in the status of the benefice, it being a reduction of the beneficiary's income—a kind of diminution or dismemberment,—the just cause for reserving a pension coincides with the canonical causes objectively required for alteration of benefices, i. e., necessity of or usefulness to the Church.[16]

Subjectively the final cause of all pensions, as formerly, is *alimentorum suppeditatio*—the provision of decent maintenance. Among the occasional or motivating causes authors mention resignation or removal because of age or serious disability, an exchange of benefices (when the new benefice does not provide sufficient revenue),[17] settlement of litigation, and the pursuit of studies in preparation for orders.[18] D'Angelo mentions as a just cause the financial assistance needed by those engaged in the advanced study of theology or canon law; but he counsels that permission of the Holy See should be sought before a pension is reserved for this cause.[19]

The cause need not necessarily be grave, but it ought to be such that in conscience the case admits no other practical economic solution, except a pension.[20] This means, first of all, that the income remaining after deducting the pension will be sufficient for the

[13] Canon 1429, § 2. Cf. also the pre-Code observation of Wernz, cited in a previous note.

[14] Canon 1429, § 1: " . . . ex iusta causa."

[15] Blat, *Commentarium*, III, part. II-VI (*De rebus*), n. 236.

[16] Pistocchi, *De re beneficiali*, pp. 141-143.

[17] V. *supra*, p. 103-104.

[18] Cocchi, *Commentarium*, VI, n. 105, p. 229. Cf. also Blat, *Commentarium*, V, p. 225, n. 177.

[19] "A cautela però noi consiglieremmo ai Vescovi, ad evitare fastidi, di chiederne sempre la venia alla S. Sede."—*Tasse e pensioni*, p. 122, nota 2.

[20] D'Angelo, *op. cit.*, p. 122, d).

beneficiary, and, secondly, that the prospective pensioner cannot be satisfactorily provided for in another manner, be it by a (another) parish, benefice, or office,[21] or other source of honorable support that he may have. For, while Christian charity, at least, seems to require that an ecclesiastic, and certainly a priest, be not left without means of livelihood, as also the dignity of the clerical state demands, yet the ecclesiastic cannot insist that precisely a pension be given to him. In treating of the provision to be made for a removed pastor, for instance, the law mentions the pension as the last specific mode of provision, adding that it is to be reserved as the case requires and circumstances permit.[22]

With regard to resignation approved by the ordinary for the good of souls, there arose after the promulgation of the Code, a question whether this could be done with the "condition" of reserving a pension. In a case submitted to the Sacred Congregation of the Council [23] it was pleaded that a certain pension imposed on a parish in behalf of a resigned pastor as a condition of the resignation, was invalid, since canon 2150, § 3 states that a conditional resignation can be made only if the ordinary can lawfully accept it;[24] but canon 1486 expressly mentions that he cannot accept the resignation of a benefice with a condition affecting its revenues.[25] The Sacred Congregation decided that the "condition" was not truly and properly such. As to the facts of the case, it was noted that the pension was

[21] Cf. canon 2154, § 1.

[22] Canon 2154, § 1. Cf. Suarez, *De remotione parochorum*, n. 75, p. 88; Coronata, *Institutiones*, III, p. 521, n. 1593; Connor, *The administrative removal of pastors*, The Catholic University of America Canon Law Studies, n. 104 (Washington, D. C.: The Catholic University of America, 1937), p. 125. D'Angelo (*Tasse e pensioni*, p. 122, e) and Creusen (Vermeersch-Creusen, *Epitome*, III, n. 354, 3, 1°) believe that the enumeration is exhaustive; Noval (*De processibus*, II, nn. 585-586, pp. 510-511), however, disagrees.

[23] S. C. C., *Dioecesis N.*, "Renuntiationis paroeciae," 11 nov. 1922—*AAS*, XV (1923), 151-156.

[24] "Renuntiatio fieri potest . . . etiam sub conditione, dummodo haec ab Ordinario legitime acceptari possit . . . "

[25] "Dimissionem beneficiorum . . . sub aliqua conditione, quae . . . beneficii . . . redituum erogationem attingat, Ordinarius admittere nequit . . . "

first proposed by the bishop; the pastor merely accepted it. Retirement was demanded and was to follow in any event. Hence, speaking accurately, it was not the resigning pastor who reserved a pension for himself, but rather the bishop who established it for him. In point of law, the pastor could not posit the pension as a condition of his resignation, even if he had wished to do so, for the law commands that provision by pension and removal should be so distinct and separate that they cannot be included in one act of consent, and, therefore, may not depend one upon the other.[26] Finally, it was argued, with regard to the reservation of pensions as alleged to be forbidden by canon 1486: the reason therefor seems to be the prevention of simony arising under ecclesiastical law; but in the case of resignation of a parish for the good of souls, danger of simony is already removed, as appears from the decree "*Maxima cura*" which explicitly permitted the ordinary "in the invitation to resign, or . . . while the process of removal is pending, . . . to propose this provision and to inform the pastor thereof, if he deems it expedient." [27]

The conclusion reached was that there was no cause for declaring the particular resignation null; but that it is more advisable that ordinaries refrain from these and similar arrangements with their subjects in matters of removal, since no necessity calls for them, and at the same time they somehow seem to do harm to the dignity of the office.

The Sacred Congregation of the Council, in explaining the application of canon 1486 to the reservation of pensions had considered only the case of resignation in the administrative process of removal, implying, as it seems, that in every other resignation

[26] "In quolibet casu quaestio de provisione futura sacerdotis non debet commisceri cum quaestione de praesenti amotione a paroecia . . . "—S. C. Consist., decr. "Maxima cura," 20 aug. 1910, can. 28, § 3.—*AAS*, II (1910), 646; *Fontes*, n. 2074; Suarez, *De remotione parochorum*, p. 275.

[27] Can. 28, § 2, of which the complete text is: "Sed potest [Ordinarius] etiam in ipsa invitatione ad renuntiandum vel separatis litteris, pendente amotionis negotio, vel in ipso amotionis decreto provisionem hanc proponere et indicare, si expediens iudicaverit."—*AAS*, II (1910), 646; *Fontes*, n. 2074; Suarez, *De remotione parochorum*, p. 275.

not requested or suggested by the ordinary, the prohibition of canon 1486 remains in force.[28] Six months later the Pontifical Code Commission not only confirmed the decision of the Sacred Congregation, but extended it, when it declared that the ordinary of the place can lawfully accept the resignation of a parish with a reservation of a pension for the life of the pensioner to be drawn from the parochial benefice in favor of the resigning pastor.[29] It will be seen immediately that this reply of the Commission is more extensive than the conclusion of the Sacred Congregation.

One writer[30] acknowledged difficulty in discerning the juridical reasons whereby such a reservation amounting even to a condition should be considered as a general exception to the express prohibition of canon 1486 rather than a case falling outside that prohibition. As an explanation he proposed that, strictly speaking, it is not the resigning pastor who reserves the pension for himself, but rather the bishop, who establishes it for him;[31] or again, it is not right that the ordinary's general power to establish pensions be restricted by the resigner's placing a condition affecting the exercise of this power.[32] In any event, the practical purpose of this reply in its broad lines is clear: the legislator thereby offered a means to encourage resignation of a parish for the sake of the good of souls.

[28] Cf. *Il Monitore ecclesiastico*, XXXV (1923), p. 295.

[29] "Utrum loci Ordinarius possit admittere renuntiationem paroeciae cum reservatione pensionis ad vitam pensionarii super beneficio paroeciali in favorem parochi renuntiantis. Resp. *Affirmative*, firmo praescripto canonis 1429 § 2."—20 maii, 1923, ad IX.—*AAS*, XVI (1924), 116.

[30] *Il Monitore ecclesiastico*, XXXVI (1924), 81.

[31] "Resignatio cum reservatione pensionis nonnisi auctoritate Episcopi licita est; accurate enim loquendo non tam cedens sibi reservare, quam Episcopus eam reservare valet." Aichner, § 95, not. 13, *apud Il Monitore ecclesiastico*, XXXV (1923), 294-295.

[32] This argument is also developed in *Ius pontificium* [IV (1924), 114-115]: "Et ratio iuridica responsionis videtur nobis requirenda esse: . . . 2° in facto quod non apparet, quare Ordinarius, qui ex can. 1429 § 2 potest beneficio paroeciali pensionem imponere in commodum cuiusvis parochi a munere abeuntis, non possit amplius eandem pensionem admittere si haec fuerit tanquam conditio reservata: ad summum namque reservatio esset inutilis; sed utile per inutile minime vitiatur." Cf. also Doheny, "The removal of irremovable pastors"—*AER*, XCIII (1935), p. 497, note 19.

As a solution to the difficulty of why resignation from a parish is not included in canon 1486 Vermeersch [33] explains that, while in other instances of resignation the affair is of a private nature, and a condition affecting the appointment to the benefice or the distribution of its revenue is suspected of simony arising at least under ecclesiastical law, the resignation of a parish is often necessary for the spiritual good of the parishioners, being advised by the bishop rather than merely accepted by him. The purpose of providing sustenance for the retiring priest removes all danger of simony from the reservation of a pension. Nor does such reservation constitute a suspensory or resolutory condition, properly so-called; if accepted, it merely gives the resigner peace of mind in the assurance that the bishop will impose this pension. There is therefore no bargaining between successor and predecessor.

According to one opinion [34] a cleric who freely retires from a parochial benefice, the reason therefor being approved by the ordinary, has the right to demand a pension,[35] and the ordinary cannot give him another benefice or office against his will and without his consent;[36] but one who is removed from his parochial office [37] is unable to demand a pension, and the ordinary has the right to assign another office or benefice in place of a pension. For there is a juridical difference between spontaneous resignation and removal for reasons even though not due to any personal fault of the incumbent but which render his ministry harmful or at least ineffective.

[33] *Periodica*, XIII (1925), 87.

[34] *Apollinaris*, IV (1931), 602, being a summary of Vito, "De pensione paroeciali,"—*Palestra del clero*, (Regio, 1930), 530-531. Unfortunately the original article is not available; consequently the opinion is considered as it is expressed in the secondary source, with all respect to the author.

[35] Cf. canon 1429, § 2.

[36] Cf. what the same author wrote on previous occasions: "Pertanto, come il parroco rinunciante ha il diritto di riservarsi una pensione, e nessuno può spogliarlo di tale diritto . . . "—"Il can. 1429 § 2 dà facoltà agli Ordinari di imporre, e quindi di accettare, le riserva di pensione sui benefici parocchiali . . . Con l'accettazione della rinunzia, il Vescovo ha anche accettato il diritto di riserva alla pensione a norma del citato canone [1429 § 2], ma non praeter, perchè non era in sua facoltà." Vito, *Questioni canoniche*, III, 169-170; IV, 147, 148.

[37] Cf. canon 2147.

"Those who freely retire" very probably are those who present their resignation of their own accord or at most upon private invitation of the ordinary, but not those who resign in compliance with the canonical invitation of the administrative process;[38] for this resignation by canonical invitation is one of the steps leading to removal, and by prolepsis can be referred to as removal.[39]

Even when the category of "those who freely retire" has been thus restricted, the opinion as reported appears rather liberal, in that it gives an absolute right to a pension. In any event, however, the "right to demand a pension," according to the opinion, depends on the ordinary's approval of the cause alleged for retiring, which by common law must be just and proportionate before the ordinary may accept the resignation.[40] The ordinary is, moreover, forbidden to accept the resignation of a benefice by a cleric in major orders unless he has an income necessary for decent livelihood from another source;[41] and, furthermore, if the benefice was his title of ordination the resignation cannot be validly accepted unless this fact is expressly mentioned and another lawful title of ordination has been substituted.[42] To say that the future pension to which the retiring pastor automatically acquires a "right" when the ordinary accepts his resignation constitutes either the "other source" which he *has* for necessary income or the title of ordination which *has been substituted*, seems to be begging the question and to be a restriction of the ordinary's liberty beyond that warranted by canons 1484 and 1485.

If the ordinary, having approved the cause for retiring, accepts the resignation and gives or at least promises a pension to the pastor, then, of course, the pastor acquires a right to the pension, acquired not by the ordinary's approval of his reason for retiring but in virtue of the ordinary's having provided the pension for him. Canon 1429, § 2 states that ordinaries *can* reserve pensions for pastors or vicars

[38] Canon 2148, § 1.

[39] E. g., canon 2154, § 1: "Amoto parocho . . ." Cf. Suarez, *De remotione parochorum*, n. 80, p. 96.

[40] Canon 185.

[41] Canon 1484.

[42] Canon 1485.

going out of office; it does not say that ordinaries *must* reserve pensions for them.

For mission countries the only cause mentioned in the apostolic faculties as warranting a pension for a retiring priest is resignation because of infirmity, from a quasi-parish or mission in which the prospective pensioner was incumbent for ten years.[43] Removal is not admitted.[44] Advanced age accompanied by weakening or failing strength is included under the term infirmity. The ten years of service in the quasi-parish or mission need not be a continuous period, but may be an aggregate period of interrupted service.[45] The faculty expressly requires service in the precise quasi-parish or mission assessed. It seems clear, therefore, that no pension could be reserved on a quasi-parish or mission if the resigning incumbent's service in that quasi-parish or mission did not add up to ten years, even though he may have spent many more years in the vicariate or prefecture. Some other mode of provision would have to be arranged.

ARTICLE 3. FORMALITIES

An ecclesiastical pension is a right to a part of the fruits of the benefice. Quite logically the Code treats of pensions in the chapter dealing with the changes of which benefices may be the object.[46]

One of the innovations mentioned is dismemberment, which the legislator describes as a withdrawal of a part of the territory or of the *property* of some benefice and the allotment thereof to another benefice, pious cause, or ecclesiastical institute.[47] Ecclesiastical pensions, then, apparently partake of the nature of dismemberment.[48]

[43] " . . . ex infirmitate resignantibus quasi-paroecias vel missiones in quas per decem annos incubuerunt . . . "

[44] " . . . quod poenam sapit." Vromant, *De bonis Ecclesiae*, p. 117.

[45] Vromant, *op. cit.*, p. 118.

[46] Lib. III, pars V, caput II, *De unione, translatione, divisione, dismembratione, conversione et suppressione beneficiorum.*

[47] Canon 1421. Cf. Schmalzgrueber (Lib. III, pars. I, tit. V, n. 201): "Dismembratio tunc fieri dicitur, quando manente unitate beneficii, pars bonorum, vel fructuum ab eo aufertur, et alteri beneficio, vel ecclesiae, quae tenues reditus habet, ad hujus fabricam, vel ministrorum sustentationem applicatur."

[48] "Pensiones . . . dismembrationibus affines . . . "—Blat, *Commentarium*, III, part. II-VI (*De rebus*), n. 325, p. 448.

It is necessary, however, to bear in mind that dismemberment may be considered with relation to the property of a benefice, to its territory, or to its revenues.[49] In the first instance a part of the very property of a benefice or its endowment is withdrawn. This withdrawal is reserved to the Holy See by prescription of canon 1422. Again, a portion of the territory may be removed, as provided in canons 1427 and 1428 for the dismemberment of parishes; as to this dismemberment the ordinary is competent, but subject to the same conditions and formalities expressly outlined for the division of parishes. Finally, a part of the income of a benefice may be withdrawn from a benefice in the form of taxes,[50] or ecclesiastical pensions as outlined in canon 1429.[51] It is well to note also that dismemberment as to property, territory, and even revenues by way of ordinary taxes is a procedure perpetual in its effects;[52] and in this it differs fundamentally from the ecclesiastical pension that can be reserved by local ordinaries according to canon 1429, because the latter may never last beyond the lifetime of the pensioner. An absolutely perpetual pension would indeed be tantamount to dismemberment of Church property or even division, and this is reserved to the Holy See.[53]

Having treated fully of innovation by union, transfer, division, and dismemberment of benefices, the legislator adds by way of corollary, as it were, the canon on ecclesiastical pensions. The canon immediately preceding the law on pensions prescribes certain formalities to be observed in uniting, transferring, dividing, or dismembering benefices, concluding in the final paragraph with the appeal that is permitted against the decree of the ordinary effecting such innovations. The treatise on innovation properly so-called is

[49] Cf. De Meester, *Juris canonici . . . compendium*, III, p. 332, n. 1408.

[50] Canons 1355-1356; 1504-1506.

[51] Cf. De Meester, *ibid.*, pp. 332-339, nn. 1409-1411.

[52] Cf. Wernz-Vidal [*Ius canonicum*, II (*De personis*), n. 169]: "Dismembratio beneficii ecclesiastici sensu stricto habetur: 1° si manente unitate beneficii pars substantiae bonorum beneficialium aut saltem redituum beneficialium ab eo *in perpetuum* separetur . . . " (Italics inserted.)

[53] " . . . Species quaedam divisionis est *pensio* in perpetuum *beneficio* imposita."—Wernz-Vidal, *Ius canonicum*, II (*De personis*), n. 154, II, c; cf. also n. 169, 1°.

evidently completed before the question of ecclesiastical pensions is taken up. Consequently, the formalities required for union, transfer, division, or dismemberment are not strictly applicable to the reservation of ecclesiastical pensions according to canon 1429. Hence, when canon 1429 is silent about certain formalities to be observed in the reserving of pensions, one cannot insist that a norm of action be taken from the formalities required for dismemberment; it is to be taken rather "from the general principles of law applied with the equity proper to Canon Law, from the manner and practice of the Roman Curia, and from the common and constant teaching of approved authors." [54]

a) Interested parties

In a consideration of formalities prescribed for the reserving of pensions the question arises whether the consent or advice of certain parties is required.

One of the reasons which formerly prohibited ordinaries from reserving perpetual pensions (since they were real and not merely personal burdens), was that the pension was regarded as a kind of alienation of ecclesiastical property in no small matter. With reference to even those pensions which ordinaries were empowered to impose it was required that the ordinary should obtain the consent of the cathedral chapter before he could reserve the pension.[55] The Code does not require that this consent be obtained, for it nowhere prescribes it. The ordinary can, therefore, reserve pensions in those cases permitted by law, observing the prescribed requirements, exclusive of the pescriptions laid down for alienation.[56]

[54] Canon 20. Translation taken from Cicognani-O'Hara, Brennan, *Canon Law* (2. ed., Philadelphia: The Dolphin Press, 1935), p. 620.

[55] Cf. Wernz, *Ius decretalium*, II, n. 321.

[56] Suarez, "De pensionibus beneficiis paroecialibus imponendis,"—*Angelicum*, VI (1929), 225; *idem.*, *De remotione parochorum*, n. 79, nota 62. D'Angelo, *Tasse e pensioni*, p. 123, f. Vito (*Questioni canoniche*, II, 109, nota 2): "*Etsi constitutio ecclesiasticae pensionis non sit proprie alienatio eiusque naturam imitatur*, ciò non ostante, il Codice non richiede, per la sua costituzione, il *Consensus Capituli Ecclesiae Cathedralis*, come si richiedeva ex iure Tridentini." Cocchi (*Commentarium*, 1. ed., 1924, VI, n. 106) stated: ". . . requiritur quoque consensus Capituli si pensio imponatur ab Ordinario;

When the bishop freely confers benefices or canonries (other than dignities) in a cathedral or collegiate church, he is to seek the advice of its respective chapter.[57] Indirectly, the matter on which the chapter is to be heard includes also the reservation of a pension on one of the canonries or lesser benefices, as it may result in an appreciable reduction of the beneficial or prebendary income, particularly in the case of a chapter whose membership is not limited to a definite number (*capitulum non numeratum*), and whose members are provided for out of one general capitular fund.[58]

Citing a decree of Innocent III (1130-1143),[59] Pistocchi states that a pension reserved by the ordinary without the consent of the beneficiary is null and void.[60] While the Code reaffirms the principle that benefices are to be conferred without diminution, it makes an express exception in favor of ecclesiastical pensions;[61] but canon 1429 makes no mention of the consent of the beneficiary as requisite to validity or lawfulness.

In those places, however, where the competitive examination (*concursus*) of candidates for a parish is still prescribed,[62] the ordinary ought to mention the fact of the pension when he announces the competitive examination.[63] Where the examination is not required,

haec enim impositio habet speciem alienationis"; but in 3. ed., 1933, *loc. cit.*, he writes: " . . . non autem requiritur amplius consensus Capituli, si pensio imponatur ab Ordinario, licet enim impositio habet speciem alienationis, tamen Codex absolute decernit casus in quibus Episcopi possunt imponere pensiones."

[57] Canon 403; C. P. I., 10 nov. 1925, ad III.—AAS, XVII (1925), 582.

[58] Cf. canon 394, § 1.

[59] C. un., X, *ut ecclesiastica beneficia sine diminutione conferantur*, III, 12.

[60] *De re beneficiali*, p. 143.

[61] "Beneficia ecclesiastica sine deminutione conferantur, salvo praescripto can. 1429, §§ 1, 2."—Canon 1440.

[62] Canon 459, § 4. In the United States this examination had been required for valid appointment to irremovable rectorships by decree of the Third Plenary Council of Baltimore, nn. 36, 40-60; but on June 24, 1931 the Sacred Congregation of the Council by a decree transmitted to the archbishops and bishops of the country through the Apostolic Delegate abrogated this provision of the Council of Baltimore. Cf. Bouscaren, *Canon Law Digest*, I, 249-250; *The Homiletic and Pastoral Review*, XXXII (1931-1932), 189-190.

[63] D'Angelo, *Tasse e pensioni*, p. 122, nota 1.

mention of the reservation of a pension ought to be made in proposing or at least in conferring the benefice, in order that it will be clear to the new titular that he accepts this benefice with a diminution lawfully imposed, and that subsequent refusal to pay the pension will not be admissible,[64] because of the implicit consent given by the acceptance of the benefice known to be burdened with a pension. Payment of the pension also indicates implicit consent.

Must the consent of the beneficiary be obtained in order to impose a pension on a benefice that is occupied? Cocchi [65] states simply that if the benefice is not vacant, the consent of the beneficiary is required; for a benefice cannot be diminished, the beneficiary being unwilling. Canon 1429, § 1, however, expressly prescribes that a pension can be reserved only at the time of conferring a benefice. Consequently, to reserve a pension on an occupied non-parochial benefice would require the special authority of the Holy See, and even then the consent of the titular is usually sought.[66] The second paragraph of canon 1429 refers only to pensions reserved on parochial benefices for pastors or vicars retiring from them. As a pension can probably be reserved for a retiring vicar even while the pastor is in office, his consent ought to be obtained, but if he should demur unreasonably, it would seem that a pension could be reserved notwithstanding, as long as the other necessary conditions are fulfilled.

Authors generally agree that a procurator (*defensor*) ought to be appointed if any change or innovation is to be wrought upon the benefice while it is vacant.[67] Although the reservation of a pension according to canon 1429 is not properly an innovation in the status

[64] Cf. Vito, *Questioni canoniche*, IV, 149.

[65] *Commentarium*, VI, n. 106, p. 229.

[66] Vito, *Questioni canoniche*, IV, 149, quoting Pirhing (*Ius canonicum*, III, 12, n. 15): "Etsi Papa possit imponere pensionem, etiam sine consensu Rectoris Beneficij, non tamen id facere solet, ut constat ex *Reg*. 43 *Cancellariae Apostolicae apud Cochier*, ubi habetur, quod Litterae resignationis, vel assignationis, etiam motu proprio, cujusvis pensionis annuae, super alicuius Beneficij fructibus expediri non possunt, nisi de consensu illius, qui dictam pensionem persolvere tunc debebit."

[67] De Meester, *op. cit.*, III, n. 1410, d; Coronata (*Institutiones*, II, p. 370, n. 979), suggests that the promoter of justice could exercise this office. Cf. also Wernz-Vidal, *Ius Canonicum*, II (*De personis*), n. 154, nota 13.

of a benefice, nevertheless Cocchi believes that here, too, a procurator ought to be heard if there is question of reserving a pension on a vacant benefice.[68]

If the benefice is one upon which there is a right of patronage, the consent of the patron is required according to Cocchi (if the benefice is not vacant),[69] and D'Angelo;[70] but, as Vito observes, the law does not require his consent, even for pensions on parochial benefices, although it would be quite proper to notify him at least on grounds of decency—"*tantum ex quadam honestate.*" This is the general rule, although there can be cases where the consent of the patron is required, as, for instance, if this has been reserved to him as a special privilege, if custom has established this right, or if the pension is immoderate and excessively burdensome, in which case the patron can demand that it be limited to the merely necessary amount or the proportion allowed by law.[71]

In providing for a pastor removed by administrative process, the ordinary is required to consult either the examiners, and, if recourse has been taken against the decree of removal, the pastor consultors, who took part in the removal proceedings.[72] It seems, however,

[68] *Commentarium,* VI, n. 106, p. 230, citing Ferrari, n. 535, and Pirhing, III, 12, n. 15.

[69] *Commentarium,* VI, n. 106, pp. 229-230.

[70] *Tasse e pensioni,* p. 123, nota 1.

[71] *Questioni canoniche,* IV, 149-150, nota 1. Schmalzgrueber (Lib. III, tit. 12, n. 15) distinguished between pensions imposed on the beneficiary alone and not on his successor (cf. canon 1429, § 1), which, aside from privilege or custom, could be granted without the consent of the patron, except that if they were immoderate, he was entitled to ask for the extinction or a reduction of the same,—and pensions imposed on the benefice and binding the succeeding incumbent (cf. canon 1429, § 2), for which the consent of the patron was required unless he objected unreasonably and in opposition to great usefulness to the Church anticipated from the grant. Cf. also Ferraris, "Pensio," append. 1, III. The opinion held by St. Alphonsus (*Theologia moralis,* IV, n. 138, 3°) probably referred to the reservation only of temporary pensions: "Ad pensionem non requiri consensum patroni, ut quidam volunt; quia id nullo jure statutum est. Neque ullum fit praejudicium per impositionem pensionis; cum is fructus non percipiat ex beneficio, sed tantum habeat jus instituendi et praesentandi, quod ei non adimitur."

[72] Canon 2154, § 1: "Amoto parocho Ordinarius, examinatoribus vel pa-

that the ordinary is required to seek counsel only as to the kind of provision in general which is to be made for the removed pastor. If a pension is deemed advisable, he very likely is not bound to seek their counsel further as to the specific amount.[73]

The Third Plenary Council of Baltimore had decreed that the advice of the diocesan consultors be had with reference to the amount of the "*pensio congrua.*"[74] The procedure set down by the Council for the removal of irremovable rectors was abrogated on March 13, 1911, when the Holy See declared that the decree "*Maxima Cura*" of August 20, 1910 applied to the Church in the United States.[75] It will be noted that those who assist the bishop in the administrative process of removal according to the common law in force at the present time are not the diocesan consultors, as the Third Plenary Council of Baltimore had prescribed, but the synodal or prosynodal examiners or the pastor consultors. The latter office was not known prior to the decree "*Maxima Cura.*" [76]

b) The decree

The reservation of a pension should normally be executed in legal written form, either in Latin or in the vernacular,[77] specifying the recipient, the causes justifying the pension, the fact of the hearing granted interested parties if the hearing was required, the period for which the pension is to run, the amount of the pension and the source whence it is to be derived. It should be dated, signed by the ordinary and the chancellor or a notary, and authenticated with the

rochis consultoribus, qui partem habuerunt in amotione decernenda, in consilium adscitis . . . " Cf. Connor, *The administrative removal of pastors,* pp. 126-127; Noval, *De processibus,* II, n. 585. Cf. also formularies in Cappello, *Praxis processualis* (Taurini, Romae: Marietti, 1940), nn. 187, 194.

[73] Cf. Suarez, *De remotione parochorum,* n. 76; Connor, *op. cit.,* p. 127.

[74] N. 38, VII: "Sive autem amoto sive sponte renuntianti [rectori inamovibili] procurabit [Episcopus] pensionem, quae ex consultorum consilio congrua censebitur . . . "

[75] *AAS,* III (1911), 313; *AAS,* II (1910), 636. Cf. Barrett, *A comparative study of the Councils of Baltimore and the Code of canon law,* pp. 95-96; 208, note 21; Connor, *The administrative removal of pastors,* pp. 41-43.

[76] Cf. Connor, *The administrative removal of pastors,* p. 92.

[77] Cf. Ojetti, *Synopsis,* "Pensio," III, p. 2963, n. 3108.

seal of the episcopal curia. The document should be filed in the chancery archives. A certified copy can be given to the pensioner and also to the incumbent of the benefice on which the pension is drawn.

The reason for preserving the acts of the reservation of a pension in writing is obvious: to provide evidence in the external forum. The imposition of a burden ought to be capable of being known in a juridical way by both him who is to bear it and him who is to profit by it; for it is an act which determines and regulates the diminution of a right of the beneficiary and the acquisition of a right by the pensioner. All uncertainty and misunderstanding that could result in harm to the peace of society, the good of souls, and, one might add, even the stability of the economic order, ought to be removed.[78]

The law states explicitly that the reservation of pensions on non-parochial benefices is to be expressed in the very act of conferring the benefice, and rightly so; for, since it is a separation of a part of the income of the benefice, it ought to be set forth in the very instrument which gives the beneficiary the right to that income, in such manner, however, that the two acts remain distinct.[79]

When a pension is reserved on a parochial benefice for a retiring pastor or vicar, the same rule should be observed and mention made of the pension in the decree of the new appointment as in the previous paragraph, for where the nature of the case is the same the application of the law ought to be the same.[80] There is a difference between the two cases, however, in that the first paragraph of canon 1429 expressly permits ordinaries to reserve pensions only when they confer the benefice. It would be extending the parallel too far to infer that no pension on a parochial benefice can be established until the successor is appointed. On the contrary, as has been pointed out, a pension can be rightfully established with the acceptance of the resignation,[81] or in the very decree of administrative removal

[78] Cf. Vito, *Questioni canoniche*, III, 161; IV, 148, nota 1.
[79] Pistocchi, *De re beneficiali*, p. 142.
[80] Vito, *Questioni canoniche*, III, 161.
[81] C. P. I., 20 maii 1923, ad IX—*AAS*, XVI (1924), 116.

or as soon as possible thereafter.[82] When the successor to the parish is appointed, the fact of the pension ought to be mentioned in his letter of appointment.

In the document proclaiming the establishment of a pension the person to receive the pension must be clearly specified, to eliminate suspicion of simony.[83]

The cause which moved the ordinary to reserve the pension must be set down, as expressly prescribed in canon 1429, § 1, and even as a condition for the valid reservation of the pension, at least on non-parochial benefices.[84]

For the protection of the pensioner as well as of the person who is to pay the pension the time for which the pension is reserved ought to be specified in the decree of establishment. Maximum terms are indeed clear from the common law, viz., the tenure of office of the holder of a non-parochial benefice,[85] death of the retired pastor or vicar holding a pension on his former parish,[86] death of the holder of any pension whatsoever when conferred by the Roman Pontiff;[87] but cases may arise when the ordinary does not intend the pension to run its fullest possible term, as in the case of pensions for students of the sacred sciences, or of those whose continuance would be an unnecessary burden on the benefice, because given to provide for temporary disability or to complement a period of inadequate maintenance from other sources which, as can be foreseen, will prove sufficient of themselves after a certain time.

Article 4. The Amount of the Pension

The most important item, the amount of the pension, must be determined with precision in the decree of its establishment, so much

[82] Canons 2154, § 1; 2155. Cf. formularies in Cappello, *Praxis processualis*, pp. 150; 157.

[83] Cf. Pius V, const. "*Intolerabilis*", 1 iun. 1569, §§ 3-8—*Bull. Rom. Taur.*, VII, n. 131. Pistocchi, *De re beneficiali*, p. 142.

[84] Cf. Vito, *Questioni canoniche*. IV, 148. nota 1.

[85] Canon 1429, § 1.

[86] Canon 1429, § 2.

[87] Canon 1429, § 3.

so that the reservation of a pension the amount of which is contrary to the law is very probably invalid.[88]

Pensions on non-parochial benefices can never be so large as to deprive the beneficiary of his adequate portion of the income of his benefice.[89] The amount which will constitute the adequate portion that must remain for the incumbent of the benefice is left to the ordinary's prudent judgment. The law being couched in general terms, the latter will be guided to a great extent by principles of equity. "Adequate portion" implies sufficient means for the livelihood of the titular, his needs varying with various circumstances of person, benefice, place, time, and the like.[90] In investigating the individual case the ordinary will take into consideration on the one hand the beneficiary's personal needs and obligations, his obligations toward the benefice arising out of his duty to manage the property and to pay all ordinary expenses connected with its maintenance,[91] and the possible rights of a patron;[92] and on the other hand, the merits of the prospective pensioner, the services he has rendered, the strength of the reasons making the reservation lawful, the degree to which it is necessary to assist him by means of the pension.[93] Besides the norms of equity there is need to consider also those general principles derived from laws enacted for similar cases. Normally, according to the doctrine under the former law, two-thirds of the revenue should remain for the beneficiary, so that a pension not exceeding one-third of the revenue may be considered just.[94]

[88] Pistocchi, *De re beneficiali*, p. 143; Vito, *Questioni canoniche*, IV, 148, nota 1.

[89] ". . . salva huic [beneficiario] congrua portione."—Canon 1429, § 1.

[90] D'Angelo, "De 'taxatione' in pensionibus definiendis"—*Apollinaris*, II (1929), 215.

[91] Canon 1477. Pistocchi, *De re beneficiali*, p. 145.

[92] Canon 1455, 2°.

[93] Vito, *Questioni canoniche*, IV, 148, nota 1. D'Angelo, *Tasse e pensioni*, pp. 123-124.

[94] "Verum in beneficiis semplicibus [simplicibus] hodie ex stylo Curiae regulariter imponi pensionem usque ad medietatem fructuum tradit Parisius, L. P. de resig. Benef. q. 2. n. 26. Garc. De benef., p. 1, n. 371."—Vito, *Questioni canoniche*, IV, 148, nota 1. Cf. also canon 1429, § 2. D'Angelo, "De 'taxatione' in pensionibus definiendis"—*Apollinaris*, II (1929), 216.

These two-thirds are regularly to be computed on the strictly beneficial income. Not to be included are free will offerings, stole fees, or the distributions in connection with a prebend.[95] If the entire revenue is derived from offerings or distributions, a third is regarded as personal income, and two-thirds, as income of the benefice.[96] Furthermore, the computation ought to be on the net income after all expenses have been subtracted.[97]

Since an adequate portion must always remain for the titular, it can be said from a practical standpoint that pensions can hardly be reserved except on the superfluous revenue of a benefice, and even then they should be moderate.[98]

The present law for determining the amount of pensions on parochial benefices is more explicit, abrogating the prescription of the Council of Trent,[99] and also settling many questions formerly discussed by canonists.[100] Today the maximum amount of the pensions is not to be more than one-third of the income of the parish, to be computed after all expenses and uncertain revenues have been deducted from the gross income.[101] It will be noted that the computation is to be made on the income of the parish and not on the pastor's income, for the law here contemplates relatively perpetual pensions, resulting in a real obligation. The computation is based on the income of the parish, for which the written annual report

[95] " . . . nisi a Papa concedente dicatur expresse. Et hoc ex citato cap. 14, *de ref.*, sess. XXIV, Trid."—Pistocchi, *De re beneficiali*, p. 146, citing Moneta, *Ius eccl.*, lib. IV, q. II; S. C. C., *Toletana*, 1565; Barbosa, *Praxis exigendi pensiones*.

[96] D'Angelo, *Tasse e pensioni*, p. 124, nota 1. Cf. canons 421, § 2; 1356, § 3.

[97] D'Angelo, *Tasse e pensioni*, p. 124. Cf. canon 1429, § 2.

[98] Pistocchi, *De re beneficiali*, p. 146. "In ogni caso la pensione sia modica al possibile."—D'Angelo, *Tasse e pensioni*, p. 125.

[99] Sess. XXIV, *de ref.*, c. 13: "Ad haec in posterum omnes hae cathedrales ecclesiae, quarum reditus summam ducatorum mille, et parochiales, quae summam ducatorum centum secundum verum annuum valorem non excedunt, nullis pensionibus aut reservationibus fructuum graventur."

[100] Pistocchi, *De re beneficiali*, p. 148.

[101] " . . . quae [pensiones] tamen ne excedant tertiam partem reditus paroeciae, quibusvis deductis expensis et incertis reditibus." Canon 1429, § 2.

of the parish can be used as a standard. A merely oral statement ought not to be accepted.

Among the items to be considered as forming the income of the parish are especially the following:[102]

1) Natural fruits accruing from parish lands, fields, orchards, mines, quarries and the like; stable and reliable income from rents or leases on parish property; returns on investments of the parish in the form of interest, dividends, annuities.

2) Tithes, where they exist,[103] as also income from reliable, voluntary offerings of the faithful, stabilized by law or custom, even though the exact amount is not determinable in advance.[104] In the United States, where the endowment and support of the parish is ordinarily constituted in this manner,[105] parish income consists largely of pew rent, subscriptions, membership dues, collections, assessments, tuition for the parish school, sale of books, religious articles, periodicals, papers and the like, votive offerings, activities of parish societies. Collections for diocesan and other extraordinary needs, however, cannot be included as parish income strictly speaking, for they merely pass through the parish and are applied to the respective cause as soon as they are received.

3) Payments to supply or complete the adequate requirements

[102] Cf. D'Angelo, *Tasse e pensioni*, p. 125; *idem*, "De 'taxatione' in pensionibus definiendis"—*Apollinaris*, II (1929), 215-216; Suarez, "De pensionibus beneficiis paroecialibus imponendis"—*Angelicum*, VI (1929), 225-226 or *De remotione parochorum*, pp. 95-96, nota; Vito, *Questioni canoniche*, III, 170, nota 3; IV, 149, nota 1; Ayrinhac, *Administrative Legislation*, p. 329; Augustine, *Canonical and Civil Status of Catholic Parishes*, p. 219; *idem*, *Commentary*, VI, 515.

[103] Canon 1502. The tithing system was adopted in St. Vincent's parish, Elkhart, Indiana, in 1915, and about nine years later in the diocese of Des Moines. In 1927 the faithful of the Seattle Diocese were asked to give four per cent of their income.—F. J. Jansen, "Church Support"—*The Homiletic and Pastoral Review*, XXVIII (1927-28), 267.

[104] Vermeersch-Creusen, *Epitome*, II, n. 743.

[105] Doheny, *Practical Problems in Church Finance*, (Milwaukee: Bruce, 1941), p. 35. Cf. also, "De recenti quaestione circa bona ecclesiastica"—*Periodica*, XIII (1924), (11)-(15).

of the benefice (*supplementum congruae*), particularly pensions paid by the government.[106]

4) Provision for the payment of the expenses for worship, if paid by the state or some other moral or physical person.

5) Stole fees, if they actually constitute the endowment of the benefice (canon 1410), to be computed according to norms of equity on a five or ten year average.[107]

After the gross parish income has been ascertained, the law directs that all expenses and uncertain income are to be deducted. According to the mind of the legislator the expenses contemplated are those which pertain to the parish, certain and more or less fixed, regarded in law as real obligations as distinguished from personal expenses.[108] Among items to be deducted can be mentioned:

1) Expenses involved in the necessary and normal maintenance of the parish plant, insurance, fuel, light, water, communication, salaries,[109] and at least the interest on debts of the parish.

2) Expenditures in connection with divine worship, such as payments for altar breads, wine, candles, sacristy equipment, choir

[106] Cf. De Meester, *Compendium*, III, n. 1424, p. 348; Vito, *Questioni canoniche*, IV, 150.

[107] D'Angelo, "De 'taxatione' in pensionibus definiendis"—*Apollinaris*, II (1929), 216.

[108] Vito, *Questioni canoniche*, IV, 149, nota.

[109] The salary of the pastor as incumbent of the parochial benefice should not be deducted as an expense item. Ordinarily the incumbent receives the entire income of a benefice (cf. c. 1472) over which he has the right of usufruct for what is necessary for his honorable subsistence, and the obligation to pay the ordinary expenses of the benefice and to devote the superfluous to charity (c. 1473; 1477, § 2). Even if not the entire income of the parochial benefice accrues to the pastor as beneficiary but only a certain part thereof is set aside as his fitting share by way of salary, nevertheless the "net income" on which the pension is to be computed should be the amount remaining after all parish expenses have been deducted but without deducting the amount of the pastor's salary. Thus, if the net income of a parish is $12,500 and the pastor's annual salary is $1,500, the pension is to be computed on the $12,500 and not on the $11,000 that would remain if the pastor's salary were regarded as deductible expense. Connor (*The administrative removal of pastors*, p. 130) holds a different view. Cf. Augustine, *The Canonical and Civil Status of Catholic Parishes*, p. 217.

maintenance (organ, music), bells. In the United States also the disbursements for materials and supplies for various parish activities.

3) The stipends of founded Masses; legacies and income from legacies. Stipends of Masses for the people (*pro populo*), however, are not deductible, for they are personal obligations of the pastor.

4) Civil taxes on the parish and ecclesiastical assessments for the seminary and cathedral, pensions already on the parish. It is not repugnant that a parish should be burdened with more than one pension, provided always that their sum total does not exceed the third permitted by law.[110]

As personal obligations, and therefore not deductible, mention can be made of certain personal taxes (property, income, inheritance).[111] The tax imposed on the beneficiary on the occasion of his taking possession of the benefice is not in itself deductible, but in equity it ought to be considered, and some allowance made in the first year of payment.[112] Chancery fees due for the reservation of the pension are to be paid either by the beneficiary or the pensioner, according to the nature of the case. With regard to perpetual pensions it would seem that expenses should be sustained by the pensioner; for the obligations of the beneficiary do not extend beyond that of paying the pension.[113]

Besides the deductible expenses the Code states that uncertain income be also excluded in computing the net income on which a pension can be levied. To be truly uncertain the income must be such not only as to the quantity or amount, but also as to its pay-

110 Noval, *De processibus*, II, n. 589, p. 516. Suarez, "De pensionibus beneficiis paroecialibus imponendis"—*Angelicum*, VI (1929), 224. Cf. e. g., S. C. C. *Firmana*, "Onera et Pensionum", 29 feb. 1896—*Analecta Eccl.*, (Romae, 1893-1911), IV (1896), 57-59. The case involved a parochial and abbatial church on which there were four pensions.

111 Cf. S. C. Ep. et Reg., *Calatajeronen.*, "Pensionis," 8 maii 1896—*Analecta Eccl.*, IV (1896), 385-386.

112 D'Angelo, "De 'taxatione' in pensionibus definiendis"—*Apollinaris*, II (1929), 217; *idem*, *Tasse e pensioni*, p. 126, nota 1. Cf. S. C. Ep. et Reg., *loc. cit.*

113 D'Angelo, "De 'taxatione' in pensionibus definiendis"—*Apollinaris*, II (1929), 217; *Tasse e pensioni*, p. 127; Gennari, *Quistioni canoniche*, (2. ed., Roma, 1908), q. 206, p. 258.

ment.[114] According to Pistocchi,[115] the income can be uncertain in two ways: as depending on the piety or generosity of the faithful and as received from the exercise of parochial rights. Specifically, stole fees (*iura stolae*) ought not to be computed as income of the parish, unless it is clear that they were assigned by lawful authority to constitute or supplement the endowment of the benefice. If this is not the case, by far the majority of canonists are of the opinion that stole fees, even aside from the question of whether they are uncertain income in the strict sense, have the character of emoluments for personal labor, constituting casual or occasional income (*casualia*)[116] or quasi-patrimonial property.[117] D'Angelo, without distinguishing, puts stole fees with the income of the parish, on the contention that only their amount is uncertain.[118] Choir distributions are regarded in the same category as stole fees.[119]

Further items to be deducted are not only purely adventitious and unexpected income of the parish, such as occasional donations and bequests (a notable amount would, however, be reckoned with the fixed capital of the parish) but also so-called "bad debts", worthless or uncollectible obligations, income due, but for the payment of which there is little hope, e. g., outlawed or prescribed taxes and

[114] Cf. Blat, *Commentarium*, III, part. II-VI (*De rebus*), n. 336, p. 464.

[115] *De re beneficiali*, p. 148, quoting Manacorda [*Iuris et Discip. Eccles. specimen*, cap. I], n. 631.

[116] "Recens quaestio de reditibus ecclesiasticis,"—*Periodica*, XIII (1924), (11)-(15).

[117] Thus Noval, *De processibus*, II, n. 589, p. 516. Vito, *Questioni canoniche*, III, 171, nota 1; IV, 147, nota 1. Coronata, *Institutiones*, I, n. 1017, p. 416. Wernz-Vidal, *Ius canonicum*, II (*De personis*), n. 320. Vermeersch-Creusen, *Epitome*, II, n. 798. De Meester, *Compendium*, III, n. 1424, p. 348. Pistocchi, *De re beneficiali*, p. 415-416. Chelodi, *Ius poenale* (4. ed., Tridenti: Libreria Moderna Editrice A. Ardesi, 1935), p. 108. Cappello, *De censuris* (3. ed., Taurinorum Augustae: Marietti, 1933), n. 334, p. 294. Fanfani, *De iure parochorum*, n. 10, p. 16.

[118] *Tasse e pensioni*, p. 125, nota 1; "De 'taxatione' in pensionibus definiendis"—*Apollinaris*, II (1929), 216. Cf. also Blat, *Commentarium*, III, part. II-VI (*De rebus*), n. 336, p. 464.

[119] Cocchi, *Commentarium*, VI, n. 105 and nota 3, p. 229; Wernz-Vidal, *Ius canonicum*, II (*De personis*), n. 320.

subsidies which had been constituted as part of the endowment.[120]

Is the pension to be determined from year to year on the basis of the current net annual income of the parish?[121] The Code does not expressly demand this. To insist on it would seem to leave the pensioner's right to receive a portion of the income in terms somewhat too general, in view of the variation of the annual income. It would weaken the sense of security which the pension is intended to provide. Such an annually computed pension would apparently amount to scarcely more than an ecclesiastical dole. Moreover, to require this annual computation would entail seemingly unnecessary labor. Practically, then, the average income of a parish over five or ten years[122] can be taken as a basis of computation, prudently taking into account possible future vicissitudes of the parish and allowing a safe margin for normal fluctuation of the annual parish income, though even these precautions are derived from equitable principles rather than from the law itself.

The former difference of opinion about the manner in which the actual amount of the pension is to be described, whether in quota or in quantity, has not been settled by the Code. Nor can it be invoked to disprove the less common pre-Code opinion that the pension should be assigned in a certain quota or proportionate part of the net income of the parish. The percentage basis postulates the annually repeated computation; for, once the proportion is reduced to a fixed amount, the quantitative method obtains. Among the reasons advanced under the former law against the reservation of a pension in a percentage of the income of the benefice was the principle that benefices are to be conferred without diminution; but the Code permits an exception precisely in the matter of pensions (canon 1440). It was further declared that to set aside a certain quota of the income was equivalent to division or dismemberment of a benefice; but the definition of the Code in canon 1429 refutes

[120] Cf. Vito, *Questioni canoniche*, III, 171, IV, 147 and nota 1.

[121] "Ogni anno il parroco renderà coscienzioso conto all'Ordinario delle rendite del beneficio; saranno levate le spese; si faranno tre parti; due resteranno al parroco, la terza sarà passata al pensionario." Vito, *Questioni canoniche*, III, 170.

[122] Cf. Ferraris, "Pensio," n. 139.

the objection as far as pensions for retiring pastors or vicars are concerned, while pensions on other benefices, for the life of the beneficiary, are not directly burdens on the benefices but rather personal obligations of the incumbent. Again, the contention was made that by determining pensions in a fixed amount instead of on a percentage basis, frauds and quarreling would be avoided; but it does not follow that they ensue inevitably in the other system: proper steps can be taken to eliminate them. On the other hand, if the pension is constituted in a fixed sum, other hardships for the pensioner are avoided, as when the income for one or the other year is subnormal. The Code does not decide the matter beyond the provision that a fitting portion must remain for the incumbent of a non-parochial benefice and that the maximum amount of pensions on parochial benefices is not to exceed one-third of the net parish income.[123]

It must be admitted that a pension in a predetermined amount puts the beneficiary at a disadvantage in adverse, as it does the pensioner in prosperous years, due to the emerging disproportion between the pension of fixed amount and the income of the benefice. The abnormal situation is usually only temporary, but if the condition persists, steps must be taken to reduce or increase the pension, as will be considered later.

The danger of exceeding the amount lawfully permitted on the basis of a percentage of the income can be avoided if the amount is fixed not too closely to the maximum, and the pension can then be established just as well in a definite sum. Indeed, this latter method appears to be preferable. The beneficiary is thereby made aware of the precise extent of his obligation; and the pensioner's right, being stated in terms of an absolute amount, is likewise rendered more definite and stable.[124] This also seems to be the more common prac-

[123] "Quod quidem iam usu seu praxi ita intelligitur." Thus, Suarez, "De pensionibus beneficiis paroecialibus imponendis"—*Angelicum*, VI (1929), 226-227. Pistocchi (*De re beneficiali*, p. 153) speaks of a "*quota determinata.*"

[124] "Licet tamen constitutio *in quota* in se fieri possit, in praxi suadendum fiat semper in quantitate ad omnes quaestiones evitandas inter beneficiatum et pensionarium." D'Angelo, "De 'taxatione' in pensionibus definiendis"—*Apollinaris*, II (1929), 217.

tice, beginning with that juridic keystone of the law of pensions set by Pope Innocent III in the renowned "*Nisi essent*" of 1207,[125] and continuing down to recent times.[126]

When the income of the benefice is in the form of natural fruits, the pension can be designated in terms of such fruits. The Code does not forbid it; hence, when the pension is established on a percentage basis, if the income consists entirely of either fruits or money it might be better to provide that the pension may be paid either in fruits or money respectively, and when the income is in the form of both fruits and money, the pension could be established as payable in proportionate parts of fruits and money.[127] The preferable method, however, both before the Code[128] and after it,[129] seems to be the one favoring payment in money, especially when the pension is determined according to a fixed sum. The procedure is more definite and less apt to open the way to altercations.

Although the reservation of a clerical pension by competent ecclesiastical authority is sufficient for its validity, the Code adopts the provisions of local civil law with reference to payments even in strictly ecclesiastical matters.[130]

[125] C. 21, X, *de praebendis et dignitatibus*, III, 5: ". . . ad praestationem quadraginta librarum. . . ."

[126] E.g., S.R.R., *Maioricen.*, "Pensionis," 2 dec. 1675.—*Recent.*, pars XIX, tom. I, decis. 379, n. 11. S.C.C., *Faventina*, "Pensionis," 17 dec. 1836.—Pallottini, "Pensio," n. 11. S.C.C., *Firmana*, "Onera et pensionum," 29 feb. 1896.—*Analecta Ecclesiastica* (Romae, 1893-1911), IV (1896), 57. S.C. Ep. et Reg., *Calatajeronen.*, "Pensionis," 8 maii 1896—*Analecta Ecclesiastica*, IV (1896), 385. S. R. R., *Vercellen.*, "Pensionis," 18 dec. 1928—S.R.R. *Decisiones*, XX (1928), 412. Cf. Noval, *De processibus*, II, n. 589, p. 517; Cocchi, *Commentarium*, VI, n. 105, p. 229; D'Angelo, "De 'taxatione' in pensionibus definiendis"—*Apollinaris*, II (1929), 217; Cappello, *Praxis processualis*, p. 157; Vromant, *De bonis Ecclesiae*, p. 116.

[127] Suarez, "De pensionibus beneficiis paroecialibus imponendis"—*Angelicum*, VI (1929), 227-228.

[128] Vecchiotti, *Institutiones canonicae* (Taurini, 1867-1868), III, c. 3, § 39: ". . . pensio non in fructibus ipsis sed in pecunia constituitur, ut evitentur discordiae, quae inter beneficiarium et pensionarium oriri possint."

[129] D'Angelo, "De 'taxatione' in pensionibus definiendis"—*Apollinaris*, II (1929), 217.

[130] "Quae ius civile in territorio statuit de . . . solutionibus, eadem iure

Provisions in existing concordats between the Church and the State may refer to the observance of such matters as giving official notice to the State before the installation of incumbents in benefices[131] or seeking the approval of the government before certain alien, non-naturalized citizens can be appointed to parochial benefices.[132]

The right of the royal placet or *exsequatur* is an infringement of the rights and liberties of the Church, and as such contradicts the principles of external public ecclesiastical law.[133] It is utterly opposed to the divine institution of the Church and cannot be granted to the State even by concession of the Holy See. Where such rights are actually asserted, it is, however, advisable from a practical standpoint and to avoid greater evils to observe the demands of civil law, thereby giving the parties concerned juridic standing under that system.[134]

A pension is defined as the right to receive *each year* a portion of the income of a benefice. The amount is based on the annual income; yet there seems to be nothing to forbid the ordinary from decreeing payment of the amount in installments, monthly, quarterly, or semi-annually, as long as the total amount is paid within the year.[135] In practice this would be more in conformity with

canonico in materia ecclesiastica iisdem cum effectibus serventur, nisi iuri divino contraria sint aut aliud iure canonico caveatur."—Canon 1529.

[131] E.g., *Inter Sanctam Sedem et Italiae Regnum Conventiones*, 11 feb. 1929, *Concordato fra la Santa Sede e l'Italia*, art. 19, 21, 22.—*AAS*, XXI (1929), 282, 283-284. Similar provisions were made in the concordats with Poland in 1925, art. 11, 19 [*AAS*, XVII (1925), 277, 280] and Roumania in 1929, art. 5 [*AAS*, XXI (1929), 443].

[132] Such provisions appeared in the Concordats with Poland, art. 10, 19 (*ibid.*, p. 277, 180) and Roumania, art. 12 (*ibid.*, p. 446).

[133] Cf. Ottaviani, *Institutiones iuris publici ecclesiastici* [2. ed., (Civitate Vaticana): Typis Polyglottis Vaticanis, 1935-1936], II, n. 348-351, p. 254-262.

[134] ". . . per evitare fastidii e pericoli, massime per le pensioni perpetue, come sappiamo aver fatto alcuni vescovi." Gennari, *Quistioni canoniche*, n. 191, p. 244, nota 1. D'Angelo, *Tasse e pensioni*, p. 123, g. Vito, *Questioni canoniche*, III, 162; 164; 171, nota 3. The *exsequatur* and placet were abolished in the Lateran Concordat, art. 24 [*AAS*, XXI (1929), 284].

[135] "Hic enim est Datariae Apostolicae perantiquus mos, annuae pensionis solutionem in duos terminos distribuere assignando dies festos Beatae M.

general business methods, to which the pensioner has probably been accustomed. At the same time, the final cause of the pension would possibly be better realized, inasmuch as the means for fitting maintenance would be provided at more frequent intervals. Obviously, this intra-annual payment may become involved in difficulties outweighing the advantages when the pension is established on a percentage basis.

Virginis solemniores, nempe diem 8 septembri et 25 martii; aut duos Nativitatis dies festos, nimirum Nativitatis D. N. I. Ch. et Ioannis Bapt. aut festum S. Ioannis Evangelistae loco Nativitatis D. N."—S. C. C., *Romana*, "Pensionis," 2 maii 1896.—*Analecta ecclesiastica*, IV (1896), 214. Cappello, (*Praxis processualis*, p. 150) in a formula suggests a monthly payment. The pension in this formula is paid out of the general chancery funds ("ex capsa Curiae Nostrae").

Chapter IX

RIGHTS AND OBLIGATIONS OF THE PENSIONER

As a general rule, the pensioner has the right to be paid at the time and in the manner and amount established in the decree of reservation. If, in order to vindicate his right, it should be necessary for him to take his grievances to court, his standing is that of a payee or creditor, exercising a personal action against the holder of the benefice.[1] The obligation on the incumbent to pay the pension becomes operative on the day when he accepts the benefice or, if he is already in possession, when the decree is issued, unless the latter should expressly provide otherwise. The obligation is not postponed until possession is taken of the benefice.[2]

Some difficulties may arise when the right to the pension ceases, but previous payments are still due. The former law ought to be observed in these situations. Thus, in the case of a temporary pension,[3] if the beneficiary dies before having paid the full amount due, the balance should be deducted from the income of the benefice. If there is none, the successor in the benefice ought to pay, because he accepts the obligation with the benefice. Although the obligation is personal in the sense that it ceases with the incumbency, yet it is also, in a certain sense, real inasmuch as it is imposed on the incumbent as such and indirectly burdens the benefice until paid.[4] A relatively perpetual pension,[5] being a real obligation, is equally collectible whether the benefice is occupied or not, and the obligation passes to the successor. If a payment becomes due during a vacancy, it ought to be paid by the administrator.[6] If the pensioner dies

[1] Cf. Pistocchi, *De re beneficiali*, p. 149; canon 1922, § 2.

[1] Cf. Pistocchi, *De re beneficiali*, p. 149; canon 1922, § 2.

[2] D'Angelo, *Tasse e pensioni*, p. 127. D'Annibale, *Summula theologiae moralis*, III, p. 76, n. 73, nota 42. Ojetti, *Synopsis rerum moralium et iuris pontificii*, I, p. 414, n. 588; III, p. 2964, n. 3112.

[3] Canon 1429, § 1.

[4] Cf. Vito, *Questioni canoniche*, IV, 151, nota 1.

[5] Canon 1429, § 2.

[6] Cf. Vito, *Questioni canoniche*, IV, 150, nota 4.

before having received full payment or before a term has been completed, his heirs seem ordinarily to be entitled to the amount due up to the day of death of the pensioner, prorated for the period elapsed since the last payment was made in its relation to the period elapsed at the date of death.

A pension is a favor, conferred gratuitously. Accordingly, it is the common opinion among canonists and also chancery practice that, unless otherwise specified, a pension should be regarded as conferred free from taxes and without obligations toward the benefice or its incumbent as far as the usual levies by ecclesiastical authority are concerned, but not as regards contributions to a cause whereby the very source of the pension is sustained.[7] Thus, pensions are not mentioned in the Code as being subject to the seminary tax,[8] the cathedraticum,[9] and any extraordinary although moderate periodic levy for some special need of the diocese.[10]

When there is question, however, of repairing and furnishing the the cathedral and other churches, the ordinary, outside of particular arrangements and special obligations, can appeal if need be to all his subjects,[11] including, therefore, those receiving pensions, to contribute to the fund necessary, provided the contribution leaves some portion of the income remaining beyond what they need for fitting sustenance.

When a cleric has a pension on a parish church in need of renovation or necessary furnishings, his obligation is more clearly expressed in the common law, when it states that the burden falls successively on the goods of the church (*fabrica ecclesiae*), on the patron, and then on those who receive some income from the church. The latter are to be taxed according to the judgment of the ordinary in proportion to the income.[12]

[7] Cf. Pistocchi, *De re beneficiali*, pp. 139-140; 150-151, quoting De Luca, *De pensionibus*, Pars II, disc. XXXIII, n. 14.

[8] Canon 1356, § 1.

[9] Canon 1504. Cf. Vito, *Questioni canoniche*, II, 89 and nota 3.

[10] Canon 1505.

[11] Canon 1186, 1°, 3°.

[12] Canons 1186, 2°; 1297. "La dottrina del can. 1186, 2° è la medesima dottrina insegnata dalle Decretali." Vito, *Questioni canoniche*, II, 162, nota 1.

Similarly, when the residence belonging to the benefice is in need of extraordinary repair, but not mere embellishment, the pensioner has the same obligations as he has towards the church of the benefice, unless the charter of foundation or lawful agreements and customs provide otherwise.[13]

The former apostolic privilege of transferring pensions, which was accorded to cardinals, conclavists, and others, is not recognized by the Code.[14] Nor can there be question of the survival of this privilege as a vested right;[15] for in 1899 Pope Leo XIII (1878-1903) declared all such privileges to be abrogated and abolished.[16]

With regard to conclavists, who had been frequent recipients of such pensions, it may be noted that since Pope Leo XIII no such privilege of transfer has been conferred upon them as a group. It is interesting to note that Pius X (1903-1914) was the last pope to grant pensions to conclavists, but he did not include the privilege of transferring them.[17] Both Benedict XV (1914-1922)[18] and Pius XI (1922-1939)[19] awarded a single remuneration to the conclavists.[20]

[13] Canon 1477. Cf. Fanfani, *De iure parochorum*, n. 23, p. 28; Vito, *Questioni canoniche*, I, 23; II, 162-163; III, 171-172.

"Quae normae huc usque de aedificatione et reparatione ecclesiarum statuta, servata proportione etiam ad domos parochiales, alia aedificia ecclesiastica, utensilia ecclesiae, coemeteria sunt applicandae."—Wernz, *Ius decretalium*, III, n. 434.

[14] Cf. canon 1429, § 3.

[15] Canon 4: ". . . in usu adhuc sunt nec revocata. . . ."

[16] "Che sieno abrogati ed aboliti i privilegi dei quali, in virtù di pontificie concessioni, hanno fin qui usato i Cardinali S. Romana Chiesa, i Conclavisti, altre persone o collegi di persone, di trasferire ad altri le pensioni ad esse conferite." Ex S. Dataria Ap., *Litt. Emi. Card. a Secretis Status, ad Emum. Pro-Datarium, quoad Beneficia et pensiones ecclesiasticas*, 24 maii 1899, 4°—ASS, XXXIII (1900-1901), 122.

[17] Motu propr., *Gratiae et privilegia Clericis Conclavistis postremi conclavis concessa*, 19 kal. ian. 1904—ASS, XXXVI (1903-1904), 584-586.

[18] Motu propr., *Gratiae et privilegia clericis conclavistis postremi conclavis concessa*, 16 oct. 1914—AAS, VI (1914), 533-535.

[19] Motu propr., *Gratiae et privilegia clericis conclavistis concessa*, 12 mart. 1922—AAS, XIV (1922), 177-179.

[20] "Quoniam vero clericis Conclavistis, qui adfuerunt S. R. E. Cardinalibus in Urbe commorantibus aut dioeceses Italiae regentibus, pro Apostolicae Sedis tenuitate non licet Nobis, quod decessores Nostri consueverunt, perpetuas

The present Holy Father, Pope Pius XII, made no mention of any sort of monetary remuneration whatever.[21]

With regard to cardinals there can be little question about the existence of any privilege of transferring pensions they might have had; for Pope Leo XIII declared that upon their elevation to the dignity they lose even whatever pensions they may have had,[22] and canon 235 of the Code repeats the same rule.

The lawful reservation of a pension gives to the parties concerned certain acquired rights. This means that without the consent of the interested parties no increase or reduction in the amount of the pension can be introduced, at least by an authority inferior to the Holy See, whose ordinary practice is to preserve intact the rights of the parties concerned.[23]

It can happen that the benefice because of increased expenses or diminished income is no longer able to provide the amount for the pension without depriving the incumbent of the fitting portion to which he is entitled. The incumbent, however, cannot at his own discretion reduce a pension because of diminished net income; the authority of the Holy See is required.[24]

On the other hand, if the income of the benefice increases considerably, should not a pension established in a fixed amount be increased proportionately to meet adequately the changed conditions

constituere pensiones, iisdem ut in hoc etiam genere aliqua voluntatis Nostrae significatio ne desit, trecentas libellas singulis, semel tantum, attribuimus." The formula of the two documents is identical.

[21] Motu propr., *De privilegiis conclavistis ecclesiasticis concessis,* 31 mart. 1939—AAS, XXXI (1939), 141-142.

[22] Ex S. Dataria Ap., *ibid.*, n. 1°.

[23] Cf. e.g., S. C. C., *Firmana,* "Onera et Pensionum," 29 feb. 1896—*Analecta eccl.*, IV (1896), 57-59; S. C. Ep. et Reg., *Posnanien.*, "Pensionis," 18 maii 1906.—ASS, XXXIX (1906), 458-461.

[24] S. C. Ep. et Reg., decr. "*Cum nuperrimis,*" 28 ian. 1871—ASS, VII (1872), 325-326; S. C. C., *Aversana,* "Reductio pensionis," 27 feb. 1904—ASS, XXXVII (1904-1905), 172-179. But S. C. C., *Viglevanen.*, "Exonerationis taxae," 24 aug. 1907, 25 ian., 1 feb. 1908—*Analecta eccl.* XV (1907), 382-384, XVI (1908), 53-54: "Taxam vulgo 'ricchezza mobile' sustinendam esse a parocho loci Castri Ugoniae." Cf. Gennari, *Quistioni canoniche,* q. 85, p. 121; D'Angelo, *Tasse e pensioni,* p. 127; *idem,* "De 'taxatione' in pensionibus definiendis,"—*Apollinaris,* II (1929), 217-218.

of living? The amount by which a pension is increased is equivalent to a new pension, and hence the same conditions must be verified, the same rules of law must be observed. A new burden is placed on the incumbent or on the benefice, as the case may be. Only the Sovereign Pontiff can take away acquired rights, because of the supreme power he has over benefices. The power of subordinate ordinaries is restricted because, since their limited faculty of reserving pensions is an exception to the common law requiring the conferring of benefices without diminution,[25] and especially since it prejudices the acquired rights of the incumbent, it is subject to strict interpretation.[26]

Another factor that may affect the amount of the pension is a change in monetary value. This condition should be considered according to the usual rules governing the payment of obligations when the value of money has changed. The judge is competent in such cases to render a decision. The value of money can be considered under two aspects: its intrinsic or natural value and its extrinsic or legal value. The former is based on the inherent worth of the metal or other monetary substances; the latter is established by public law or by act of the government.

If the value of money is changed intrinsically, payment is to be made according to the former standard of value, current at the time of the reservation of the pension; and if this former standard cannot be ascertained, payment should be according to an estimate thereof. This is the rule whether the intrinsic value has increased or decreased. If on the other hand, the value has changed extrinsically, payment is to be made according to its value at the time of payment, the reason being that not the intrinsic worth of the money, but only its extrinsic, i. e., its legal value, has changed. If the value must be estimated, the time of payment is also consulted as the basis of the estimate.[27]

[25] Canon 1440.

[26] Canons 19 and 50. S. R. R., *Vercellen.*, "Pensionis," 18 dec. 1928, n. 4—*S. R. R. Decisiones*, XX (1928), 492. It was decided in this case that the judge is incompetent to increase a pension, and that the ordinary can not do so when the benefice is occupied and the incumbent is unwilling.

[27] S. R. R., *ibid.*, n. 7, citing Fagnanus, in c. "Olim," 20, X, *de censibus*, III, 39, n. 4 ss.; Ferraris, "Moneta," nn. 5-13, "Pensio," n. 119.

The former law had imposed on all those who received pensions the obligation of reciting the little office of the Blessed Virgin (unless they were already otherwise obliged to pray the divine office), and if their pensions amounted to sixty ducats in gold, of wearing the clerical garb and tonsure. Under the present common law the pensioner is not bound by these obligations, for the Code makes no mention of them.[28]

The pension is generally not exempt from taxes levied by the civil government, for instance, patrimonial and mortmain taxes. The pension, being income for the pensioner, may sometimes and in some countries be regarded as taxable income by the State. In countries where the State levies pro rata taxes on the benefice on which a pension is drawn, the Holy See has decided in a number of cases that the pensioner ought to contribute his proportionate share toward the payment of such taxes.[29]

Lawful ecclesiastical authority—the Holy See, or probably the local ordinary if the pensioner consents, not, however, the incumbent of the benefice—can then deduct from the pension the portion which the pensioner ought to contribute. Such conditions will usually remain somewhat permanent, and steps may wisely be taken to reduce the pension.

Scholion. The superfluous income of the pension

What canon 1473 says of the obligation of the beneficiary, who has the right to the usufruct of all the income of his benefice, to distribute the superfluous income, cannot be applied to the pensioner. The pension is not a benefice,[30] nor does its income constitute beneficial income; it is classed rather with quasi-patrimonial goods, de-

[28] Wernz-Vidal, *Ius canonicum*, II *(De personis)*, n. 181, IV, p. 204. Coronata, *Institutiones*, II, n. 985, p. 381. Cf. canon 6, 6°.

[29] S. C. Ep. et Reg., decr. "*Cum nuperrimis*," 28 Ian. 1871—*ASS*, VII (1872), 325-326. S. C. C., *Aversana*, "Reductio pensionis," 27 feb. 1901—*ASS*, XXXVII (1904-1905), 172-179. It was decided that the entire *tassa di ricchezza mobile* was to be paid by the seminary receiving the pension in the case. S.R.R., *Romana*, "Crediti," 21 iun. 1923—*AAS*, XV (1923), 515. Cf. *Il Monitore ecclesiastico*, XXXV (1923), 155; Gennari, *Quistioni canoniche*, q. 85, p. 121; D'Angelo, *Tasse e pensioni*, p. 127.

[30] Canon 1412, 4°.

rived indeed from a spiritual title, as distinct from purely patrimonial property acquired from a secular source, e. g., inheritance or donation; but it is not granted by title of actual incumbency. The canon states only that the income of the benefice, as accruing to the incumbent, comes under this obligation of ecclesiastical law requiring its distribution to charity. Nowhere does the Code mention a corresponding obligation for the recipient of a pension. Divine law may, of course, intervene and require that some of the pension be expended in charity, depending on individual cases and particular circumstances.

Formerly the question was disputed and arguments were advanced for both sides. One camp maintained that as long as the pension is an ecclesiastical one, or one given to clerics for services other than those of a purely temporal or secular character, the recipient thereof is bound to dispose of the superfluous income for pious uses, in the same way as the incumbent of the benefice is bound. The reason is that, since the pension is derived from the income of a benefice, it passes to the pensioner with the same obligations upon it. The contrary opinion was held by a large number of authors. They contended that since the Pope for a just cause separates pensions from the beneficiary income, he thereby directs them to pious causes; wherefore there is no further obligation of devoting them to charity. This opinion was, according to St. Alphonsus Liguori (†1787), sufficiently probable.[31]

[31] *Theologia moralis*, Lib. III, n. 491, q. 6, mentioning authors for both sides. This is also the opinion embraced at the present time by Ferreris (*Compendium theologiae moralis*, I, p. 409, n. 695), citing, besides St. Alphonsus, Lugo (d. 4, n. 32) and Gury (n. 562).

D'Annibale (†1892) (*Summula theologiae moralis*, III, n. 73, nota 46, p. 77) preferred the affirmative opinion: "Quaestionis est, utrum teneatur superfluum erogare in pias causas, quia sunt fructus beneficii; an minus, quia ipsamet pensione addicti sunt in pios usus, quos proinde non oportet in alios pios usus deinceps invertere? Illud mihi verius hoc longe communius, et satis probabile (S. Alph., III, 491)."

CHAPTER X

THE TERMINATION OF ECCLESIASTICAL PENSIONS

In the past the Pope and subordinate ordinaries authorized by the Roman Pontiff sometimes reserved absolutely perpetual pensions (obliging all successive incumbents of a benefice so that upon the death of one pensioner the pension would be transferred to another).[1] By common law today even pensions reserved by the Roman Pontiff are declared to cease with the death of the pensioner.[2]

The most extensive power granted by the present law is that of reserving a relatively perpetual pension (for the life of the pensioner). This kind of pension, however, can be reserved only in behalf of a pastor or vicar and can be imposed only on the parochial benefice from which he has retired.[3]

Pensions imposed on all non-parochial benefices are to be temporary, terminating with the incumbency of the beneficiary.[4] This temporary pension may, as a matter of fact, last longer than a relatively perpetual pension on a parochial benefice, if the retired pastor or vicar predeceases his first successor or if the assistant dies before the pastor.

The termination of pensions may be regarded under a twofold aspect. Improperly speaking, pensions terminate with reference to the original pensioner by alienation or by a suspension of the full right of the pension (*dominium radicale et utile*), through simple profession or by way of penal privation of the income of a pension.

[1] Cf. e.g. Pallottini, "Pensio," n. 127; *supra*, pp. 40, 47, 98, 131.

[2] Canon 1429, § 3.

[3] Canon 1429, § 2; S. C. C., *Dioecesis N.*, "Renuntiationis paroeciae," 11 nov. 1922—*AAS*, XV (1923), 454-456; C. P. I., 20 maii 1923, ad IX.—*AAS*, XVI (1924), 116.

[4] ". . . pensiones temporarias, quae durent ad vitam beneficiarii. . . ." Canon 1429, § 1. They terminate with the death of the beneficiary, and also with his resignation of or removal from the benefice. Cf. D'Angelo, *Tasse e pensioni*, p. 119; Pistocchi, *De re beneficiali*, p. 144, quoting Antonellus (*De regimine Eccles.*, Lib. III, c. 11): ". . . . ideoque mortuo beneficiario, *vel a beneficio amoto*, pensionis onus existinguitur."

Properly speaking, pensions terminate objectively, (e. g., by a diminution or cessation of the benefice on which the pension is drawn, or the expiration of the term of its duration as set by the agent reserving it) and subjectively by the pensioner's resignation, promotion, or death either canonical (e. g., arising from his return to the lay state or from penalties) or physical.

a) Alienation

The Code states explicitly that unless expressly empowered to do so, a cleric drawing an ecclesiastical pension, cannot alienate the same.[5] By alienation is understood in general any act whereby the title of ownership (*dominium radicale*) is conveyed to another.[6]

A pension is a personal right which cannot exist apart from the person on whom it has been conferred.[7] Moreover, to alienate a clerical pension would be simony arising at least under ecclesiastical law, since it is given either in recognition of some spiritual service rendered in the past or as subsistence to one actually engaged in the performance of spiritual services.[8]

The canon uses only the term "alienation"; but a decree of the Sacred Congregation of Bishops and Regulars, cited by Cardinal Gasparri in the footnotes to the canon as the source of the present law, declares that every kind of cession, transfer, or alienation of ecclesiastical pensions is forbidden, unless special apostolic permission

[5] ". . . qui [pensionarius] tamen nequit eas [pensiones] alienare, nisi id expresse concessum sit." Canon 1429, § 3.

[6] "Alienare hic intelligitur generatim, pro quocumque ex modis quibus ius possessum *in re* potest transferri."—Pistocchi, *De re beneficiali*, p. 155. "The transfer of direct ownership of an object to another."—E. Heston, *The alienation of Church property in the United States*, The Catholic University of America Canon Law Studies, n. 132 (Washington, D. C.: The Catholic University of America Press, 1941), p. 169, citing Ferraris, "Alienatio," art. 1, n. 2. "Alienare autem est transferre dominium: proinde, vendere, donare, permutare, in solutionem dare, in emphyteusim concedere."—Cappello, *De censuris*, n. 410, p. 357 and Chelodi, *Ius poenale*, n. 79, p. 109.

[7] Wernz-Vidal, *Ius canonicum*, II (*De personis*), n. 180, b, III, p. 203.

[8] Cf. Pistocchi, *De re beneficiali*, p. 155, quoting Sebastianelli, (*Praelectiones juris canonici*, n. 252): "Pensiones vendi nequeunt absque crimine simoniae, nec etiam locari ad longum tempus. . . ."

has been previously obtained.[9] As forbidden alienation must, then, be regarded all acts whereby the right to the pension is sold or redeemed, conveyed by donation, exchanged, relinquished in payment of debts, posted as collateral or security, loaned or leased for a long term.[10]

Not only is it forbidden to alienate the right of pension, but to assign the income in its entirety and at least for an extended period is equally unlawful.[11]

A pension is a personal right, and intended to be used personally by the cleric to maintain himself in a condition becoming to the dignity of the clerical state. The income derived from the pension is intended to enable him to defray ordinary personal expenses, to provide becoming hospitality, and to practice a measure of charity. The aforementioned decree of the Sacred Congregation of Bishops and Regulars gives two other reasons for the prohibiting of the alienation of pensions: the elimination of any appearance of unseemly trafficking to the disedification of the faithful, and the prevention of law suits to the disgrace of the Church.[12]

Canon 1429, § 3 does not mention who is empowered to grant the permission to alienate a pension. Pistocchi states that local ordinaries, whose faculties with regard to alienation of ecclesiastical property are considerably restricted, cannot grant this permission.[13]

[9] ". . . quovis cessionis, translationis, alienationis titulo de pensionibus Ecclesiasticis . . . nisi habita prius de ea re speciali Apost. beneplacito."—Decr. "*Cum ad SSm̃um,*" 12 mart. 1840—Bizzarri, *Collectanea in usum Secretariae Sacrae Congregationis Episcoporum et Regularium* (Romae, 1863), p. 99; *Fontes*, n. 1926. Cf. Augustine, *The Canonical and Civil Status of Catholic Parishes*, p. 223.

[10] Pistocchi, *De re beneficiali*, p. 155. Cf. also Chelodi, *Ius poenale*, n. 79, p. 109; Cappello, *De censuris*, n. 410, p. 357; Fanfani, *De Iure parochorum*, n. 179, p. 180.

[11] " contractus, quibus unice etiam, quam dicunt, commoditas pensionis percipiendae in alium transferatur. . . ." S. C. Ep. et Reg., decr. "*Cum ad SSm̃um,*" 12 mart. 1840—Bizzarri, *Collectanea S. C. Ep. et Reg.*, p. 99. Blat, *Commentarium*, III, part. II-VI *(De rebus)*, n. 336, p. 464.

[12] S.C. Ep. et Reg., *Loc. cit.* Cf. Blat, *Commentarium*, III, part. II-VI *(De rebus)*, n. 336, p. 464; Augustine, *The Canonical and Civil Status of Catholic Parishes*, p. 222.

[13] "Ordinarius autem, qui, can. 1532, sat limitatas habet a iure facultates,

The argument seems to be based on the fact that coalescing payments place the capitalized value of the pension outside the competence of the local ordinary. It is further doubted whether the ordinary can indirectly and through the pensioner transfer ecclesiastical property in such an aggregate amount even though it comes to the latter in annual payments. The total amount depends on the duration of the pension, which, however, in the more common pensions is unpredictable, while in pensions for a predetermined number of years it might be within the ordinary's competence. A further and more direct argument is based on the former law,[14] found in the decree of the Sacred Congregation of Bishops and Regulars, explicitly stating that *apostolic* permission must be obtained.[15]

b) Termination by default of the benefice

If the benefice on which a pension is reserved ceases to exist, the pension likewise ceases.[16] Again, the income of the benefice may become so attenuated that after the prior right of the incumbent to fitting support has been attended to, nothing or but very little remains for the pensioner. It may then become necessary not only to reduce the pension but even to declare it entirely extinguished. For this the authority of the Holy See is required.[17]

c) Prescription

Can the rules of prescription be invoked to bring about the termination of canonical pensions? Pensions are not mentioned in canon

circa bonorum ecclesiasticorum alienationes, ceteris, hoc loco, pensionariis, has concedere nequit." *De re beneficiali*, p. 156.

[14] Cf. e.g., Pyrrhus, Corradus (*De beneficiis*, P. I, c. 2), quoted by Pistocchi (*loc. cit.*) to confirm his own argument: "Clarum est apud omnes, quod pensio non potest redimi seu emi pecunia, vel pretio aut eodem modo transferri sine auctoritate Papae; alias enim redemptio, emptio seu translatio, erit simoniaca et nulla."

[15] "Nisi habito prius de ea re speciali Apost. beneplacito." *Loc. cit.*

[16] Cocchi, *Commentarium*, VI, n. 108, p. 233; Vromant, *De bonis Ecclesiae*, n. 93, p. 116. "Accesorium naturam sequi congruit principalis." Reg. 42, R. J., in VI°.

[17] Cf. S. C. Ep. et Reg., decr. "*Cum nuperrimis*," 27 ian. 1871—ASS, VI (1872), 325-326. Vromant, *De bonis Ecclesiae*, p. 116. V. *supra*, p. 153.

1509 as being immune to prescription.[18] Hence, the civil law of the respective country as canonized by the Code must be consulted.[19] It is doubtful, in view of the divergent opinions held prior to the Code, whether the right itself can be prescribed. Probably only the individual payments can be outlawed.[20]

An argument in favor of prescription is drawn from canon 1446,[21] which states: "If a cleric who actually holds a benefice proves that he has been in undisputed and *bona fide* possession of a benefice for a space of fully three years of time, though perhaps his title to the benefice was invalid, he obtains the benefice by legitimate prescription, provided simony was not committed in securing possession of the benefice."[22] Consequently three years of peaceful possession give rise to the right of retaining the benefice in the state in which it was held in good faith and with the same rights and obligations or freedom from obligations. Hence, even when there was a lawful pension on the benefice, if the incumbent in peaceful possession and in good faith, being unaware of such reservation, never paid the pension, after said three years he seems no longer obliged to recognize the existence of such pension.[23] One might add that fail-

18 Pensions conferred by indult of the Holy See would be immune; cf. canon 1509, 2°.

19 Canon 1508.

20 *V. supra*, p. 70.

21 Vito, *Questioni canoniche*, III, 161-164.

22 "Si clericus qui beneficium possidet, probaverit se in eiusdem beneficii possessione pacifice per integrum triennium fuisse bona fide, etsi forte cum titulo invalido, dummodo absit simonia, beneficium ex legitima praescriptione obtinet." Translation by Woywod, *A Practical Commentary on the Code of Canon Law*, II, n. 1452, p. 150.

23 "Dalla dottrina di detto canone possiamo ricavare i sequenti principi: a) Un triennio di pacifico possesso di un qualsiasi beneficio dà il diritto a ritenere il beneficio *sicut antea;* b) Il triennio ha la forza, nel diritto, di rendere valido un titolo invalido; c) In forza della triennale prescrizione si ha diritto a possedere il beneficio, percepirne gli utili e sopportarne i pesi *quo antea sc. ut per integrum triennium.* Riteniamo che, anche quando la pensione fosse stata legalmente imposta sul beneficio parrocchiale, se tale pensione non fu nota al nuovo beneficiato, mai a lui fu chiesta *per integrum triennium,* se visse sempre in buona fede ed in tale fede ritenne sempre come suo, completamente suo tutto il frutto del beneficio parrocchiale, passato il triennio di

ure on the part of the pensioner to seek payment, who thereby left undisturbed the good faith of the incumbent, may give rise to a presumption of tacit renunciation of the pension.

The possibility of prescription suggests another reason for stating the fact of the existence of the pension in the decree of appointment to the benefice, when the pension has been established previously and is to continue in force.

d) Expiration of the term of the pension

When a pension has been reserved for a certain period, it terminates upon the expiration of the time set down. The term can be fixed absolutely for a definite number of years explicitly or implicitly, e. g., a term of preaching, a course of studies, or conditionally either by law, e. g., until the beneficiary paying the pension dies or leaves office,[24] or by decree, e. g., until a certain benefice or office suitable for the cleric now holding a pension becomes vacant, until his health is sufficiently restored.

e) Cessation of poverty

The simple cessation of poverty of the pensioner because other income, such as the income from a legacy or the reward of his industry and talents, is now coming to him does not seem to be sufficient of itself to terminate the pension. The cleric has a right to the pension which cannot be taken from him without his consent save by supreme ecclesiastical authority. The matter would be different if he accepted the pension under a condition which is now verified.[25]

legittimo possesso, *vi praescriptionis,* ha diritto a ritenere, esclusivamente, per se tutta la rendita, compresa la pensione che è prescritta in suo esclusivo vantaggio, ed in danno di qualsiasi altro anche *se munitus titulo legali et valido.*" Vito, *Questioni canoniche,* III, 163-164 and nota 1. Cf. St. Alphonsus (*Theologia moralis,* III, q. 513): "Per bonam fidem potest quisque praescribere libertatem a solvendo debito, si invincibiliter illud ignoret," citing Lugo, *De iustitia et iure,* Disp. 7, n. 49, La-Croix, *Theologia moralis,* Lib. III, pars 2, n. 493.

[24] Canon 1429, § 1.

[25] Cf. Giovanni Lardone, "Pensione perpetua o temporanea?" — *Perfice Munus!* VIII (1933), 300.

f) Resignation of pension

When a pension is no longer necessary to provide adequate maintenance for him, and if the money paid by way of pension would be more useful, not to say necessary, for other needs of the Church, the ordinary could invite the pensioner to resign his right. The ordinary may lawfully accept the resignation of a pension, but if such is the cleric's title of ordination, he may not accept it unless his decent support is assured in some other way.[26]

g) Promotion of pensioner

The present law states that all pensions cease by promotion to the cardinalate, unless the Holy See provides otherwise in particular cases.[27] The cessation of pensions by promotion to the cardinalate is not mentioned in the two papal constitutions cited as sources of this canon. Prior to the Code, however, Pope Leo XIII (1878-1903) had already made a similar pronouncement, but more rigid and extensive; for no mention was made of possible exceptions for particular cases. The Leonine regulation, furthermore, mentioned not only those advanced to the cardinalate, but included also residential bishops, nuncios of the first and second class,[28] secretaries of the Sacred Congregations of Bishops and Regulars,[29] of the Council, of the Propagation of the Faith, assessors of the Holy Office, and the majordomo of His Holiness.[30] None of the aforementioned, with the ex-

[26] Canon 980, § 1.

[27] Canon 235. Cf. Pruemmer, *Manuale iuris canonici*, p. 134.

[28] "There are four Nunciatures of the first class: Paris, Madrid, Vienna, and Lisbon; we find Nuncios of the second class in Argentina, Bavaria, Belgium, Brazil, Chile, Columbia, etc."—Ayrinhac, *The Constitution of the Church*, pp. 89-90. Cf. *Annuario pontificio*, 1940, pp. 766-771.

[29] This Congregation was suppressed by Pius X, const. "*Sapienti Consilio*," 29 iun. 1908.—*AAS*, I (1909), 7-19. Cf. Wernz-Vidal, *Ius canonicum*, II (*De personis*), n. 494, p. 501; Coronata, *Institutiones*, I, p. 412, n. 343. The S. Cong. de Religiosis was established to transact some of the business formerly committed to the S. C. of Bishops and Regulars.

[30] "Che a partire da questo giorno, nell' atto stesso della loro promozione debbano perdere tutte e singole le pensioni, delle quali per avventura si trovino al possesso, tutti coloro i quali siano promossi alla dignità cardinalizia, a Vescovi residenziali, a Nunzi di prima e seconda classe, a Segretarii delle

ception of cardinals, is mentioned by the Code as losing pensions upon appointment. It would seem, therefore, that pensions are not thereby automatically terminated by the mere promotion to such office.[31]

Obviously, promotion to the benefice upon which a pension is being drawn will result in the termination of the pension.[32]

h) Solemn religious profession

Before pronouncing solemn vows, the religious, unless excused by special indult of the Holy See, is directed to renounce to whomever he chooses all the property actually owned by him, the renunciation to become effective upon subsequent profession.[33] Indeed, without an indult of the Holy See, a person solemnly professed is incapable of retaining and acquiring temporal goods.[34]

Pensions are viewed by authors as being uniquely and strictly personal in character.[35] They are inalienable rights and as such can-

Sacre Congregazioni dei Vescovi e Regolari, del Concilio, di Propaganda, non che ad Assessore del S. Uffizio ed a Maggiordomo della Santità Sua." Dataria Ap., *Litterae Eminentissimi Cardinalis a Secretis Status, ad Emum Pro-Datarium quoad Beneficia et pensiones ecclesiasticas*, 24 maii 1899, ad 1°.—ASS, XXXIII (1900-1901), 121.

[31] Cf. canon 4.

[32] Cocchi, *Commentarium*, VI, n. 108, p. 232.

[33] Canon 581, § 1. "Abdicat proinde etiam dominium radicale, immo per professionem sollemnem regulariter incapax fit dominii in bona temporalia proprio nomine possidenda."—Genicot-Salsmans, *Institutiones theologiae moralis* (13. ed., 6. post Cod., Bruxelles: L'Edition universelle, S. A., 1936), II, p. 80, n. 91.

[34] Vermeersch-Creusen, *Epitome*, I, n. 736, § 7, p. 534. Cf. also Claeys-Bouuaert-Simenon, *Manuale iuris canonici*, I, n. 657, p. 386; Blat, *Commentarium*, II *(De religiosis et laicis)*, n. 469-470, p. 410-412; Wernz-Vidal, *Ius canonicum*, III (*De religiosis*), n. 329, VIII, p. 319; Fanfani, *De iure religiosorum* (2. ed., Taurini-Romae: Marietti, 1925), n. 229, p. 246; n. 261, p. 297.

[35] Cf. Goyeneche, "Consultatio 26 a: Premium bellicum quod redeuntibus e militia nunc obveniat," etc.—*CpR*, I (1920), 341, citing Suarez (*De religione*, t. III, l. VIII, cap. XIV, n. 14), Passerini (*De hominum statibus et officiis*, t. I, q. 186, art VII, n. 325 sq.), De Luca (*De regularibus* [*Theatrum Veritatis*, Tom. III, pars I], disc. 57, n. 19), Vermeersch (*De religiosis*, I, n. 278, p. 180), Wernz (*Ius decretalium*, III, 650), and others.

not be renounced or ceded at will to a third party.[36] Hence either they continue vested in the solemnly professed religious or they terminate upon profession. The basic cause for the pension and the fundamental reason forbidding alienation thereof—provision of fitting subsistence primarily and proximately for himself—for all practical purposes ceases to exist; for solemn vows are always perpetual. Hence, there is not the same need, as in the case of those taking temporary vows, for the legislator to make any general provisions for his fitting maintenance should the regular return to the world.[37] Religious profession effects a change in the status of personality,[38] and solemn profession formally adds firmness and immutability to this new state for the attainment of Christian perfection.[39] The reason for the canon which bids the religious about to make solemn profession to renounce all his property is self-evident when viewed in the light of the vow of poverty. The common law states only that pensions cease with the death of the pensioner,[40] thereby indicating that it admits no pension greater than a relatively perpetual one; but it is obviously not the intent of the legislator to restrict the termination of pensions to this one mode.[41] The general law forbidding alienation and decreeing the termination of ecclesiastical pensions by death is modified by the special law for regulars.[42]

In the light of the considerations outlined as well as of the teaching of the former law, it must be concluded that, aside from an express concession of the Holy See permitting him to alienate pen-

[36] "L'essere la pensione inalienabile impedisce che il pensionato possa venderla o commutarla con altro diritto; e impedisce anche, a mio parere, che egli possa privarsi per rinuncia o cessione del diritto stesso. Il diritto alla pensione è un diritto personalissimo e inalienabile per diritto positivo canonico." Coronata, "Pensione e religiosi"—*Perfice Munus!* VIII (1933), p. 212.

[37] Cf. canons 580; 569; 583, 1°; *infra*, p. 166-167.

[38] Cf. canon 487.

[39] Cf. Wernz-Vidal, *Ius canonicum*, III (*De religiosis*), n. 4-5, p. 3-5; Fanfani, *De iure religiosorum*, n. 1-2, p. 1-4.

[40] Canon 1429, § 3.

[41] " . . . *cessant semper morte pensionarii*, uti modo peculiari praeter alios modos amittendi iura, aliasque pensiones." Blat, *Commentarium*, III, part. II-VI (*De rebus*), n. 336, p. 464.

[42] "Generi per speciem derogatur." Reg. 34, R. J., in VI°.

sions[43] or particular indults of the Holy See permitting him to retain them,[44] the ecclesiastical pensions which a cleric may have been holding terminate when he pronounces solemn vows.[45]

Scholion. Simple religious profession

Simple religious profession does not cause the extinction of the right to a pension previously held by the candidate. The religious professed of simple vows retains the ownership of his property, but in accordance with the vow of poverty he is required to entrust the administration of the pension to a person of his choice, and to dispose according to his own choice (unless the constitutions provide otherwise) of the use and usufruct of the pension.[46] Indeed, the constitutions of congregations cannot demand that their professed members renounce their property;[47] for such religious are explicitly forbidden to abdicate gratuitously the ownership (*dominium radicale*) of their property by a voluntary deed of conveyance.[48] This certainly includes ecclesiastical pensions, which as was seen, cannot be alienated in any way whatsoever, save by special permission. The survival of the right to the pension is postulated in the intent

[43] Canon 1429, § 3.

[44] Canon 581, § 1.

[45] Cocchi (*Commentarium*, VI, n. 108, p. 232) states: "Pensio exstinguitur . . . per . . . professionem religiosam," and in a footnote he refers to Ferraris ("Pensio," n. 63), who wrote: "Sicut per professionem *regularem* in religione approbata vacant beneficia . . . ita vacant etiam pensiones." (Italics inserted.) Cf. also *supra*, p. 51.

Coronata ["Pensione e religiosi"—*Perfice Munus!* VIII (1933), 211-212] arrives at a somewhat different conclusion: the right of pension being inalienable, it cannot be renounced but is retained even by a regular; only the use of the pension is ceded either to persons of his choice before solemn profession or to the institute if he fails to make the cession or the persons chosen in the cession predecease him; and if he returns to the world he regains full rights.

[46] Cf. canons 580; 569. V. *supra*, p. 165.

[47] Vermeersch-Creusen, *Epitome*, I, n. 734, 2, b, p. 532.

[48] "Professis a votis simplicibus in Congregationibus religiosis non licet: 1.° per actum inter vivos dominium bonorum suorum titulo gratioso abdicare."—Canon 583. To attempt to convey a pension by testament would be impossible, for death terminates all pensions (canon 1429, § 3). Cf. Pistocchi, *De re beneficiali*, p. 155, nota 2.

of this law: that the religious may have at hand means of decent support, should he leave the congregation.[49]

The question might become practical in the case of a simply professed religious in major orders[50] who legitimately leaves the institute after the expiration of temporary vows without subsequent renewal,[51] or by reason of an indult of secularization,[52] or because of dismissal. (If dismissal is for penal reasons the crime may be such that the loss of pension is part of the penalty.) Full rights over the pension, including full use of its fruits, then revert to him, although obviously he cannot claim the income realized from the pension while he was in the institute, unless his administrator failed to collect it.[53]

i) Departure from the clerical state

One of the effects of a cleric's return to the lay state is the automatic loss of rights proper to clerics,[54] among which is the right to ecclesiastical pensions.[55] Therefore, laicized clerics lose whatever ecclesiastical pensions they may have had.

The Code in outlining the departure from the clerical state, distinguishes between clerics in major orders and those in minor orders.[56]

Clerics in major orders can be laicized: 1) by rescript of the Holy See, issued through the Sacred Congregation of Religious[57] or the Sacred Congregation of the Sacraments;[58] 2) in cases of reception

[49] Cf. Blat, *Commentarium*, II *(De religiosis et laicis)*, n. 475; Wernz-Vidal, *Ius canonicum*, III *(De religiosis)*, n. 327, V, p. 315-316; Creusen-Garesché-Ellis, *Religious Men and Women in the Code* (3. English ed., Milwaukee: The Bruce Publishing Company, 1940), pp. 183-184; Coronata, *Institutiones*, I, p. 762, n. 593, 2°, a.

[50] Clerics in minor orders are automatically reduced to the lay state. Canon 648.

[51] Canon 637.

[52] Canon 640, § 1.

[53] Cf. canon 643, § 1.

[54] "Omnes qui e clericali statu ad laicalem legitime redacti aut regressi sunt, eo ipso amittunt . . . iura . . . clericalia." Canon 213, § 1.

[55] "Soli clerici possunt . . . pensiones ecclesiasticas obtinere." Canon 118.

[56] Canon 211, §§ 1-2.

[57] Cf. canon 251, § 3.

[58] Cf. canon 249, § 2.

of orders under grave fear[59] by administrative or extra-judicial decree of the Sacred Congregation of the Sacraments or of the Sacred Congregation of the Holy Office,[60] or by judicial sentence of an ecclesiastical tribunal to which the case has been remitted by the respective Sacred Congregation; 3) by degradation either verbal or real;[61] 4) indirectly through lawful dispensation for marriage from the diriment impediment of subdiaconate or diaconate granted in danger of death according to canons 1043 and 1044.[62]

Clerics in minor orders return to the lay state: 1) automatically, according to the provisions in law as a result of *a)* marriage, except it be null because of force or fear,[63] *b)* failure to wear the clerical garb and tonsure within a month after the ordinary's warning,[64] *c)* voluntary enlistment in the armed forces of the State,[65] *d)* dismissal from a religious institute,[66] *e)* or judicial declaration of an admittedly deceitful profession;[67] 2) by their own free will, after they have notified the ordinary; 3) by decree of the ordinary;[68] 4) by way of penalty to be inflicted for more serious crimes against the sixth commandment;[69] 5) by degradation.[70]

Marriage attempted with full knowledge by a cleric in major orders does not directly and immediately bring about the loss of pensions. The crime is punished by automatic excommunication reserved to the Holy See in a simple manner, and by degradation to be inflicted if the delinquent does not repent within the time set by the ordinary.[71] In the first stage preceding the act of degradation,

[59] Cf. canon 214.

[60] Cf. canon 1993, § 1.

[61] Cf. canon 2305.—Canon 211, § 1.

[62] Coronata, *Institutiones*, I, p. 361, n. 298. Cf. Wernz-Vidal, *Ius canonicum*, II *(De personis)*, n. 394, pp. 384-385.

[63] Cf. canon 132, § 2.

[64] Cf. canon 136, § 3.

[65] Cf. canon 141, §§ 1-2.

[66] Cf. canons 648; 699, § 3.

[67] Cf. canon 2387.

[68] Canon 211, § 2.

[69] Cf. canon 2358.

[70] Cf. canon 2305. Cf. Wernz-Vidal, *Ius canonicum*, II *(De personis)*, n. 392, pp. 383-384; Coronata, *Institutiones*, I, p. 361, n. 299.

[71] Canon 2388, § 1.

forfeiture of the income of the pension would become effective only after a declaratory sentence of excommunication would have been rendered; should he be declared *vitandus*, he would lose the pension itself.[72] In the latter stage the pension would be lost through the implied deposition and reduction to the lay state.[73]

j) Penalties

Whereas every censure of excommunication, suspension, and personal interdict has the effect of rendering a cleric incapable of acquiring pensions,[74] yet, in the matter of depriving a cleric of a pension actually held, the law inflicts this penalty only in the gravest delinquencies, decreeing privation of only the fruits in less extreme cases. Thus, not until a condemnatory or declaratory sentence has been rendered, is the excommunicate deprived of the income of any pensions he may have, and only a *vitandus* loses the pension itself.[75] The Code does not decree any loss of pension or its income as a consequence of personal interdict.[76] Nor is there any common law censure of suspension from a pension or its income.[77]

Among the vindicative penalties to which all the faithful are liable there is the explicit privation or temporary suspension of a pension paid by the Church or out of Church property.[78] This, however, does not refer to strictly ecclesiastical pensions on benefices, reserved exclusively in favor of clerics.

Only the Holy See can inflict the penalty of incapacity to acquire ecclesiastical pensions; and the right of pension once acquired is not lost because of a supervening disability, unless such loss is decreed as a new and distinct penalty.[79]

[72] Canon 2266.

[73] Canon 2305.

[74] Canons 2265; 2275, 3°; 2283.

[75] "Post sententiam condemnatoriam vel declaratoriam excommunicatus manet privatus fructibus . . . pensionis . . . si quod habeat in Ecclesia; et vitandus ipsamet . . . pensione."—Canon 2266.

[76] Cf. canon 2275.

[77] Cf. canons 2278-2283.

[78] Canon 2291, 7°. Cf. canon 2322, 1°, which expressly decrees that a lay person who simulates the celebration of Mass or the hearing of sacramental confession is to be deprived of any pension he may have in the Church.

[79] Cf. canon 2296 together with canon 118. Cf. Wernz-Vidal, *Ius canonicum, VII (Ius poenale ecclesiasticum)*, n. 342, 9, p. 359.

Among the vindicative penalties to be inflicted on delinquent clerics is the penal privation of a benefice or office with or without "pension," [80] i. e., the income derived from the benefice or office. The pension in this case belongs to the class known as spiritual pensions. If the privation of the benefice or office is *ipso facto,* the privation of the "pension" becomes effective immediately; but if a condemnatory sentence of a judge must intervene, the "pension," or right to income, is not lost until such sentence has been rendered.[81]

A cleric who has been ordained by title of pension cannot be deprived of the same even as a special penalty unless other provision is made for his fitting support.[82]

Deposition is attended with the loss of pensions which the defendant may have, even if such were his title of ordination; but in this case, if the deposed cleric is in grave want, the ordinary is bound in charity to provide for him in the best way possible.[83] Even this obligation of providing for a deposed cleric ceases when he is deprived of the ecclesiastical garb.[84]

Finally, the extreme penalty of degradation includes not only deposition and permanent loss of the ecclesiastical garb, but also

[80] Canon 2298, 6°: "Privatio poenalis beneficii vel officii cum vel sine pensione."

[81] Cf. Wernz-Vidal, *Ius canonicum,* VII *(Ius poenale ecclesiasticum),* n. 349, VII, b, pp. 369-370; Blat, *Commentarium,* V, n. 131, 6°, p. 182; Chelodi, *Ius poenale,* n. 51, p. 67.

According to canon 2299, § 1 a cleric who holds an irremovable benefice cannot be deprived of it by way of penalty except in the cases stated expressly in law; one who holds a removable benefice can be deprived of it also for other reasonable causes. *Privati ipso facto*: canons 2396; 2397; 2398; 2266. *Privandi*: canons 2314, § 1, 2°; 2331, § 2; 2340, § 2; 2343, § 2, 3°; 2345; 2346; 2350, § 2; 2354, § 2; 2359, §§ 1-2; 2368, § 1; 2381, 2°; 2180 et 2181 una cum 2177. *Privari possunt*: canons 2324; 2336, §§ 1-2; 2355; 2359, § 3; 2360, § 2; 2394, 2°; 2403; 2405. Cf. Chelodi, *ibid.*, nota 2; Coronata, *Institutiones,* IV, p. 259, n. 1830.

[82] Canon 2299, § 3.

[83] Canon 2303, §§ 1-2. Cf. Findlay, *Canonical norms governing the deposition and degradation of clerics,* The Catholic University of America Canon Law Studies, n. 130 (Washington, D. C.: The Catholic University of America Press, 1941), pp. 167-171.

[84] Canon 2304, § 2.

reduction to the lay state,[85] thereby terminating ecclesiastical pensions by a twofold cause.

Besides these general penalties which induce loss of pensions the Code mentions several crimes, which, although they may not possibly effect the loss of pensions implicitly,[86] nevertheless are explicitly sanctioned with the loss of pensions. Thus apostasy from the faith, as well as heresy and schism, after the delinquent's failure to heed the warning of the ordinary, must be punished by deprivation of pensions.[87] Again, clerics who interfere with the liberty, rights, and jurisdiction of the Church, as well as those who join masonic or similar societies, must be deprived of ecclesiastical pensions.[88] Similarly, clerics who lay violent hands on cardinals or legates of the Roman Pontiff must be punished with privation of pensions, if they have any.[89] Encroachments upon the rights and property of the Roman Church must likewise be punished with privation of clerical pensions.[90] Forgery or deliberate use of pontifical documents known to be forged may be punished even with privation of pensions, if the gravity of the circumstances warrants.[91]

k) Death

Pensions imposed by local ordinaries on non-parochial benefices cease with the death of the incumbent.[92] All pensions drawn on benefices, not excluding pensions imposed by the Roman Pontiff, terminate, according to the prescription of the Code, with the death of the pensioner. Common law today recognizes no absolutely perpetual pensions.[93]

85 Canon 2305, § 1.

86 Cf. canon 2266.

87 Canon 2314, § 1, 2°.

88 Canons 2336; 2334; 2335.

89 Canon 2343, § 2, 3°. By the first clause of the preceding paragraph persons laying violent hands on the person of the Pope are by that very fact *vitandi*, and hence, according to canon 2266, lose any pensions they may have.

90 Canon 2345.

91 Canon 2360, § 2.

92 Canon 1429, § 1.

93 "Pensiones beneficiis sive a Romano Pontifice sive ab aliis collatoribus impositae, cessant morte pensionarii. . . ." Canon 1429, § 3.

Scholion. The effects of canonical irregularity on the capacity to retain ecclesiastical pensions

In themselves canonical irregularities can never cause the loss of pensions. Indeed, if an irregularity does not even hinder a cleric from retaining the benefice already obtained,[94] much less does it prevent a cleric from retaining whatever pensions he may be holding and from receiving the income thereof.

Indirectly, however, irregularities arising from crime may bring about deprivation of pensions through the penalty inflicted in punishment of the crime.[95] The loss of pension would have to be clear from the law, for a pension is an acquired right and not to be taken away without due authority.

Certain irregularities because of defect, however, far from causing the loss of a pension, present all the more reason for the establishment of the pension and its income as not only desirable but necessary, as in the case of a cleric who should become seriously disabled physically or mentally.[96]

[94] Cappello, *De Sacramentis,* II, pars III (*De sacra ordinatione*), n. 435, 5°, p. 417.

[95] E.g., in apostasy, heresy, and schism after an ineffectual warning (canons 2314, § 1, 2°; 985, 1°), loss of pension is expressly prescribed; in the procuring of abortion (canons 2350, § 1; 985, 4°), through prescribed deposition; in attempted marriage on the part of clerics in sacred orders (canons 2388, § 1; 985, 3°), through prescribed deposition and reduction to the lay state; in conviction of homicide (canons 2354; 985, 4°, 6°), through prescribed degradation; in the celebration of Mass, and the hearing of confession by those not ordained to the priesthood (canons 2322, 1°; 985, 7°), through prescribed deposition.

[96] "Speciatim *beneficio ecclesiastico* legitime iam acquisito irregularis ipso iure non privatur, etsi irregularitas superveniat ex delicto; si autem irregularitas *ex defectu contrahatur,* irregularis beneficiatus multo minus suo beneficio spoliari non debet."—Wernz-Vidal, *Ius canonicum,* IV, pars I (*De rebus*), n. 234, p. 311. What is said of irregularities as affecting the capacity of a beneficiary is applicable *a fortiori* to a pensioner.

CONCLUSIONS

1. Pensions can be reserved only by those who can confer benefices or accept resignations; but when the bishop is physically impeded, the powers of the vicar general are greater than those of a vicar capitular; he can reserve pensions on all benefices even without a special mandate, and before the expiration of a year's quasi-vacancy of the see.

2. Clerics removed from their benefices by penal administrative process are not qualified to receive pensions.

3. Religious after simple profession cannot lawfully acquire pensions for themselves; after solemn profession they cannot do so validly.

4. Religious of simple vows retain the right to pensions acquired before profession.

5. Pensions held by regulars before solemn profession terminate with such profession.

6. Canonical irregularity in itself and directly does not disqualify a cleric from obtaining or retaining pensions.

7. Pensions on parochial benefices can be reserved not only at the time of the conferring of the benefice, but also during its vacancy, or during the time that it is occupied.

8. By the mere fact that the resignation of his benefice has been accepted, the retiring beneficiary cannot claim to have acquired a strict right to a pension.

9. The pension should be established in a determined amount rather than in a percentage of the income of the benefice.

10. The local ordinary can reserve relatively perpetual pensions only on parochial benefices but for the benefit exclusively of pastors or vicars retiring from the same.

11. Permission to transfer pensions can be granted only by the Holy See.

12. A pensioner can be deprived of the income or of the very right of pension by the Holy See, by provisions and *ipso facto* sanctions of the common law, and by authorities subordinate to the Holy See when this is expressly decreed in the law.

BIBLIOGRAPHY

Sources

Acta Apostolicae Sedis, Commentarium Officiale, Romae, 1909-

Acta Conciliorum et Epistolae Decretales ac Constitutiones Summorum Pontificum, Ed. Regia, 10 vols., Parisiis, 1774-1775.

Acta Conciliorum Oecumenicorum, iussu atque mandato Societatis scientiarum Argentoratensis edidit Eduardus Schwartz, Strassburg, 1914, deinde Berolini et Lipsiae: Walter de Gruyter & Co., 1922-

Acta et Decreta Concilii Plenarii Baltimorensis III, A. D. MDCCCLXXXIV, Baltimorae, 1886.

Acta Sanctae Sedis, 41 vols., Romae, 1865-1908.

Baluzius, Stephanus, *Nova Collectio Conciliorum*, 1 tom., Parisiis, 1683.

Berger, Elie, *Les Registres d'Innocent IV, d'après les manuscrits originaux du Vatican et de la Bibliothèque Nationale*, 4 vols., Paris, 1884-1897.

Bizzarri, A., *Collectanea in usum Secretariae Sacrae Congregationis Episcoporum, et Regularium*, cura A. Bizzarri Archiepiscopi Philippensis secretarii edita, Romae, 1863.

Bullarii Romani Continuatio, Summorum Pontificum Clementis XIII, Clementis XIV, Pii VI, Pii VII, Leonis XII et Pii VIII . . . collegit Andreas Advocatus Barbèri, . . . additis . . . adnotationibus . . . opera et studio . . . Alexandri Spetia [et Rainaldi Segreti], 13 vols., Prati, 1840-1849.

Bullarum diplomatum et privilegiorum sanctorum Romanorum Pontificum taurinensis editio, studio Al. Tomasetti et Card. Francisci Gaudé, 24 vols. in 25, Augustae Taurinorum, 1857-1872.

Codex Iuris Canonici Pii X Pontificis Maximi iussu digestus Benedicti XV auctoritate promulgatus, Petro Card. Gasparri, ed., Romae: Typis Polyglottis Vaticanis, 1917, reimpressio, 1934.

Codex Theodosianus, ed. Krueger-Mommsen-Meyer, 3 vols., Berolini, 1905.

Codicis Iuris Canonici Fontes cura Em̃i. Petri Card. Gasparri editi, 9 vols., Romae (postea Civitate Vaticana): Typis Polyglottis Vaticanis, 1923-1939. Vol. VII, VIII, et IX ed. cura et studio Em̃i. Iustiniani Card. Serédi.

Concilia Provincialia, Baltimori habita ab anno 1829 usque ad annum 1849, 2. ed., Baltimori, 1851.

Concilium Tridentinum, Diariorum, Actorum, Epistularum, Tractatuum, nova collectio, ed. Societas Goerresiana, Friburgi Brisgoviae: Herder, 1901-

Corpus Iuris Canonici, ed. Lipsiensis 2., post Aemilii Ludouici Richteri curas instruxit Aemilius Friedberg, 2 vols., Lipsiae: ex officina Bernhardi Tauchnitz, 1879-1881. Editio anastatice repetita, Lipsiae: Tauchnitz, 1928.

Corpus Iuris Civilis, ed. Krueger-Mommsen-Schoell-Kroll, 3 vols., Berlin: Weidmann, 1928-1929.

D'Achery, Lucas, *Spicilegium sive collectio veterum aliquot scriptorum*, Parisiis, 1723.

Decisiones Sacrae Romanae Rotae coram . . . Bartholomaeo Olivatio, 8 vols., Romae, 1784.

Decretales Gregorii Papae IX, una cum Glossa restitutae, Romae, 1582.

Farinacius, Prosper, *Sacrae Romanae Rotae decisionum* . . . 19 partes in 25 vols., Francofurti, 1623.

Gaius, *Institutionum commentarii quattuor*, ed. B. Kuebler, Lipsiae: B. G. Teubner, 1928.

Hardouin, Jean, *Acta Conciliorum et Epistolae Decretales ac Constitutiones Summorum Pontificum*, 12 vols., Parisiis, 1714-1715.

Jaffé, Philippus, *Regesta Pontificum Romanorum ab condita Ecclesia ad annum post Christum natum MCXCVIII*, 2. ed. corr. et aucta, 2 vols. in 1, Lipsiae, 1885-1888. *Ab condita Ecclesia ad annum DXC*, ed. F. Kaltenbrunner; *ab anno DXC ad annum DCCCLXXXII*, ed. P. Ewald; *ab anno DCCCLXXXII usque ad annum MCXCVIII*, ed. S. Loewenfeld.

Journel, M. J. Rouët de, *Enchiridion Patristicum*, ed. 8. et 9., Friburgi Brisgoviae: Herder & Co., 1932.

Le Plat, Judocus, *Monumentorum ad Historiam Concilii Tridentini . . . Amplissima Collectio*, 7 vols., Lovanii, 1781-1787.

Lex Romana canonice compta, testo di leggi romano-canoniche del sec. IX, ed. Carlo Guido Mor, Pavia: Tipografia cooperativa, 1927.

Liber Pontificalis, Le, Introduction et commentaire par l'abbé L. Duchesne, 2 vols., Paris, 1886-1892.

Magnum Bullarium Romanum a Beato Leone Magno usque ad S. D. N. Benedictum XIII, ed. Laertius Cherubini, . . . Angelo Maria Cherubini, et al., 8 vols., Luxemburgi, 1727.

Mansi, Ioannes Dominicus, *Sacrorum Conciliorum Nova et Amplissima Collectio*, 53 vols. in 60, Florentiae, Parisiis, Lipsiae, Arnhem, 1901-1927.

Monumenta Germaniae Historica, edidit Societas aperiendis fontibus rerum germanicarum medii aevi, Berlin: Weidmann; Hannover: Hahn; Leipzig: Karl W. Hiersemann, 1824- . *Epistolae*, Tom. I, pars 1, *Gregorii I Papae registrum epistolarum, Libri I-IV*, ed. Paulus Ewald, Berolini: Weidmann, 1887; Tom. I, pars 2, *Gregorii I Papae registrum epistolarum, Lib. V-VII*, post Pauli Ewaldi obitum ed. L. M. Hartmann, Berolini: Weidmann, 1891. Tom. II, pars 2, *Gregorii I Papae registrum epistolarum, Lib. X-XIV*, post Pauli Ewaldi obitum edidit Ludovicus M. Hartmann, Berolini: Weidmann, 1895.

Leges, sect. II, *Capitularia Regum Francorum*, I, ed. A. Boretius, 1883; II, ed. A. Boretius et V. Krause, 1897; sect. III, *Concilia*, tom. I, *Concilia aevi Merovingici*, rec. F. Maassen, 1893; tom. II, *Concilia aevi Karolini I*, rec. Albertus Werminghoff, 2 part., 1904-1908.

Scriptores rerum merovingicarum, ed. W. Arndt et B. Krusch, I, *Gregorii Turonensis opera*, 1884.

Epistolae selectae, tom. II, fasc. 1, *Gregorii VII regestrum*, ed. E. Caspar, pars I, lib. I-IV, 1920, pars II, lib. V-IX, 1923.

Pallottini, Salvator, *Collectio omnium Conclusionum et Resolutionum quae in causis propositis apud Sacram Congregationem Cardinalium S. Concilii Tridentini interpretum prodierunt ab eius institutione anno MDLXIV ad annum MDCCCLX, distinctis titulis alphabetico ordine per materias digestas*, 18 vols., Romae, 1868-1895.

Potthast, Augustus, *Regesta Pontificum Romanorum inde ab A. post Christum natum MCXCVIII ad A. MCCCIV*, 2 vols., Berolini, 1874-1875.

S. *Romanae Rotae Decisiones seu Sententiae quae . . . prodierunt anno 1909*- Romae: Typis Vaticanis, 1912-

Schroeder, H. J., *Canons and Decrees of the Council of Trent*, original text with English translation, St. Louis, Mo.: B. Herder Book Co., 1941.

Thesaurus Resolutionum Sacrae Congregationis Concilii, 167 vols., Romae, 1718-1908.

Reference Works

Abbas, cf. Nicolaus de Tudeschis.

Aichner, Simon, *Compendium juris ecclesiastici ad usum cleri*, Brixinae, 1887.

Amydenius, Theodorus, *Tractatus de officio et iurisdictione Datarii et de stylo Datariae*, 2 vols., Venetiis, 1653.

André, Michel, *Cours Alphabétique et Méthodique de Droit Canonique*, Paris, 1844-46.

Angelis, Philippus Canonicus de, *Praelectiones Juris Canonici, ad methodum Decretalium Gregorii IX exactas*, 4 vols. in 6, Romae, 1877-1887.

Annuario Pontificio per l'anno 1940, Città del Vaticano, Tipografia poliglotta vaticana, 1940.

Augustine, *pseud*; cf. Bachofen, Charles Augustine.

Ayrinhac, H. A., *Administrative Legislation in the New Code of Canon Law (Lib. III., can. 1154-1551)*, London, New York, etc.: Longmans, Green and Co., 1930.

————, *Constitution of the Church in the New Code of Canon Law (Lib. II, can. 215-486)*, London, New York, etc.: Longmans, Green and Co., 1930.

————, *General Legislation in the New Code of Canon Law, General Norms (can. 1-86), Ecclesiastical Persons in General (can. 87-214)*, London, New York, etc.: Longmans, Green and Co., 1933.

Azpilcueta, cf. Navarrus.

Bachofen, Charles Augustine, *A Commentary on the New Code of Canon Law*, 3.-5. ed., 8 vols., St. Louis: Herder, 1925-1938. Vol. VI: *Administrative Law* (can. 1154-1551), 3. ed., 1931.

————, *The Canonical and Civil Status of Catholic Parishes in the United States*, St. Louis: B. Herder Book Co., 1926.

Barbosa, Augustinus, *Collectanea doctorum qui in suis operibus Concilii Tridentini loca referentes illorum materiam incidenter tractarunt, & varias quaestiones, in foro ecclesiastico versantibus maxime utiles deciderunt,* Lugduni, 1657.

————, *Iuris ecclesiastici universi libri tres,* 3 lib. in 2 vol., Lugduni, 1660.

————, *Pastoralis solicitudinis sive de officio et potestate Episcopi tripartita descriptio,* 4 part. in 2 vols., Lugduni, 1628.

————, *Summa apostolicarum decisionum extra ius commune vagantium,* Lugduni, 1645.

————, *Tractatus de canonicis et dignitatibus,* Lugduni, 1658.

Baronius, Caesar, *Annales ecclesiastici* auctore Caesare Baronio, una cum critica historica-chronologica P. Antonii Pagii, 11 vols., Lucae, 1738-1742.

————, *Annales ecclesiastici,* denuo excusi et ad nostra usque tempora perducti ab Augustino Theiner, 37 vols., Barri-Ducis, Parisiis, 1864-1883.

Barrett, John D., *A comparative study of the Councils of Baltimore and the Code of canon law,* The Catholic University of America Canon Law Studies, n. 83, Washington, D. C.: The Catholic University of America, 1932.

Berardi, Aemilius, *De parocho compendium,* Faventiae, 1887.

Bersano, Bartholomaeus, *Tractatus de compensationibus,* Mediolani, 1691.

Blat, Albertus, *Commentarium textus codicis iuris canonici,* 1.-3. ed., 6 vols. and appendix, Romae: Collegio Angelico, 1921-1938. I: *Normae generales,* 1921; II: *De personis,* 2. ed., 1921; appendix ad II: *De personis,* 1924; II: *De religiosis,* 3. ed., 1938; III, pars 1: *De rebus,* 2. ed., 1924; III, part. 2-6: *De rebus,* 2. ed., 1934; IV: *De processibus,* 1927; V: *De delictis et poenis,* 1924.

Bonacina, Martinus, *Opera omnia,* 3 vols., Venetiis, 1687.

Bouscaren, T. L., *The Canon Law Digest,* 2 vols. and supplement, Milwaukee: Bruce, 1934-1941.

Buckland, W. W., *A Text Book of Roman Law from Augustus to Justinian,* 2. ed., Cambridge: University Press, 1932.

Buonocore, Giuseppe, *Il "Titulus Canonicus,"* Napoli: Enrico Maria Muca, 1933.

Calamita, F. P., *I capitoli canonicali nel Codice del Diritto canonico,* Napoli: Gennaro Tavassi, 1923.

Campagna, Angelo, *Il Vicario Generale del Vescovo,* The Catholic University of America Canon Law Studies, n. 66, Washington, D. C.: The Catholic University of America, 1931.

Cappello, Felix, *De Curia Romana iuxta reformationem a Pio X sapientissime inductam,* 2 vols., Romae, 1911-1912.

————, *Praxis processualis ad normam Codicis et peculiarium S. Sedis instructionum,* Taurini, Romae: Marietti, 1940.

————, *Tractatus Canonico-Moralis de Censuris iuxta Codicem Iuris Canonici,* 3. ed., recogn. et emend., Taurinorum Augustae: Marietti, 1933.

————, *Tractatus Canonico-Moralis de Sacramentis,* 1.-4. ed., 3 vols. in

6, Taurinorum Augustae: Marietti, 1932-1939. I, 3. ed., 1938; II, pars 1, 3. ed., 1938; II, pars 2, 1932; II, pars 3, 1935; III, pars 1, 4. ed., 1939; III, pars 2, 4. ed., 1939.

Chelodi, Ioannes, *Ius de personis iuxta Codicem iuris canonici praemisso tractatu de principiis et fontibus I. C.*, 2. ed. a Sac. Ernesto Bertagnoli . . . recog. et aucta, Tridenti: Libr. edit. tridentinum, 1927.

———, *Ius poenale et ordo procedendi in iudiciis criminalibus iuxta C. I. C.*, 4. ed., recogn. et aucta a Vigilio Dalpiaz, Tridenti: A. Ardesi, 1935.

Chockier, Ioannes A., *Tractatus de commutationibus beneficiorum . . . et de beneficiorum ecclesiasticorum, et officiorum saecularium coadiutoriis*, auctore Nicolao Remocampio, Romae, 1700.

Cicognani, Amleto G., *Canon Law*, authorized English version by Joseph M. O'Hara and Francis Brennan, 2. rev. ed., Philadelphia: Dolphin Press, 1935.

Claeys-Bouuaert, F. et Simenon, G., *Manuale Juris Canonici ad usum seminariorum*, Vol. I and III, 3. ed.; vol. II, 1. ed.; 3 vols., Gandae et Leodii: apud auctores, 1930-1931.

Cocchi, Guidus, *Commentarium in Codicem iuris canonici ad usum scholarum*, 3.-5. ed., 8 vols., Taurinorum Augustae: Marietti, 1931-1940. Vol. 6: *Lib. III, De rebus*, part. IV-VI, 3. ed. recogn., 1933.

Connor, Maurice, *The Administrative Removal of Pastors*, The Catholic University of America Canon Law Studies, n. 104, Washington, D. C.: The Catholic University of America, 1937.

Coronata, Matthaeus Conte a, *Institutiones iuris canonici ad usum utriusque cleri et scholarum*, 5 vols., Taurini: Marietti, 1933-1939. Vols. I, II, 2. ed., auct. et emend., 1939; Vols. III-V, 1933-1936.

Creusen, Joseph, Garesché, Edward F., Ellis, Adam C., *Religious Men and Women in the Code*, 3. English ed. rev. and ed. to conform with the 5. French ed. by Adam C. Ellis, first transl. by Edward F. Garesché, Milwaukee: The Bruce Publishing Company, 1940.

Cuiacius, Jacobus, *Opera*, ad parisiensem fabrotianam editionem diligentissime exacta in tomos XIII distributa auctiora et emendatiora, 13 vols. in 12, Prati, 1836-1843.

Cutts, Edward L., *Parish Priests and their People in the Middle Ages in England*, publ. under the direction of the Tract Committee, London: Society for promoting Christian Knowledge; New York: E. & J. B. Young and Co., 1898.

D'Angelo, Sosio, *Tasse e pensioni nel Codice di diritto canonico*, 2. ed., corr. ed ampl., Torino: L. I. C. E., 1927.

D'Annibale, Ioseph, *Summula theologiae moralis*, 5. ed., 3 vols., Romae, 1908.

De Meester, Alphonsus, *Juris canonici et juris canonico-civilis compendium, olim a Revmo. de Brabandere et Rdo. adm. Dom. .Van Coillie editum, nova ed. ad normam Codicis juris canonici*, 4 vols. in 3, Brugis: Desclée de Brouwer et Si, 1921-1928.

Dirksen, Henricus, *Manuale latinitatis fontium juris civilis Romanorum*, Berolini, 1837.

Doheny, William J., *Practical Problems in Church Finance*, Milwaukee: The Bruce Publishing Company, 1941.

Du Cange, Carolus F., *Glossarium ad scriptores mediae et infimae latinitatis*, nova ed., 6 vols., Parisiis, 1733-1736.

Eichmann, Eduard, *Lehrbuch des Kirchenrechts*, 4. verb. u. verm. Aufl., 2 vols., Paderborn: Ferdinand Schöningh, 1934.

Engel, Ludovicus, *Collegium universi juris canonici*, Beneventi, Venetiis, 1760.

Fagnanus, Prosper, *Commentaria in quinque libros decretalium*, 4 vols., Romae, 1661.

Fanfani, Ludovicus I., *De iure parochorum ad normam Codicis iuris canonici*, 2. ed., rev. atque notabiliter aucta, Taurini-Romae: Marietti, 1936.

————, *De iure religiosorum ad normam Codicis iuris canonici*, 2. ed., rev. atque notabiliter aucta, Taurini-Romae: Marietti, 1925.

Ferraris, F. Lucius, *Bibliotheca canonica, iuridica, moralis, theologica necnon ascetica, polemica, rubricistica, historica*, 9 vols., Romae, 1885-1899. (Vol. 9: *Supplementum*, ed. by Ianuarius Bucceroni.)

Ferreris, Ioannes B., *Compendium theologiae moralis ad normam Codicis iuris canonici*, 14. ed., Barcinone: Eugenius Subirana, 1928.

————, *Institutiones canonicae iuxta novissimum Codicem Pii X a Benedicto XV promulgatum iuxtaque praescripta Hispanae disciplinae et Americae Latinae*, 2. ed., correctior et auctior, 2 vols., Barcinone: Eugenius Subirana, 1920.

Filsjean, l'Abbé,*Dictionnaire des conciles, suivi d'une collection des canons les plus remarquables, par* Alletz, nouvelle ed., Paris, 1829.

Findlay, Stephen W., *Canonical Norms Governing the Deposition and Degradation of Clerics*, The Catholic University of America Canon Law Studies, n. 130, Washington, D. C.: The Catholic University of America Press, 1941.

Frey, Wolfgang N., *The Act of Religious Profession*, The Catholic University of America Canon Law Studies, n. 63, Washington, D. C.: The Catholic University of America, 1931.

Garcias [Garcia], Nicholaus, *De beneficiis ecclesiasticis amplissimus et doctissimus tractatus, in quo continentur declarationes Cardinal. S. Congr. Concil. Trid. & decisiones Rotae*, 2 vols. in 1, Venetiis, 1618.

Genicot, E.,—Salsmans, I., *Institutiones theologiae moralis*, 13. ed. (6. post Codicem), 2 vols., Bruxelles: L'Edition universelle, S. A., 1936.

Gennari, Casimiro, *Quistioni canoniche di materie riguardanti specialmente i tempi nostri*, 2. ed., Roma, 1908.

Gigas, Hieronymus, *Tractatus de pensionibus ecclesiasticis*, Venetiis, [1542?].

Golden, Henry F., *Parochial Benefices in the New Code*, The Catholic University of America Canon Law Studies, n. 10, Washington: The Catholic University of America, 1921.

Gudelinus, Petrus, *Commentarium de Iure Novissimo libri sex*, Florentiae, 1839.

Guérin, P., *Les conciles généraux et particuliers*, 3 vols., Bar-le-Duc, 1868-1869.

Guilday, Peter, *A History of the Councils of Baltimore (1791-1884)*, New York: The Macmillan Company, 1932.

Hannan, Jerome D., *The Canon Law of Wills*, Philadelphia: The Dolphin Press, 1935.

Haring, Johann B., *Grundzuege des katholischen Kirchenrechtes*, 3. ed., 1 vol. in 2, Graz: Ulrich Moser, 1924.

Hefele, J. C., *Conciliengeschichte*, nach den Quellen bearbeitet, 2. ed., 9 vols., Freiburg im Breisgau, 1873-1890.

Hefele, J. C.,—Leclerq, H., *Histoire des conciles*, tr. de la XII. éd. allem., par M. Leclerq, 10 vols. in 19, Paris: Letouzey et Ané, 1907-1938.

Heston, Edward L., *The Alienation of Church Property in the United States*, The Catholic University of America Canon Law Studies, n. 132, Washington, D. C.: The Catholic University of America Press, 1941.

Hilling, Nikolaus, *Das Personenrecht des Codex Iuris Canonici*, Paderborn: Schöningh, 1924.

Hinschius, Paul, *Das Kirchenrecht der Katholiken und Protestanten in Deutschland*, 6 vols., Berlin, 1869-1897. Vols. I-IV, *System des katholischen Kirchenrechts*, 1869-1888.

Hohenlohe, Konstantin, *Grundlegende Fragen des Kirchenrechts*, Wien: Kommissionsverlag, 1931.

Iglesias, Antonius, *Brevis commentarius in Facultates, quae Sacra Congregatio de Propaganda Fide dare solet missionariis*, Taurini-Romae: Marietti, 1924.

Jaeger, Leo A., *The Administration of Vacant and Quasi-Vacant Dioceses in the United States*, The Catholic University of America Canon Law Studies, n. 81, Washington, D. C.: The Catholic University of America, 1932.

Kearney, Raymond A., *The Principles of Delegation*, The Catholic University of America Canon Law Studies, n. 55, Washington, D. C.: The Catholic University of America, 1929.

Kienitz, Erwin von, *Generalvikar und Offizial auf Grund des Codex Iuris Canonici*, Freiburg im Breisgau: Herder & Co., 1931.

La-Croix, Claudius, *Theologia moralis antehac breviter concinnata a R. P. Herrmanno Busenbaum,—postremo vero multis locupletata & studiosis proposita a R. P. Francisco Antonio Zacharia*, 3 vols., Venetiis, 1761.

Layman, Paulus, *Theologia moralis in V lib. partita*, Lutetiae Parisiorum, 1627.

Lesne, Emile, *Histoire de la propriété eccléstiastique en France*, Mémoires et travaux, publiés par des professeurs des facultés catholiques de Lille, Lille: R. Girard, 1910.

Leurenius, Petrus, *Forum beneficiale sive quaestiones et responsa canonica*, 4 vols. in 2, Venetiis, 1742.

Liguori, St. Alphonsus, *Theologia moralis, editio nova cum antiquis editionibus diligenter collata in singulis auctorum allegationibus recognita notisque criticis et commentariis illustrata cura et studio P. Leonardi Gaudé, C. SS. R.*, 4 vols., Romae: ex Typographia Vaticana, 1905-1912.

Lotterius, Melchior, *De re beneficiaria*, 2 vols. in 1, Patavii, 1700.

Luca, Ioannes B. de, *Theatrum Veritatis*, 16 vols. in 9, Coloniae Agrippinae, 1706.

Maiolus, Simon, *De irregularitatibus, et aliis canonicis impedimentis*, Romae, 1575.

Maroto, Philippus, *Institutiones iuris canonici ad normam novi Codicis*, 2 vols., Matriti, Romae, 1919.

Maupied, Franciscus, *Juris canonici universi . . . compendium*, 2 vols., Paris, 1863.

Mayr, Robertus, *Vocabularium Codicis Iustiniani*, Prague: Ceská Grafická unie, 1923.

McDonough, Thomas J., *Apostolic Administrators*, The Catholic University of America Canon Law Studies, n. 139, Washington, D. C.: The Catholic University of America Press, 1941.

Migne, Jacques Paul, *Patrologiae cursus completus, series latina*, 221 vols., Parisiis, 1844-1864.

Monacelli, *Formularium legale practicum fori ecclesiastici*, 3. ed., 4 vols. in 3, Romae, 1844.

Moroni, Gaetano, *Dizionario di erudizione storico-ecclesiastica*, 109 vols., Venezia, 1840-1879.

Navarrus [Azpilcueta], *Opera omnia*, 6 vols., Venetiis, 1618-1621.

Nicolaus de Tudeschis [Abbas Siculus, Modernus, Panormitanus], *Commentaria in Quinque Libros Decretalium*, 5 vols. in 7, Venetiis, 1588.

Noval, Ioseph, *De Processibus*, Romae, Augustae Taurinorum: Marietti [1932]. (Vol. II of *Commentarium Codicis iuris canonici, Lib. IV.*)

Ojetti, Benedictus, *Synopsis rerum moralium et iuris pontificii*, 3. ed., 4 vols., Romae, 1909-1914.

Ottaviani, Alaphridus, *Institutiones iuris publici ecclesiastici*, 2. ed. emend. et aucta, 2 vols., [Civitate Vaticana]: Typis Polyglottis Vaticanis, 1935-1936.

Panormitanus, cf.: Nicolaus de Tudeschis.

Phillips, Georg, *Kirchenrecht*, 8 vols., Regensburg, 1855-1889.

Pichler, Gui, *Jus canonicum secundum quinque decretalium titulos Gregorii IX*, 2 vols., Venetiis, 1741.

Pirhing, Ernricus, *Ius canonicum nova methodo explicatum*, ed. novissima, 4 vols., Dillingae, 1722.

Pistocchi, Marius, *De re beneficiali iuxta canones Codicis iuris canonici*, Taurini: Marietti, 1928.

Prompsault, J. H. R.,*Dictionnaire raisonné de droit et de jurisprudence en matière civile ecclésiastique*, 3 vols., Paris, 1849.

Prümmer, Dominicus M., *Manuale iuris canonici*, 6. ed. quam curavit Engelbertus M. Münch, Friburgi Brisgoviae: Herder & Co., 1933.

Pyrrhus, Corradus, *Praxis beneficiaria*, Venetiis, 1735.

Reiffenstuel, Anacletus, *Ius canonicum universum*, 5 vols. in 7, Parisiis, 1864-1882.

Richer, Thomas M., *Dictionarium juris civilis, canonici et feudalis nec non delectus legum feudalium*, Taurini, 1792.

Rittershaus [Ritterschutius], Conradus, *Expositio methodica Novellarum*, Florentiae, 1839.

Schaefer, Timotheus, *De religiosis ad normam Codicis iuris canonici*, 3. ed., aucta et emend., Roma, S. A. L. E. R., Rappresentante della casa editrice Herder [1940].

————, *Die Kirchenämter nach dem Codex Iuris Canonici, II: Pfarrer und Pfarrvikare*, 1. u. 2. Aufl., Münster i. W.: Aschendorff, 1922.

Scherer, Rudolf Ritter von, *Handbuch des Kirchenrechts*, 2 vols., Graz, 1886-1898.

Schmalzgrueber, Franciscus, *Jus ecclesiasticum universum*, 5 vols. in 12, Romae, 1843-1845.

Schneider, Philip, *Die Entwicklung der bischöflichen Domkapitel bis zum vierzehnten Jahrhundert*, Mainz, 1882.

Sebastianelli, Guilelmus, *Praelectiones juris canonici quas in scholis pontificii seminarii romani tradebat . . . de rebus*, 1. ed., Roma, 1905.

Shea, John G., *A History of the Catholic Church within the Limits of the United States from the first attempted colonization to the present time*, 4 vols., New York, 1886-1892.

Sherman, Charles P., *Roman Law in the Modern World*, 2. ed., 3 vols., New York: Baker, Voorhis & Co., 1922-1924.

Shumaker, Walter A. and Longsdorf, George F., *The Cyclopedic Law Dictionary*, 2. ed., by James C. Cahill, Chicago: Callaghan and Company, 1922.

Sipos, Stephanus, *Enchiridion iuris canonici*, Pécs, "Haladás R. T.," 1926.

Stephanus, Matthias, *Commentarius in Novellas Justiniani imperatoris*, ed. novissima, Florentiae, 1843.

Stutz, Ulrich, *Geschichte des kirchlichen Benefizialwesens von seinen Anfängen bis auf die Zeit Alexanders III*, Berlin, 1895.

Suarez, Emmanuel, *De remotione parochorum aliisque processibus tertiae partis lib. IV Cod. iur. can.*, Romae: Angelicum, 1931.

Suarez, Franciscus, *Opera omnia*, ed. nova a Carolo Berton, 30 vols., Parisiis, 1856-1878.

Thomassinus, Ludovicus, *Vetus et nova Ecclesiae disciplina circa beneficia et beneficiarios*, 10 vols., Magontiaci, 1787.

Tondutus, Petrus F., *Tractatus de pensionibus ecclesiasticis ad stylum Curiae romanae et ad praxim tribunalium Galliae accommodatus*, Lugduni, 1661.

Van Hove, A., *Commentarium Lovaniense*, Vol. I, tom. 1, *Prolegomena*, Mechlinae, Romae: A. Dessain, 1928.

Vecchiotti, Septimius, *Institutiones canonicae ex operibus Ioannis Card. Soglia excerptae*. 4 vols. in 2, Taurini, 1867-1868.

Ventriglia, Ioannes B., *Praxis rerum notabilium praesertim fori ecclesiastici*, Venetiis, 1694.

Vermeersch, A.,—Creusen, J., *Epitome iuris canonici cum commentariis ad scholas et ad usum privatum*, 3 vols., Mechliniae-Romae: H. Dessain, Vol. I, 6. ed., 1937, Vol. II, 5. ed., 1934, Vol. III, 5. ed., 1936.

Vito, Pasquale, *Questioni canoniche di materie riguardanti i nostri tempi secondo il Codice di diritto canonico*, 4 vols., Napoli: Raffaele Picone, 1926-1930.

Vocabularium Iurisprudentiae Romanae, 5 vols., Berlin: Walter de Gruyter, 1894-1936.

Vromant, G., *De bonis Ecclesiae temporalibus, ad usum praesertim missionariorum et religiosorum*, Louvain: Editions du Museum Lessianum, 1927.

————, *Facultates Apostolicae quas Sacra Congregatio de Propaganda Fide delegare solet Ordinariis Missionum*, Supplementum ad Commentaria in ,Formulam tertiam, Louvain: Editions du Museum Lessianum, 1930.

Wernz, Franciscus, *Ius decretalium*, 6 vols., Romae et Prati, 1898-1905.

Wernz, Franciscus—Vidal, Petrus, *Ius canonicum*, 7 vols. in 8, Romae: Universitas Gregoriana, 1927-1938. Vols. II, V, 2. ed., 1928.

Winslow, Francis J., *Vicars and Prefects Apostolic*, Maryknoll, N. Y.: Catholic Foreign Mission Society of America, Inc., c1924.

Woywod, Stanislaus, *A Practical Commentary on the Code of Canon Law*, 4. rev. ed., 2 vols., New York: Joseph F. Wagner, 1932.

Note: Mention should be made of Fedele, Pio, *Delle pensioni ecclesiastiche*, Milano: Giuffrè, 1937, which, however was unavailable due to the present international situation.

Articles

Borovy, Clemens, "Die Prager Diöcesan-Synode vom Jahre 1873"—*AKKR*, XXXI, (1873), 198-208.

Claeys-Bouuaert, F., "Du droit de l'évêque d'imposer des taxes à son clergé à propos d'une décision récente"—*NRT*, XLVIII (1921), 195-200; 225-232.

Coronata, Matteo da, "Pensione e religiosi"—*Perfice Munus!* VIII (1933), 211-212.

D'Angelo, Sosio, "De pensione super beneficio paroeciali"—*Apollinaris*, II (1929), 320-322.

————, "De 'taxatione' in pensionibus definiendis"—*Apollinaris*, II (1929), 215-218.

Doheny, William J., "The Removal of Irremovable Pastors"—*AER*, XCIII (1935), 490-503.

Ehses, Stephanus, "Kirchliche Reformarbeiten unter Papst Paul III,"—*Römische Quartalschrift*, XV (1901), 153-174.

Goyeneche, S., "Annotationes in S. C. de Rel. 16 mar. 1922"—*CpR*, IV (1923), 34-39.

————, "Consultationes: 26a: Praemium bellicum quod redeuntibus e militia nunc obvenit, religiosi simpliciter professi acquirunt sibi ad normam can. 580 § 1, vel potius religioni ad normam eiusdem can. 580 § 2"—*CpR*, I (1920), 340-343.

Hilling, Nikolaus, "Die Iurisdiktion des Generalvikars"—*AKKR*, CIV (1924), 199-205.

Jansen, F. J., "Church Support"—*The Homiletic and Pastoral Review*, XXVIII (1927-1928), 266-271.

Kinane, J., "The Resignation of a Parish with the Reservation of a Pension for the Lifetime of the Pensioner"—*IER*, V ser., XXIX (Jan.-June 1927), 632-634.

Kroll, Anselm, "The Support of Sick, Aged, and Delinquent Clergy"—*American Ecclesiastical Review*, XXIII (1910), 458-474.

Lardone, Giovanni, "Pensione perpetua o temporanea?"—*Perfice Munus!* VIII (1933), 300.

Larraona, Arcadius, "De paupertate simplici"—*CpR*, I (1920), 333-340.

Lesne, Emile, "Les diverses acceptions du terme 'beneficium' du VIIIe au XIe s."—*Nouvelle revue historique de droit français et étranger*, 4e sér., t. III (1924), 5-56.

Maroto, Philippus, "De iuribus Capituli Cathedralis in casu sedis impeditae"—*Apollinaris*, II (1929), 210-215.

Stutz, Ulrich, "Der Geist des Codex iuris canonici"—*Kirchenrechtliche Abhandlungen*, XCII-XCIII (1918).

Suarez, Emmanuel, "De pensionibus beneficiis paroecialibus imponendis"—*Angelicum*, VI (1929), 217-228.

Toso, Albertus, "Summa de Officio ac Potestate Vicarii Generalis"—*Jus Pontificium*, VII (1927), 143-144.

Vermeersch, Arthurus, "Commentaria de Formulis Facultatum quas S. Congr. de Propaganda Fide concedere solet"—*Periodica*, XI (1922), (33)-(144).

Periodicals

Analecta Ecclesiastica seu Romana Collectanea de disciplinis speculativis et practicis circa theologiam, ius canonicum, administrationem in foro contentioso et gratioso, sacram liturgiam, historiam, etc., Romae, 1893-1911.

Angelicum, Romae, 1924-

Apollinaris, Romae, 1928-

Archiv für katholisches Kirchenrecht, Innsbruck, 1857-1861; Mainz, 1862-

Commentarium pro Religiosis (later [1935] *Commentarium pro Religiosis et Missionariis)*, Romae, 1920-

Ecclesiastical Review, The (originally *The American Ecclesiastical Review)*, Philadelphia, 1889-

Homiletic and Pastoral Review, The, New York, 1900-
Irish Ecclesiastical Record, Dublin, 1864-
Jurist, The, Washington, D. C., 1941-
Jus Pontificium, Romae, 1921-
Kirchenrechtliche Abhandlungen, Stuttgart, 1902-
Monitore ecclesiastico, Il, Romae, 1876-
Nouvelle Revue Théologique, Tournai, 1869-
Perfice Munus! Torino, 1926-
Periodica de re morali, canonica, liturgica, Brugis et Romae, 1905- [*De religiosis institutis et personis supplementa et monumenta*, I-VIII (1905-1919); *Periodica de re canonica et morali*, IX-XV (1920-1927)].
Römische Quartalschrift für christliche Altertumskunde und für Kirchengeschichte, Freiburg, Rom, 1886-

Abbreviations

AAS—*Acta Apostolicae Sedis.*
AER—*American Ecclesiastical Review.*
AKKR—*Archiv für katholisches Kirchenrecht.*
ASS—*Acta Sanctae Sedis.*
Bull. Rom. cont.—*Bullarii Romani continuatio.*
Bull. Rom. Taur.—*Bullarum diplomatum et privilegiorum sanctorum Romanorum Pontificum taurinensis editio.*
C.—Codex Iustiniani.
C. P. I.—Commissio Pontificia ad Codicis Canones authentice Interpretandos.
CpR—*Commentarium pro Religiosis.*
CpRM—*Commentarium pro Religiosis et Missionariis.*
C. Th.—Codex Theodosianus.
D.—Digesta (Pandecta) Iustiniani.
Fontes—*Codicis Iuris Canonici Fontes cura . . . Gasparri, ed.*
I.—Institutiones Iustiniani.
JE—Jaffé, *Regista Pontificum*, 2. ed., pars II, A.D. 590-882, ed. P. Ewald.
JK—Jaffé, *Regista Pontificum*, 2. ed., pars I, Ab condita Ecclesia ad annum 590, ed. F. Kaltenbrunner.
JL—Jaffé, *Regista Pontificum*, 2. ed., pars III, A. D. 882-1198, ed. S. Loewenfeld.
Magn. Bull. Rom.—*Magnum Bullarium Romanum.*
MGH—*Monumenta Germaniae Historica.*
MPL—Migne, *Patrologiae . . . series latina.*
N.—Novellae Iustiniani.
NRT—*Nouvelle Revue Théologique.*
S. R. R., *Recent.*—Farinacius, ed., *Sacrae Romanae Rotae Decisiones recentiores.*
Thesaurus—*Thesaurus resolutionum S. Congregationis Concilii.*

BIOGRAPHICAL NOTE

Sylvester Francis Gass was born on December 31, 1911, in Milwaukee, Wisconsin. He received his elementary training at Saint Anne parish school of that city. In 1927 he entered the Seminary of Saint Francis de Sales, Saint Francis, Wisconsin, where he received the degrees of Bachelor of Arts in 1936 and Master of Arts in 1939. He was ordained to the priesthood on June 3, 1939. In the autumn of that year he was assigned by his Ordinary to pursue a course of studies in the School of Canon Law at the Catholic University of America, where he received the degree of the Baccalaureate in Canon Law in June, 1940, and the degree of the Licentiate in Canon Law in June, 1941.

INDEX

(Superior figures indicate footnotes)

Abbey, pension on, 29, 38, 45
Abbot,
  as pensioner, 29, 30, 31, 36
  power of, to reserve pensions, 25, 80
  nullius, power of, to reserve pensions, 80, 81
Administrator Apostolic,
  power of, to reserve pensions, 80, 81, 88
  temporary, power of, to reserve pensions, 84
Administrator, diocesan, power of, to reserve pensions, 83
Agde, Council of, 10 [7]
Agapetus, 15
Age, minimum, required of pensioner, 48, 100
Aix, Synod of, 41
Alienation,
  of benefice, pension is not, 132 and [56]
  of pension, 36, 158-160
Alexander II, 11 [12], 19
Alexander III, 26, 34, 36
Alexander VII, 73
Alexander VIII, 67
Amount of pension,
  as fixed amount, 36, 61, 145-147, 173
  based on mean annual income of benefice, 38, 39, 145-147
  established in money or natural fruits, 147
  not to impoverish incumbent, 34, 35, 38, 54, 56, 60-61, 139, 140, 153
  on cathedral, 61
  on non-parochial benefice, 139-140
  on parochial benefice, 61, 140
  on percentage basis, 36, 61, 145-147, 173
Assistant, parochial, as pensioner, 106-108, 123, 173

Baltimore, I Prov. Council of, 99
Baltimore, III Plen. Council of, 108-110, 133 [62], 136
Benedict XIII, 46
Benedict XIV, 56, 65, 70
Benedict XV, 89, 152
Benefice,
  capitular, pension on, 94-95
  consistorial, pension on, 45, 80, 92
  devolved to Holy See, pension on, 92-93
  inferior in chapter, pension on, 46, 95
  non-parochial, pension on, 95
  obligations of pensioner toward, 66, 151-152
  occupied, reserving pension on, 123, 173
  origin of, 10, 18, 19 [24]
  parochial, pension on, 94, 95, 100, 102, 173
  reserved, pension on, 43, 80, 93
  vacant,
    pension on, 122-123, 173
    procurator for, 59, 123, 134-135
Benefices, parochial in U. S., iii, 108, 111
Beneficiary,
  consent of, 58-59, 133-134
  death of, 37, 171
  not to be impoverished by pension, 33-35, 38, 40, 54, 56, 60-61, 68, 139, 140, 153

obligations of, toward pensioner, 62, 150
Bishop,
residential,
as pensioner, 13, 15, 21, 30, 38, 48-49, 73, 100
power of, to reserve pensions, 21, 25, 26, 27, 41, 80, 81
titular,
as pensioner, 29, 49, 101
power of, to reserve pensions, 80
Boniface VIII, 6, 39 [72]
Bordeaux, Council of, 52 [86], 64

Camera Ap., 67
Canon, as pensioner, 49
Canonry, pension on, 45, 46, 95
Cardinal,
as pensioner, 49, 67, 73, 100, 152-153, 163
power of, to reserve pensions, 80, 91
Cathedral, pension on, 45, 54-55
Cause for reserving pension, 22, 35, 44, 59-60, 124-130
Celestine III, 31 [35], 34 [47]
Censure,
acquisition of pensions, 53, 119
privation of pensions, 77, 169
Cessation of poverty of pensioner, 71, 162
Chalcedon, Council of, 13, 21 [28]
Change of state,
acquisition of pensions, 53, 120
termination of pensions, 23, 39, 74, 75, 167
Chaplain, as pensioner, 30
Chaplaincy, pension on, 96, 97
Chapter,
abbatial, power of, to reserve pensions, 80
cathedral,
consent of, 58, 132-133
power of, to reserve pensions, 80, 84, 88
prelatial, power of, to reserve pensions, 80
proper, consent of, 58, 133
Civil law and pensions, 147-148
Clement III, 31
Clement IV, 24
Clement V, 24, 25, 29, 35, 39 [72]
Clement VII, 72
Clement VIII, 49
Clement XI, 67
Clerical aid societies, v, 108-109
Cleric,
as pensioner, 16-17, 22, 48, 100
attempted marriage in major orders, 168
delegated, *sede impedita*, power of, to reserve pensions, 85, 88
laicized, 23, 39, 53, 120, 167
married, as pensioner, 53, 74, 168
not incumbent, 33
not proper subject of bishop, 33
subordinate, power of, to reserve pensions, 27, 80
Cognac, Council of, 29 [23], 35, 39 [68]
Comm. Pontif. Interpr., 5 [29], 93 [7], 94 [13], 127, 133 [57], 137 [81], 157 [3]
Conclavists as pensioners, 49, 67, 152
Consent,
of cathedral chapter, 58, 132-133
of parochial consultors, 135-136
of parochial examiners, 135-136
of pastor, 58-59, 133-135
of patron, 57-58, 135
of proper chapter, 133
Consistory, S. Cong. of, reservation of pensions, 80, 92, 126 and [26]
Consultors,
diocesan, power of, to reserve pensions, 80, 84, 88
parochial, 135-136
Council, S. C., 7, 8, 40 [1, 3], 41 [13], 42,

43, 44, 46 [47], 47 and [49-53], 48, 51 and [78], 53, 57, 58 [118], 59 [127], 61, 63 [149], 65 [160, 163], 66 [165-166, 168], 67 [181], 68 [186-187], 69 [190], 74 [222, 225, 227], 76, 98 [2], 99 [4], 121, 122 [4], 125-126, 133 [62], 147 [126], 149 [135], 153 [23-24], 155 [29], 157 [3], 163
Crime,
  acquisition of pensions, 22, 53, 118
  termination of pensions, 39, 76, 169, 171

Dapifers as pensioners, 49, 67
Datary Apostolic, 46, 68, 73 [216], 80, 94 and [2], 152, 153, 163
Death,
  of beneficiary, 37, 171
  of pensioner, 23, 37, 171
Decree of reservation of pension, 136
Default of benefice, 160
Definition of pension,
  etymological, 1
  real, 3
Degradation, 120, 170
Deposition, 120, 170
Dignity, pension on, 45, 46, 93
Diocesan administrator, power of, to reserve pensions, 83
Dismemberment, pension a form of, 130-132
Division of pensions, 3-5

Ephesus, Council of, 14[2]
Ep. et Reg., S. C. de, 69 [190], 147 [126], 153 [23, 24], 155 [29], 159, 160 [17], 163
Examiners, parochial, 135-136
Exchange of benefice with reservation of pension, 46, 60 and [102], 103-104, 124
Excommunication,
  acquisition of pensions, 53, 119
  privation of pensions, 77, 169
Expenses, deductible, 142-143
Expiration of term of pension, 22, 23, 37-38, 162

Freedom of superior in reserving pensions, 28, 125-130
Fund, diocesan, for disabled priests, v, 109-110

Garb, clerical, obligation of pensioner, 62, 64-65, 75, 155
Gregory I, 11 [11], 15, 17, 22, 23
Gregory VII, 11 [11], 19, 20, 22
Gregory IX, 36
Gregory XIII, 7, 50, 56, 76
Gregory XV, 49

Illegitimacy and acquisition of pensions, 52, 114
Income,
  diminished, of benefice, 38, 68-69, 153-154, 155
  of parish, 140-142
  superfluous, of pension, 65, 155-156
  uncertain, 143-144
Increase of pension, 35, 153-154
Infamy
  of fact and acquisition of pensions, 119
  of law and acquisition of pensions, 114, 119
Innocent III, 6, 26, 36 and [60], 147
Innocent IV, 28, 30, 33, 38, 39 [72]
Innocent XI, 67
Innocent XII, 46
Innocent XIII, 67
Interdict, personal, and acquisition of pensions, 119
Interested parties, 77, 132
Irregularity, canonical,
  acquisition of pensions, 52-53, 112-114, 173
  retention of pensions, 76, 172, 173

John XXII, 39 [72]

Judge, power of, to reserve pensions, 26, 35, 44, 80 [6]
Julius II, 72, 99

Knights as pensioners, 51-52, 75-76

Laicized cleric, 23, 39, 53, 120, 167
Lateran, III Council of, 24, 25, 29
Lateran, IV Council of, 6, 34, 36, 60
Lateran, V Council of, 63
Laymen as pensioners, 3-4, 47, 98-99
Leo X, 63
Leo XIII, 68, 73, 152, 153, 163
Legates, power of, to reserve pensions, 44, 80
Loan of pension, 37, 70, 158

Mâcon, Council of, 15, 21
Manse, episcopal, pension on, 29, 50, 101
Meaux, Council of, 23, 39 [69]
Merida, Council of, 18
Military service, 23, 39, 53, 75, 168
Mission territory, 81-82, 88, 95, 111, 117
  just cause for pension, 130
  mission, pension on, 95-96
Monastery, pension on, 30, 31, 33
Monetary value, change in, 36, 154
Moral person as pensioner, 47, 71, 98
Mutual aid societies, clerical, v, 108-109

"*Nisi essent*"—(c. 21, X, *de praebendis et dignitatibus*, III, 5), 26, 35, 42, 43, 60 [133], 147
Nuntios as pensioners, 73

Obligations,
  of beneficiary toward pensioner, 62, 150
  of pensioner, 22, 62, 63, 151-152, 155
Office, obligation of pensioner,
  divine, 63-64
  little, of B.V.M., 64, 155
Off., S. C. S., 168
Officialis, power of, to reserve pensions, 80
Orleans, I Council of, 9 [9]
Orleans, III Council of, 16
Oxford, Council of, 37

Paris, Council of, 26
Parish,
  pension for, 47, 98
  pension on, 45, 46, 47, 54-55, 94, 95, 100, 102
Parish priest as pensioner, 17, 31-32, 47, 50, 105-106
Parochial consultors, consent of, 135-136
Parochial examiners, consent of, 135-136
Parochial vicar as pensioner, 106-108, 123, 173
Parties, interested, in reservation of pension, 57, 132
Pastor,
  as pensioner, 105-106, 173
  consent of, 58-59, 133-135
Patron,
  consent of, 57-58, 135
  lay, as pensioner, 99
Paul II, 37
Paul III, 54
Paul V, 49
Payment of pension,
  distribution, 30, 32, 33, 36, 148-149
  due after right of pension ceases, 63, 150
  in advance, 64, 70
  right of pensioner to, 62, 150
Penalties,
  medicinal,
    acquisition of pensions, 53, 119
    privation of pensions, 77, 169
  vindicative,

acquisition of pensions, 119-120
privation of pensions, 170
Pension,
absolutely perpetual, 5, 8, 25, 41, 46, 98, 157
advance payment of, 64, 70
alienation of, 36, 158-160
decree of reservation, 136
definition of,
etymological, 1
real, 3
earliest record, 13, 14 [2]
expiration of term, 22, 23, 37-38, 162
form of dismemberment, 130-132
for parish, 47, 98
increase of, 35, 153-154
in Roman law, iv, 1
loan of, 37, 70, 158
not a benefice, 5, 97, 113
not alienation of benefice, 132 and [56]
not to impoverish incumbent, 33-35, 38, 40, 54, 56, 60-61, 68, 139, 140, 153
on benefice, v, 3, 18, 28, 33, 92
on canonry, 45, 46, 95
on chaplaincy, 96, 97
on dignity, 45, 46, 93
on mission, 95-96
on other ecclesiastical revenues, 3, 13-18, 21, 28, 149 [135]
on parochial vicarship, 29, 96, 97, 107-108, 123
on quasi-parish, 95-96, 111-112
prescription of, 70, 160
reduction of, 35, 37-38, 68-69, 153-154, 155
relatively perpetual, 5, 41-43, 140, 150, 157, 173
resignation of, 163
right to, 128-130, 173
sale of, 36, 70, 158-159
superfluous income of, 65, 155-156
temporary, 5, 40, 150
termination of, 37, 38, 68, 157, 173
title of ordination, 4, 129, 170
transfer of, 37, 66-68, 72, 152, 173
upon resignation of benefice, 46, 50-51, 56-57, 60, 70, 125-130, 173
Pensioner,
death of, 23, 37, 171
definitely determined, 48-49, 83
minimum age, required of, 48, 100
obligations of, 22, 62, 63, 151-152, 155
promotion of, 71-73, 163
Pensions, divisions of, 3-5
Personal interdict, 119
Pius V, 48, 56, 63, 70
Pius VI, 67
Pius VII, 47, 50, 66
Pius X, 49, 50, 94 [12], 111 [79], 152
Pius XI, 4 [20], 99 [3], 152
Pius XII, 153
Placet, royal, 148
Popes, power of, to reserve pensions, 20, 24, 40, 79, 98
Poverty of pensioner, cessation of, 71, 162
Prebend, pension on, 45
Prefect apostolic, power of, to reserve pensions, 80, 81
Prelate, power of, to reserve pensions,
not a bishop, 44, 80
nullius, 80, 81
Prescription of pension, 70, 160
Priory, pension on, 29
Procurator for vacant benefice, 59, 123, 134-135
Profession, religious,
acquisition of pensions, 115-118, 173

retention of pensions, 73, 164, 166, 173
Promotion of pensioner, 71-73, 163
Propagation of the Faith, S. Cong. for the, 81, 89[59], 92, 95, 99[8], 108, 111, 112, 163
Pro-prefect apostolic, power of, to reserve pensions, 89, 90
Pro-vicar apostolic, power of, to reserve pensions, 89, 90
Quasi-parish, pension on, 95-96, 111-112
Quasi religious as pensioners, 118

Rector of mission as pensioner, 111-112
Reduction of pension, 35, 37-38, 68-69, 153-154, 155
Rel., S. C. de, 167
Religious, as pensioners, 51, 115-116, 173
assistants of mission churches, 117
parochial vicars, 116-117
rectors of mission churches, 117
Resignation,
of benefice with reservation of pension, 46, 50-51, 56-57, 60, 70, 125-130, 173
of pension, 163
Right of pensioner to payment, 62, 150
Roman law and pensions, iv, 1
Rota, S. R., 41[13], 47[54-55], 48[59-60], 51 and[81], 52[86, 87], 55[100-102], 58, 60[134], 61[137, 141, 142], 62[143, 145, 146], 63[149-151], 69 and[193], 70[198], 71 and[200-203], 72[210-212], 73[218], 74[222, 226], 75[233], 76[239], 80[6], 147[126], 155[29]
Rouen, Synod of, 27, 28

Sacr., S. C. de, 167, 168
Sale of pension, 36, 70, 158-159
Saumur, Council of, 25, 29[23, 24], 34
Seminary,
pension for, 47
pension on, 47, 50
Simony in pensions, 34, 48-49, 83, 126, 128, 158
Sixtus V, 48, 62, 64, 72[207], 75
State, change of,
acquisition of pensions, 53, 120
retention of pensions, 23, 39, 74, 75, 167
Superfluous income of pension, 65, 155-156
Superiors, religious, power of, to reserve pensions, 27, 44, 80
Suspension,
acquisition of pensions, 106, 119
termination of pensions, 169
Symmachus, 18

Taxes,
civil, and pensioner, 66, 155
pensioner exempt from certain, 65-66, 151
Termination of pension, 23, 37, 38, 68, 157
Term of pension, expiration of, 22, 23, 37-38, 162
Time for reserving pension, 121-123
Tonsure, wearing of, obligation of pensioner, 64-65, 75, 153
Tours, Council of, 36
Transfer of pension, 37, 66-68, 72, 152
Trent, Council of, 45[43], 52, 54-55, 61, 65, 69, 74, 76, 109, 140

Urban VIII, 49, 61[142], 66, 67, 72[207]

Vicar,
apostolic, power of, to reserve pensions, 80, 81
capitular, power of, to reserve pensions, 83, 86
delegate, power of, to reserve pensions, 89-90
general, power of, to reserve pen-

sions, 80, 82, 84-88, 173
of bishop *in pontificalibus*, as pensioner, 29
of bishop, power of, to reserve pensions, 44
of mission, as pensioner, 111
parochial, as pensioner, 106-108, 123, 173
Vicarship, parochial, pension on, 29, 96, 97, 107-108, 123
Vienne, Council of, 24, 25, 29, 35, 39[72]
Vindicative penalties, 119-120, 170
Westminster, Council of, 27

CANON LAW STUDIES

1. Freriks, Rev. Celestine A., C.PP.S., J.C.D., Religious Congregations in Their External Relations, 121 pp., 1916.
2. Galliher, Rev. Daniel M., O.P., J.C.D., Canonical Elections, 117 pp., 1917.
3. Borkowski, Rev. Aurelius L., O.F.M., J.C.D., De Confraternitatibus Ecclesiasticis, 136 pp., 1918.
4. Castillo, Rev. Cayo, J.C.D., Disertacion Historico-Canonica sobre la Potestad del Cabildo en Sede Vacante o Impedida del Vicario Capitular, 99 pp., 1919 (1918).
5. Kubelbeck, Rev. William J., S.T.B., J.C.D., The Sacred Pentitentiaria and Its Relations to Faculties of Ordinaries and Priests, 129 pp., 1918.
6. Petrovits, Rev. Joseph J.C., S.T.D., J.C.D., The New Church Law On Matrimony, X-461 pp., 1919.
7. Hickey, Rev. John J., S.T.B., J.C.D., Irregularities and Simple Impediments in the New Code of Canon Law, 100 pp., 1920.
8. Klekotka, Rev. Peter J., S.T.B., J.C.D., Diocesan Consultors, 179 pp., 1920.
9. Wanenmacher, Rev. Francis, J.C.D., The Evidence in Ecclesiastical Procedure Affecting the Marriage Bond, 1920 (Printed 1935).
10. Golden, Rev. Henry Francis, J.C.D., Parochial Benefices in the New Code, IV-119 pp., 1921 (Printed 1925).
11. Koudelka, Rev. Charles J., J.C.D., Pastors, Their Rights and Duties According to the New Code of Canon Law, 211 pp., 1921.
12. Melo, Rev. Antonius, O.F.M., J.C.D., De Exemptione Regularium, X-188 pp., 1921.
13. Schaaf, Rev. Valentine Theodore, O.F.M., S.T.B., J.C.D., The Cloister, X-180 pp., 1921.
14. Burke, Rev. Thomas Joseph, S.T.D., J.C.D., Competence in Ecclesiastical Tribunals, IV-117 pp., 1922.
15. Leech, Rev. George Leo, J.C.D., A Comparative Study of the Constitution, "Apostolicae Sedis" and the "Codex Juris Canonici," 179 pp., 1922.
16. Motry, Rev. Hubert Louis, S.T.D., J.C.D., Diocesan Faculties According to the Code of Canon Law, II-167 pp., 1922.
17. Murphy, Rev. George Lawrence, J.C.D., Delinquencies and Penalties in the Administration and Reception of the Sacraments, IV-121 pp., 1923.
18. O'Reilly, Rev. John Anthony, S.T.B., J.C.D., Ecclesiastical Sepulture in the New Code of Canon Law, II-129 pp., 1923.

19. Michalicka, Rev. Wenceslas Cyrill, O.S.B., J.C.D., Judicial Procedure in Dismissal of Clerical Exempt Religious, 107 pp., 1923.
20. Dargin, Rev. Edward Vincent, S.T.B., J.C.D., Reserved Cases According to the Code of Canon Law, IV-103, pp., 1924.
21. Godfrey, Rev. John A., S.T.B., J.C.D., The Right of Patronage According to the Code of Canon Law, 153 pp., 1924.
22. Hagedorn, Rev. Francis Edward, J.C.D., General Legislation on Indulgences, II-154 pp., 1924.
23. King, Rev. James Ignatius, J.C.D., The Administration of the Sacraments to Dying Non-Catholics, V-141 pp., 1924.
24. Winslow, Rev. Francis Joseph, A.F.M., J.C.D., Vicars and Prefects Apostolic, IV-149 pp., 1924.
25. Correa, Rev. Jose Servelion, S.T.L., J.C.D., La Potestad Legislativa de la Iglesia Catolica, IV-127 pp., 1925.
26. Dugan, Rev. Henry Francis, A.M., J.C.D., The Judiciary Department of the Diocesan Curia, 87 pp., 1925.
27. Keller, Rev. Charles Frederick, S.T.B., J.C.D., Mass Stipends, 167 pp., 1925.
28. Paschang, Rev. John Linus, J.C.D., The Sacramentals According to the Code of Canon Law, 129 pp., 1925.
29. Pointek, Rev. Cyrillus, O.F.M., S.T.B., J.C.D., De Indulto Exclaustrationis necnon Saecularizationis, XIII-289 pp., 1925.
30. Kearney, Rev. Richard Joseph, S.T.B., J.C.D., Sponsors at Baptism According to the Code of Canon Law, IV-127 pp., 1925.
31. Bartlett, Rev. Chester Joseph, A.M., LL.B., J.C.D., The Tenure of Parochial Property in the United States of America, V-108 pp., 1926.
32. Kilker, Rev. Adrian Jerome, J.C.D., Extreme Unction, V-425 pp., 1926.
33. McCormick, Rev. Robert Emmett, J.C.D., Confessors of Religious, VIII-266 pp., 1926.
34. Miller, Rev. Newton Thomas, J.C.D., Founded Masses According to the Code of Canon Law, VII-93 pp., 1926.
35. Roelker, Rev. Edward G., S.T.D., J.C.D., Principles of Privilege According to the Code of Canon Law, XI-166 pp., 1926.
36. Bakalarczyk, Rev. Richardus, M.I.C., J.U.D., De Novitiatu, VIII-208 pp., 1927.
37. Pizzuti, Rev. Lawrence, O.F.M., J.U.L., De Parochis Religiosis, 1927. (Not printed).
38. Bliley, Rev. Nicholas Martin, O.S.B., J.C.D., Altars According to the Code of Canon Law, XIX-132 pp., 1927.
39. Brown, Mr. Brendan Francis, A.B. LL.M., J.U.D., The Canonical Juristic Personality with Special Reference to Its Status in the United States of America, V-212 pp., 1927.

40. Cavanaugh, Rev. William Thomas, C.P., J.U.D., The Reservation of the Blessed Sacrament, VIII-101 pp., 1927.
41. Doheny, Rev. William J., C.S.C., A.B., J.U.D., Church Property: Modes of Acquisition, X-118 pp., 1927.
42. Feldhaus, Rev. Aloysius H., C.PP.S., J.C.D., Oratories, IX-141 pp., 1927.
43. Kelly, Rev. James Patrick, A.B., J.C.D., The Jurisdiction of the Simple Confessor, X-208 pp., 1927.
44. Neuberger, Rev. Nicholas J., J.C.D., Canon 6 or the Relation of the Codex Juris Canonici to the Preceding Legislation, V-95 pp., 1927.
45. O'Keefe, Rev. Gerald Michael, J.C.D., Matrimonial Dispensations, Powers of Bishops, Priests and Confessors, VIII-232 pp., 1927.
46. Quigley, Rev. Joseph A.M., A.B., J.C.B., Condemned Societies, 139 pp., 1927.
47. Zaplotnik, Rev. Johannes Leo, J.C.D., De Vicariis Foraneis, X-142 pp., 1927.
48. Duskie, Rev. John Aloysius, A.B., J.C.D., The Canonical Status of the Orientals in the United States, VIII-196 pp., 1928.
49. Hyland, Rev. Francis Edward, J.C.D., Excommunication, Its Nature, Historical Development and Effects, VIII-181 pp., 1928.
50. Reinmann, Rev. Gerald Joseph, O.M.C., J.C.D., The Third Order Secular of Saint Francis, 201 pp., 1928.
51. Schenk, Rev. Francis J., J.C.D., The Matrimonial Impediments of Mixed Religion and Disparity of Cult, XVI-318 pp., 1929.
52. Coady, Rev. John Joseph, S.T.D., J.U.D., A.M., The Appointment of Pastors, VIII-150 pp., 1929.
53. Kay, Rev. Thomas Henry, J.C.D., Competence in Matrimonial Procedure, VIII-164 pp., 1929.
54. Turner, Rev. Sidney Joseph, C.P., J.U.D., The Vow of Poverty, XLIX-217 pp., 1929.
55. Kearney, Rev. Raymond, A., A.B., S.T.D., J.C.D., The Principles, of Delegation, VII-149 pp., 1929.
56. Conran, Rev. Edward James, A.B., J.C.D., The Interdict, V-163 pp., 1930.
57. O'Neil, Rev. William H., J.C.D., Papal Rescripts of Favor, VII-218 pp., 1930.
58. Bastnagel, Rev. Clement Vincent, J.U.D., The Appointment of Parochial Adjutants and Assistants, XV-257 pp., 1930.
59. Ferry, Rev. William A., A.B., J.C.D., Stole Fees, V-135 pp., 1930.
60. Costello, Rev. John Michael, A.B., J.C.D., Domicile and Quasi-domicile, VII-201 pp., 1930.
61. Kremer, Rev. Michael Nicholas, A.B., S.T.B., J.C.D., Church Support in the United States, VI-1930.

62. Angulo, Rev. Luis, C.M., J.C.D., Legislation de la Iglesia sobre la intencion en la application de la Santa Misa, VII-104 pp., 1931.
63. Frey, Rev. Wolfgang Norbert, O.S.B., A.B., J.C.D., The Act of Religious Profession, VIII-174 pp., 1931.
64. Roberts, Rev. James Brendan, A.B., J.C.D., The Banns of Marriage, XIV-140 pp., 1931.
65. Ryder, Rev. Raymond Aloysius, A.B., J.C.D., Simony, IX-151 pp., 1931.
66. Campagna, Rev. Angelo, Ph.D., J.U.D., Il Vicario Generale del Vescovo, VII-205 pp., 1931.
67. Cox, Rev. Joseph Godfrey, A.B., J.C.D., The Administration of Seminaries, VI-124 pp., 1931.
68. Gregory, Rev. Donald J., J.U.D., The Pauline Privilege, XV-165 pp., 1931.
69. Donohue, Rev. John F., J.C.D., The Impediment of Crime, VII-110 pp., 1931.
70. Dooley, Rev. Eugene A., O.M.I., J.C.D., Church Law On Sacred Relics, IX-143 pp., 1931.
71. Orth, Rev. Raymond Clement, O.M.C., J.C.D., The Approbation of Religious Institutes, 171 pp., 1931.
72. Pernicone, Rev. Joseph M., A.B., J.C.D., The Ecclesiastical Prohibition of Books, XII-267 pp., 1932.
73. Clinton, Rev. Connell, A.B., J.C.D., The Paschal Precept, IX-108 pp., 1932.
74. Donnelly, Rev. Francis B., A.M., S.T.L., J.C.D., The Diocesan Synod, VIII-125 pp., 1932.
75. Torrente, Rev. Camilo, C.M.F., J.C.D., Las Processiones Sagradas, V-145 pp., 1932.
76. Murphy, Rev. Edwin J., C.PP.S., J.C.D., Suspension Ex Informata Conscientia, XI-122, pp., 1932.
77. Mackenzie, Rev. Eric F., A.M., S.T.L., J.C.D., The Delict of Heresy in its Commission Penalization, Absolution, VII-124 pp., 1932.
78. Lyons Rev. Avitus E., S.T.B., J.C.D., The Collegiate Tribunal of First Instance, XI-147 pp., 1932.
79. Connolly, Rev. Thomas A., J.C.D., Appeals, XI-195 pp., 1932.
80. Sangmeister, Rev. Joseph V., A.B., J.C.D., Force and Fear as Precluding Matrimonial Consent, V-211 pp., 1932.
81. Jaeger, Rev. Leo A., A.B., J.C.D., The Administration of Vacant and Quasi-vacant Episcopal Sees in the United States, IX-229 pp., 1932.
82. Rimlinger, Rev. Herbert T., J.C.D., Error Invalidating Matrimonial Consent, VII-79 pp., 1932.
83. Barrett, Rev. John D.M., S.S., J.C.D., A Comparative Study of the Third Plenary Council of Baltimore and the Code, IX-221 pp., 1932.

84. Carberry, Rev. John J., Ph.D., S.T.D., J.C.D., The Juridical Form of Marriage, X-177 pp., 1934.
85. Dolan, Rev. John L., A.B., J.C.D., The Defensor Vinculi, XII-157 pp., 1934.
86. Hannan, Rev. Jerome D., A.M., S.T.D., LL.B., J.C.D., The Canon Law of Wills, IX-517 pp., 1934.
87. Lemieux, Rev. Delisle A., A.M., J.C.D., The Sentence in Ecclesiastical Procedure, IX-131 pp., 1934.
88. O'Rourke, Rev. James J., A.B., J.C.D., Parish Registers, VII-109 pp., 1934.
89. Timlin, Rev. Bartholomew, O.F.M., A.M., J.C.D., Conditional Matrimonial Consent, X-381 pp., 1934.
90. Wahl, Rev. Francis X., A.B., J.C.D., The Matrimonial Impediments of Consanguinity and Affinity, VI-125 pp., 1934.
91. White, Rev. Robert J., A.B., LL.B., S.T.B., J.C.D., Canonical Ante-Nuptial Promises and the Civil Law, VI-152 pp., 1934.
92. Herrera, Rev. Antonio Parra, O.C.D., J.C.D., Legislation Ecclesiastica sobra el Ayuno y la Abstinencia, XI-191 pp., 1935.
93. Kennedy, Rev. Edwin J., J.C.D., The Special Matrimonial Process in Cases of Evident Nullity, X-165 pp., 1935.
94. Manning, Rev. John J., A.B., J.C.D., Presumption of Law in Matrimonial Procedure, XI-111 pp., 1935.
95. Moeder, Rev. John M., J.C.D., The Proper Bishop for Ordination and Dismissorial Letters, VII-135 pp., 1935.
96. O'Mara, Rev. William A., A.B., J.C.D., Canonical Causes For Matrimonial Dispensations, IX-155 pp., 1935.
97. Reilly, Rev. Peter, J.C.D., Residence of Pastors, IX-81 pp., 1935.
98. Smith, Rev. Mariner T., O.P., S.T.L., J.C.D., The Penal Law For Religious, VII-169 pp., 1935.
99. Whalen, Rev. Donald W., A.M., J.C.D., The Value of Testimonial Evidence in Matrimonial Procedure, XIII-297 pp., 1935.
100. Cleary, Rev. Joseph F., J.C.D., Canonical Limitations on the Alienation of Church Property, VIII-141 pp., 1936.
101. Glynn, Rev. John C., J.C.D., The Promoter of Justice, XX-337 pp., 1936.
102. Brennan, Rev. James H., S.S., A.M., S.T.B., J.C.D., The Simple Convalidation of Marriage, VI-135 pp, 1937.
103. Brunini, Rev. Joseph Bernard, J.C.D., The Clerical Obligations of Canons, 139 and 142, X-121 pp., 1937.
104. Connor, Rev. Maurice, A.B., J.C.D., The Administrative Removal of Pastors, VIII-159 pp., 1937.
105. Guilfoyle, Rev. Merlin Joseph, J.C.D., Custom, XI-144 pp., 1937.
106. Hughes, Rev. James Austin, A.B., A.M., J.C.D., Witnesses in Criminal Trials of Clerics, IX-140 pp., 1937.

107. Jansen, Rev. Raymond J., A.B., S.T.L., J.C.D., Canonical Provisions for Catechetical Instruction, VII-153 pp., 1937.
108. Kealy, Rev. John James, A.B., J.C.D,, The Introductory Libellus in Church Court Procedure, XI-121 pp., 1937.
109. McManus, Rev. James Edward, C.SS.R., J.C.D., The Administration of Temporal Goods in Religious Institutes, XVI-196 pp., 1937.
110. Moriarity, Rev. Eugene James, J.C.D., Oaths in Ecclesiastical Courts, X-115 pp., 1937.
111. Rainer, Rev. Eligius George, C.SS.R., J.C.D., Suspension of Clerics, XVII-249 pp., 1937.
112. Reilly, Rev. Thomas F., C.SS.R., J.C.D., Visitation of Religious, VI-195 pp., 1938.
113. Moriarty, Rev. Francis E., C.SS.R., J.C.D., The Extraordinary Absolution from Censures, XV-334 pp., 1938.
114. Connolly, Rev. Nicholas P., J.C.D., The Canonical Erection of Parishes, X-132 pp., 1938.
115. Donovan, Rev. James Joseph, J.C.D., The Pastor's Obligation in Prenuptial Investigation, VII-322 pp., 1938.
116. Harrigan, Rev. Robert J., M.A., S.T.B., J.C.D., The Radical Sanation of Invalid Marriages, VIII-208 pp., 1938.
117. Boffa, Rev. Conrad Humbert, J.C.D., Canonical Provisions for Catholic Schools, VII-211 pp., 1939.
118. Parsons, Rev. Anscar John, O.M. Cap., J.C.D., Canonical Elections, XII-236 pp., 1939.
119. Reilly, Rev. Edward Michael, A.B., J.C.D., The General Norms of Dispensation, X-156 pp., 1939.
120. Ryan, Rev. Gerald Aloysius, A.B., J.C.D., Principles of Episcopal Jurisdiction, XII-172 pp., 1939.
121. Burton, Rev. Francis James, C.S.C., A.B., J.C.D., A Commentary on Canon 1125, X-222 pp., 1940.
122. Miaskiewicz, Rev. Francis Sigismund, J.C.D., Supplied Jurisdiction according to Canon 209, XII-340 pp., 1940.
123. Rice, Rev. Patrick William, A.B., J.C.D., Proof of Death in Prenuptial Investigation, VIII-156 pp., 1940.
124. Anglin, Rev. Thomas Francis, M.S., J.C.D., The Eucharistic Fast, VIII-183 pp., 1941.
125. Coleman, Rev. John Jerome, J.C.D., The Minister of Confirmation, VI-153 pp., 1941.
126. Downs, Rev. John Emmanuel, A.B., J.C.D., The Concept of Clerical Immunity.
127. Esswein, Rev. Anthony Albert, J.C.D., Extrajudicial Penal Powers of Ecclesiastical Superiors, X-144 pp., 1941.

128. Farrell, Rev. Benjamin Francis, M.A., S.T.L., J.C.D., The Rights and Duties of the Local Ordinary Regarding Congregations of Women Religious of Pontifical Approval, V-195 pp., 1941.
129. Feeney, Rev. Thomas John, A.B., S.T.L., J.C.D., Restitution in Integrum, VI-169 pp., 1941.
130. Findlay, Rev. Stephen William, O.S.B., A.B., J.C.D., Canonical Norms Governing the Deposition and Degradation of Clerics.
131. Goodwine, Rev. John, A.B., S.T.L., J.C.D., The Right of the Church to Acquire Property, VIII-119 pp., 1941.
132. Heston, Rev. Edward Louis, C.S.C., PhD., S.T.D., J.C.D., The Alienation of Church Property in the United States, XII-222 pp., 1941.
133. Hogan, Rev. James John, S.T.L., J.C.D., Judicial Advocates and Procurators, VIII-200 pp., 1941.
134. Kealy, Rev. Thomas M. A.B., Litt.B., J.C.D., Dowry of Women Religious, IX-152 pp., 1941.
135. Keene, Rev. Michael James, O.S.B., J.C.D., Religious Ordinaries and Canon 198.
136. Kerin, Rev. Charles A., S.S., M.A., S.T.B., J.C.D., The Privation of Christian Burial, XVI-279 pp., 1941.
137. Louis, Rev. William Francis, M.A., J.C.D., Diocesan Archives, X-101 pp., 1941.
138. McDevitt, Rev. Gilbert Joseph, A.B., J.C.D., Legitimacy and Legitimation.
139. McDonough, Rev. Thomas Joseph, A.B., J.C.D., Apostolic Administrators.
140. Meier, Rev. Carl Anthony, A.B., J.C.D., Penal Administrative Procedure Against Negligent Pastors, XI-240 pp., 1941.
141. Schmidt, Rev. John Rogg, A.B., J.C.D., The Principles of Authentic Interpretation in Canon 17 of the Code of Canon Law, XII-331 pp., 1941.
142. Slafkosky, Rev. Andrew eLonard, A.B., J.C.D., The Canonical Episcopal Visitation of the Diocese, X-197 pp., 1941.
143. Swoboda, Rev. Innocent Robert, O.F.M., J.C.D., Ignorance in Relation to the Imputability of Delicts, IX-271 pp., 1941.
144. Dubé, Rev. Arthur Joseph, A.B., J.C.D., The General Principles for the Reckoning of Time in Canon Law. VIII-299 pp., 1941.
145. McBride, Rev. James T., A.B., J.C.D., Incardination and Excardination of Seculars., XX-585 pp., 1941.
146. Król, Rev. John J., J.C.L., The Defendant in Contentious Trials, IX-207 pp., 1942.
147. Comyns, Rev. Joseph J., C.SS.R., J.C.L., The Papal and Episcopal Administration of Church Property.
148. Barry, Rev. Garrett Francis, O.M.I., J.C.L., Violation of the Cloister.

149. Bolduc, Rev. Gatien, C.S.V., A.B., S.T.L., J.C.L., Les études dans les religions cléricales.
150. Boyle, Rev. David John, M.A., J.C.L., The Juridic Effects of Moral Certitude on Pre-Nuptial Guarantees.
151. Canavan, Rev. Walter Joseph, M.A., Litt.D., J.C.L., Profession of Faith.
152. Desrochers, Rev. Bruno, A.B., Ph.L., S.T.B., J.C.L., Le Premier Concile Plénier de Québec et le Code de Droit Canonique.
153. Dillon, Rev. Robert Edward, A.B., J.C.L., Common Law Marriage.
154. Dodwell, Rev. Edward John, Ph.D., S.T.B., J.C.L., The Time and Place for the Celebration of Marriage.
155. Donnellan, Rev. Thomas Andrew, A.B., J.C.L., The Obligation of the Missa pro Populo.
156. Eltz, Rev. Louis Anthony, A.B., JC.L., Cooperation in Crime.
157. Gass, Rev. Sylvester Francis, M.A., J.C.L., Ecclestiastical Pensions.
158. Guiniven, Rev. John Joseph, C.SS.R., J.C.L., The Precept of Hearing Mass on Sundays and Holy Days of Obligation.
159. Gulczynski, Rev. John Theophilus, J.C.L., The Desecration and Violation of Churches.
160. Hammill, Rev. John Leo, M.A., J.C.L., The Obligations of the Traveler according to Canon 14.
161. Haydt, Rev. John Joseph, A.B., J.C.L., Reserved Benefices.
162. Huser, Rev. Roger John, O.F.M., A.B., J.C.L., The Crime of Abortion in Canon Law.
163. Kearney, Rev. Francis Patrick, A.B., S.T.L., J.C.L., The Principles of Canon 1127.
164. Linahen, Rev. Leo James, S.T.L., J.C.L., De Absolutione Complicis in Peccato Turpi.
165. McCloskey, Rev. Joseph Aloysius, A.B., J.C.L., The Subject of Ecclesiastical Law according to Canon 12.
166. O'Neill, Rev. Francis Joseph, C.SS.R., J.C.L., The Dismissal of Religious in Temporary Vows.
167. Prince, Rev. John Edward, A.B., S.T.B., J.C.L., The Diocesan Chancellor.
168. Riesner, Rev. Albert Joseph, C.SS.R., J.C.L., Apostates and Fugitives from Religious Institutes.
169. Stenger, Rev. Joseph Bernard, J.C.L., The Mortgaging of Church Property.
170. Waldron, Rev. Joseph Francis, A.B., J.C.L., The Minister of Baptism.
171. Willett, Rev. Robert Albert, J.C.L., The Probative Value of Documents in Ecclesiastical Trials.
172. Woeber, Rev. Edward Martin, M.A., J.C.L., The Interpellations.

www.ingramcontent.com/pod-product-compliance
Lightning Source LLC
LaVergne TN
LVHW050242080826
844660LV00012B/580

* 9 7 8 0 8 1 3 2 2 3 4 6 9 *